SPORT *in* *the* FIELDS *and* WOODS

Richard Jefferies

an anthology compiled by
Rebecca Welshman

Merlin Unwin Books

This anthology first published in Great Britain by
Merlin Unwin Books Ltd, 2017

Merlin Unwin Books Ltd
Palmers House
7 Corve Street
Ludlow
Shropshire SY8 1DB
U.K.

www.merlinunwin.co.uk

ISBN 978-1-910723-40-1

Typeset in 12 point Bembo by Merlin Unwin Books
Printed by Jellyfish Solutions, UK

Contents

Introduction

by Dr Rebecca Welshman

Richard Jefferies (1848–1887) was an author and naturalist, born in Wiltshire. He wrote *The Gamekeeper at Home*, *The Amateur Poacher*, *Round About a Great Estate*, and numerous other works. Jefferies was a pioneer in countryside and nature writing, and his style has been widely embraced and replicated by writers over the last century. He wrote with great feeling and insight about the nature and landscapes of the Wiltshire Downs, and later about the natural history and human life around Surbiton, Brighton, and London.

Jefferies' writings on sport are from firsthand experience. As a teenager he spent time observing the habits and habitats of birds and animals, and through his friendship with the gamekeeper on the Burderop estate he learnt the techniques of shooting. After befriending local poachers and sportsmen, he became familiar with the methods of poaching, and the culture of rural sporting traditions. He also learnt much from his father who cultivated the land and gardens around the family home, Coate Farmhouse, near Swindon, which can still be visited and enjoyed today.

For Jefferies, sport was more than just a pastime. It gave him a reason to be out in the fields or woods, or by the water, and allowed him to enjoy and reflect upon the treasures of the natural world. Sport is present in some form in the majority of his books. We might remember the relentless physical pursuits of the two boys in *Bevis* who shoot, fish, swim, and sail, or Felix, the accomplished archer in *After London*, both of whom were modelled on Jefferies himself. In his essay 'A Defence of Sport', written for the *National Review* in 1883 as a response to the debates surrounding the cruelty of fieldsports, Jefferies refers to sport as an 'instinct' that betters mental and physical health, and suggests that a person will be better equipped in all areas of life if they are first well educated in the life of the outdoors.

This is the first anthology to focus on Jefferies' writings on sport. With extracts from well known and lesser known works, and newly discovered articles republished for the first time, the collection represents Jefferies' experiences of shooting ground game and wildfowl, hunting, poaching, fishing, and hare coursing. The selections also highlight Jefferies' interests in estate management and the lives of people who lived in the countryside. Printed alongside are seasonal pieces and some of his more reflective observations.

Jefferies' sketches of sportsmen, squires, gamekeepers, and poachers are based on people he knew and spent time with. As an agricultural journalist in the 1870s he attended events, such as fairs, markets, shows, and exhibitions. Many of the farmers and labourers who he would have met along the way would have participated in rural sports. In his notebook from 1876 Jefferies records attending the Epsom Derby, which was one of Britain's largest sporting fixtures. Horses fascinated Jefferies; their strength, endurance and beauty of form were qualities which he envied. In the *Amateur Poacher* Jefferies writes: 'The proximity of horse-racing establishments adds to the general atmosphere of dissipation. Betting, card-playing, ferret breeding and dog-fancying, poaching and politics, are the occupations of the populace.' The sporting territories of the Wiltshire Downs lay close to Jefferies' birthplace. At Lambourn, which is known as the Valley of the Racehorse, horses have been trained since the eighteenth century. Also close by is Ashdown Park, the home of the Earl of Craven, which in the nineteenth century was one of the best known venues for coursing meetings. In 'Walks in the Wheatfields' Jefferies writes that 'hares are almost formed on purpose to be good sport' and that 'coursing is capital, the harriers first-rate.' His passion for the sport is also evident in the hare-coursing scenes in *The Amateur Poacher*, which Edward Thomas called 'the finest thing in the book.'

Jefferies also appreciated fox hunting – not because it was a blood sport – but because as a rural tradition it had a unique aesthetic and atmosphere. In 1876 Jefferies made a note on the insight into social history that hunting afforded, saying that 'to hunting we owe no little knowledge of men and manners'. He bemoaned the fact that landscape painters seemed to avoid painting the gritty details of hunting scenes: 'no one paints the foggy days, the dead leaves, the soaking grass... its melancholy landscape. Why does not someone paint the natural hunt? With the cottager and his bill hook looking up, and even the scarlet dulled by the rain or splashed by a fall and the fence tearing the coat.'

In his sporting contributions Jefferies makes clear and striking observations about movement, position and individual response to the environment. These qualities are particularly evident in his contributions on shooting. Soon after his country books were serialised in the *Pall Mall Gazette* in the 1870s, Jefferies was asked by the publisher Charles Longman to write a manual on shooting. Although this project was never finished, fragments of manuscript were printed in 1957 by Samuel Looker, some of which are reproduced here in this collection. However, although he grew to be an accurate shot, Jefferies also expressed his desire to simply observe birds and animals. In *The Amateur Poacher* he describes the moment when he lets the gun go just to watch the flight of a pheasant:

My finger felt the trigger, and the least increase of pressure would have been fatal; but in the act I hesitated, dropped the barrel, and watched the beautiful bird. That watching so often stayed the shot that at last it grew to be a habit: the mere simple pleasure of seeing birds and animals, when they were quite unconscious that they were observed, being too great to be spoilt by the discharge. After carefully getting a wire over a jack; after waiting in a tree till a hare came along; after sitting in a mound till the partridges began to run together to roost; in the end the wire or gun remained unused. The same feeling has equally checked my hand in legitimate shooting: time after time I have flushed partridges without firing, and have let the hare bound over the furrow free.

I have entered many woods just for the pleasure of creeping through the brake and the thickets. Destruction in itself was not the motive; it was an overpowering instinct for woods and fields. Yet woods and fields lose half their interest without a gun – I like the power to shoot, even though I may not use it.

In 1883 Jefferies spent the summer on Exmoor researching the area. After being introduced to Arthur Heal, huntsman to the Devon and Somerset Staghounds, Jefferies experienced firsthand the finer details of the chase. These experiences became the foundation of his book *Red Deer*. In the book he refers to the 'complete catalogue of sport' that took place in Red Deer land – including salmon fishing, otter hunting, stag hunting, black game shooting, as well as pheasant and partridge shooting. For Jefferies Exmoor ways of life were refreshingly remote from the ordinary grind of urban living, and illustrated an ancient form of human occupation and relationship with the land.

Sadly, for someone who so loved the outdoors, Jefferies' failing health meant that he was confined to the indoors during his last few years. In 'Hours of Spring' he describes watching the unfurling of the season from his place by the little window of his cottage at Goring: 'Today through the window-pane I see a lark high up against the grey cloud, and hear his song. ... It is years since I went out amongst them in the old fields, and saw them in the green corn'. As his illness worsened the benefits and pleasures of sport became memories rather than realities. Yet the faculties employed in sport – instinct, precision, and focus – and the beauty and grace of animals and birds, continued to inspire Jefferies until the very end of his life. For the love of sport is often closely associated with a love of the countryside – as Jefferies writes in *The Amateur Poacher*: 'Let us get out of these indoor narrow modern days ... into the sunlight and the pure wind. A something that the ancients called divine can be found and felt there still.'

Rebecca Welshman

A Defence of Sport

A sportsman, or a sportswoman, is never forgotten. The memories of many are still green, though the grass has grown rank over them long since, and while yet one of their generation endures they will be spoken of. Never do you hear a sportsman speak ill of another sportsman. He may joke to any extent, but you will not hear an evil word of another behind his back. A true sportsman has a kind heart for his fellow men; there is no hunting country, not a village where examples may not be collected. There are instances where the inhabitants of a whole district look upon the master of the hounds as their friend and guide. The humblest cottager knows that he can get assistance – everyone speaks well of the master, and deeply would the countryside, especially the poorer population, feel any interruption to that intercourse. One pack of hounds will cause more good feeling among men than fifty pulpits resounding. Give me for a friend a man who rides. With gun, or rod, or in the saddle, a man, let me repeat, is the better, larger in heart and mind, for exercise in the field. He becomes himself; the layers of interest, self, and prejudice which circumstances have placed round about him disappear. He forgives and forgets; his vision opens, and his heart expands.

❖

A pliant rod and silken line, beguiling the footsteps away beside a trout stream, will open a new view of the world. The management of the rod and line, the art to throw it exactly where the ripple runs swiftly at the foot of the rapid, gradually takes up the mind. Intense preoccupation yields to physical effort – the turn and sway of the wrist, the lissom bend of the rod, the swish of the line, transmute thought into the pleasure of action. The very rush of the water against the fishing-boots recalls the strained brain to flesh and blood; the nerves resume their long-suspended functions, and the thrill of life courses to and fro. Sounds of ripples, and splash, the leap of trout, the soft, loving sigh of the wind in the trees, the passage and call of birds – these stroke away the heavy ache of ceaseless labour. Gleams of light reflected, shadowy pools, green meads, and hills whose very curves against the sky are soothing in their slumberous, reposeful outline – these charm the inner existence into accord with the earth. The wound-up sternness of thought melts away, and the fisherman discovers how beautiful it is simply to live.

River and meadow, sunlight and wind, have shown the fisherman his own heart; he finds that there is such a thing as friendship, as good-fellowship, as unselfish companionship. Once know these, and honour is no more an empty word – honour and truth, straightforwardness in everything, are far above the measure of the banker's book. Let us take a broader, a nobler view of this our lovely country. Let us not look at our land as merely so many acres worth so much. Let us remember the long roll of greatness which forms the real title-deed of the nation. You see the river, and the meadow, the sun, and the wind, bring to the mind a sense of reality – a grasp of the fact that this is England. Till a man has in some manner or other gone afield he does not thoroughly comprehend the meaning of his own country. In a word, it is not home to him. After knowledge of the river and the wood, the hill and mead, such knowledge as gun, rod, or saddle alone can give, he realizes that it is his country, that it is his home. I claim for sport that it makes a man feel himself an Englishman in the full sense of the word, and that it counteracts the narrowing spirit of commerce alone.

A Defence of Sport

Our fields and woods, moors and rivers, are our playgrounds, from which we emerge, strong and ready, to fight the battles of the world. Their value as playgrounds increases year after year. Their thought, heart, and body are alike recruited, and energy stored up for work. As the bees gather their honey from the broad stretches of heather, so those who go out into the open air gather up vigour of frame, and infinite nerve-power which is more valuable than muscular strength. Nothing but sport can supply it, and thus the country has a value over and above its utilitarian produce. A moor – a vast stretch of heather – may graze a few sheep: the money they represent is but little. But the grouse give an increase of strength, a renewal of nerve-force, to those who pursue them over the mountain side, not to be estimated in pounds, shillings, and pence. A little trout stream, if it were farmed on the most utilitarian principle, could only send a small tribute of fish towards feeding a town. But the same river may lead many and many a sportsman out into the meadows, insensibly absorbing the influence of the air and sunlight, the woods and hills, to his own profit individually and to the benefit of all with whom he associates.

from *Chronicles of the Hedges*, 1948

Poaching on Exmoor

The way up to the woods is beside the trout-stream; it is indeed but a streamlet, easy to stride across, yet it is full of trout. Running with a quick tinkle over red stones, the shallow water does not look as if it would float a fish, but they work round the stones and under hollows of the banks. The lads have not forgotten how to poach them; such knowledge is handed down by tradition, and will never be lost while a stream flows; it will be familiar when the school-books are dust and mildew. They tickle the fish as it lies under a stone, slightly rubbing it underneath to keep it still, and then quickly run a sharpened kitchen fork through the tail, and so secure the slippery trout. They tie a treble hook, like a grapnel, to a stout piece of twine, and draw it across the water till under the fish, when, giving a sudden snatch, one of the hooks is sure to catch it at the side. Trout can also be wired with a running loop of wire. Groping for trout (or tickling), still practised in the rivers when they are low so that the fish can be got at, is tracing it to the stone it lies under, then rubbing it gently beneath, which causes the fish to gradually move backwards into the hand till the fingers suddenly close in the gills, where alone a firm hold can be obtained.

The rivers of Somerset have stony bottoms, so that the eels can be seen moving about like black snakes. They glide over the stones at the bottom, exactly as a snake glides over the surface of the ground, and when still, remain in a sinuous form. Trout swim over and past them. All their motions can be watched, while in the brooks and streams of other counties, where the bottom is of mud or dark sandy loam, they are rarely seen. There they seem to move through the mud, or its dark colour conceals them. Getting into the water, men move the stones till they find an eel, and then thrust a fork through it, the only way to hold it.

Some distance up the streamlet in a coombe, wooded each side to a great height, are three trout ponds. Ferns grow green and thick where the water falls over the hatch, and by the shore flourishes the tall reed-mace (so rarely distinguished from the lesser bulrush). A ripple here, a circle yonder, a splash across in the corner, show where trout have risen to flies. The osprey was shot at these ponds, and once now and then the spoor of an otter is found on the shore. Leaving the water, the path goes up the steep coombe under oaks, far up to the green pasture at the summit. Across on another slope, against which the declining sun shines brightly, there are two or three white spots – quite brilliantly white. One moves presently, and it is seen that they are white wild rabbits. Their brown friends are scarcely visible except when moving. Red deer used to lie in the cover yonder till they were chased, since which none have returned to the spot. Beside the oak wood in the pasture on the summit it is pleasant walking now in the shade after the heat of the day.

It is along the side of a cover like this that the poachers set their larger rabbit-nets at night. There is one seized from poachers down at the old hall. The net is about a hundred yards long and a yard or so wide, made of bluish-green hemp, three threads to the strand, and the mesh about two inches square – just large enough for a rabbit to get his head through; a very young rabbit could go right through the mesh. There is an iron pin at each end to thrust in the ground. The poacher having pushed the iron pin in, steps a pace or two and runs a stick in the ground, twists the string at the upper part of the net round the top of the stick, leaving the net suspended, and repeats this every few steps till he comes to the iron pin at the other end of the net. In this way he can set the net almost as quickly as he walks.

Three are required to work it properly, and the net is placed along the head of a cover between nine and ten at night while the rabbits are out feeding in the pasture, so as to cut off their return to their burrows. Either one of the poachers or a lurcher next go round some distance and drive everything towards it, while the other poachers stand behind the net to take out the rabbits as they come. In a moment or two they rush from all quarters helter-skelter in the darkness, and bound into the net. The rabbit's head enters the mesh, and he rolls over, causing it to bag round him. The poachers endeavour to get them out as fast as they come to prevent their escape, and to make ready for fresh captives. They wring the rabbits' necks, killing them instantly. Sometimes the rabbits come in such numbers and all together in a crowd, so that they cannot get them out fast enough, and a few manage to escape. Once, however, the rabbit's head is well through the mesh, he is generally safe for a quarter of an hour.

Large catches are often made like this. Sometimes as many as sixty or eighty rabbits may be seen out feeding in the evening by the head of a cover – that is, where the wood joins the meadows. Besides rabbits a hare now and then runs in, and a fox is occasionally caught. Everything out in the fields, on being alarmed, scampers back to the wood, and the large net, invisible in the darkness, intercepts the retreat. Bluish-green meshes are scarcely noticeable even in daylight when laid in ferns, on bushes, or by tall grass. This net down at the hall cost the poachers two or three pounds, and was taken from them the very first night they used it. It is heavy and forms a heap rolled up – enough to fill a bushel basket. The meshes are very strong and will hold anything. A very favourite time to set these nets, and indeed for all kinds of poaching, as with wires, is after rain, when rabbits, and hares too, feed voraciously. After rain a hare will run at night twice as much as other nights; these evenings are the best for shooting rabbits out feeding.

The poacher who goes out to net hares has a net about twelve feet long, similar in shape, and takes with him a lurcher. He has previously found where hares feed at night by their tracks to and fro and the marks of their pads on the wet ground, as the sand in gateways. Hares usually go through gateways, so that he knows which way they will come. He sets the net across the gateway inside the field, stands aside and sends the dog to drive the hare into it. The dog is a cross between a sheep-dog and a collie, very fast, and runs mute; he does not give tongue on finding the scent; if he did the poacher would strangle him as useless, since barking would announce too plainly what was going forward.

The lurcher is very intelligent, and quite understands what he is wanted to do. On finding the hare he gives chase; often the hare goes straight for the net, but may of course follow another direction, when it is the lurcher's work to turn her, and not let her leave the field except by that one exit. To do this the lurcher must be swift, else the hare can distance him. If he succeeds and drives her that way, the instant she is in the net the poacher falls on it and secures her. Hares struggle hard, and if he stayed to catch hold with his hands she might be gone, but by falling bodily on the net he is certain of getting her, and prevents her too from screaming, as hares will in the most heartrending manner. By moving on from gateway to gateway, where he has previously ascertained hares are usually out at night, the poacher may catch four or five or more in a little while.

But it sometimes happens that a hare escapes from the net, not getting sufficiently entangled, and she remembers it ever afterwards, and tries hard the next time for her life. The marks of the struggle are plainly visible on the wet ground next morning – the marks of her pads as she raced round and round the field, refusing to be driven by the lurcher through the gateway, where she now suspects danger. Round and round she flies, endeavouring to gain sufficiently on the dog to be able to leap at some favourable place in the hedge, and so to get through and away. Sometimes she cannot do it; the lurcher overtakes her, and either seizes her, or forces her to the net; sometimes she increases her distance sufficiently, leaps at the hedge, is through and safe. It is the hedge and wall that trouble her so; she cannot put forth her swiftest pace and go right away; she must course in a circle. This is another reason why the poacher falls on the hare the instant she strikes the net, because if she does escape she will always remember and be so difficult to take afterwards. Several poachers often go out like this in the evening, one one way and another another, and so scour the fields.

A young fellow once, who wanted some money and had heard of the hauls made by a gang of poachers, joined them, and his first essay on the following night was with a hare net. The net being set for him in a gateway, he was instructed to instantly fall on anything that entered it. He took his stand; the poachers went on to different gateways and gaps, set their own nets, and finally despatched their dogs. The young poacher watched his net as closely as he could in the darkness, ready to obey his orders. All at once something struck the net; he fell headlong on it and got it under him right enough, but the next instant he received a terrible bite. He shouted and yelled 'Murder!' at the top of his voice, but held on groaning to the net and the creature in it, though in an agony of pain.

No one came to his assistance, for at the sound of his yell the poachers imagined the keepers were collaring him, and snatching up their nets ran off at full speed. Shouting and yelling, he struggled and held the creature down till he had kicked it to death, when he found it was a badger. Out feeding, the badger had been alarmed by the dog, and made for the gateway; so soon as he was touched, he began to bite as only a badger can. The young fellow was terribly hurt, both his arms and legs having suffered, and had to keep his bed for some time. Indignant at the faithless conduct of his associates, who had so meanly abandoned him, he renounced poaching. Besides watching the net the poacher watches to see if a keeper approaches. The keeper knows as well as the poacher where hares run, and suspects that certain gateways may be netted. If he sees the keeper coming he snatches up his net and bolts, and this he is sometimes obliged to do at the very moment the hare has entered the meshes, so that in tearing up the net he turns her out, unexpectedly free. The netting of partridges depends on a habit these birds have of remaining still on the ground at night until forced to move. Roosting on the ground, they will not rise till compelled; and the same thing may be observed of larks, who lie quiet at night till nearly stepped on. A partridge-net is held by a man at each end and dragged along the ground. It is weighted to keep one side of it heavy and close to the earth, and in action somewhat resembles a trawl. The poachers know where birds are roosting, and drag the net over them. They will not move till then, when they rise, and the instant the poachers hear anything in the net they drop it, and find the birds beneath it. Poaching varies in localities; where hares abound it is hare-poaching, or rabbits – as the case may be.

The most desperate poachers are those who enter the woods in the winter for pheasants. They shoot pheasants, and sometimes in the deep-wooded coombes, where the sound rolls and echoes for several seconds from the rocks, it is difficult to tell where the gun was fired. It might have been at one end of the valley or at the other. The gangs, however, who shoot pheasants openly declare their indifference as to whether they are detected or not.

They simply let it be known that they do not intend to be taken; they have guns and will use them, and if the keepers attack them it is at the risk of their lives. The question arises whether a too severe punishment for game-theft may not be responsible for this, and whether it does not defeat its object, since, if a poacher is aware that a heavy term of imprisonment awaits him, he will rather fire than be captured. At all events, such is the condition of things in some districts, and the keepers, for this reason, rarely interfere with such a gang. Such severe terms of imprisonment are cruel to keepers, whose lives are thereby imperilled.

The path has now led up by the oak woods to a great height, and the setting sun gleams over the hills of Red Deer Land. It is a land full of old memories. It is strange that Sir Francis Drake, like Virgil, should have acquired the fame of a magician. Sometimes in the hottest noon-tide of summer, when the sky is clear, the wood still, and the vapour of heat lying about the hillsides, there comes from unknown distances a roll and vibration like heavy thunder, fined to a tremble of the air. It is an inexplicable sound. There are no visible thunder-clouds, no forts within audible distance. Perhaps it is the implacable Drake discharging his enchanted cannon in the azure air against the enemies of England.

from *Red Deer*, 1884

The Farmer Loves his Gun

With the exception of knocking over a young rabbit now and then for household use, the farmer, even if he is independent of a landlord, as in this case, does not shoot till late in the year. Old-fashioned folk, though not in the least constrained to do so, still leave the first pick of the shooting to some neighbouring landowner between whose family and their own friendly relations have existed for generations. It is true that the practice becomes rarer yearly as the old style of men die out and the spirit of commerce is imported into rural life: the rising race preferring to make money of their shooting, by letting it, instead of cultivating social ties.

At Wick, however, they keep up the ancient custom, and the neighbouring squire takes the pick of the wing-game. They lose nothing for their larder through this arrangement – receiving presents of partridges and pheasants far exceeding in number - what could possibly be killed upon the farm itself; while later in the year the boundaries are relaxed on the other side, and the farmer kills his rabbit pretty much where he likes, in moderation.

He is seldom seen without a gun on his shoulder from November till towards the end of January. No matter whether he strolls to the arable field, or down the meadows, or across the footpath to a neighbour's house, the inevitable double-barrel accompanies him. To those who live much out of doors a gun is a natural and almost a necessary companion, whether there be much or little to shoot; and in this desultory way, without much method or set sport, he and his friends, often meeting and joining forces, find sufficient ground game and wild-fowl to give them plenty of amusement. When the hedges are bare of leaves the rabbit-burrows are ferreted: the holes can be more conveniently approached then, and the frost is supposed to give the rabbit a better flavour.

About Christmas-time, half in joke and half in earnest, a small party often agree to shoot as many blackbirds as they can, if possible to make up the traditional twenty-four for a pie. The blackbird pie is, of course, really an occasion for a social gathering, at which cards and

14

music are forthcoming. Though blackbirds abound in every hedge, it is by no means an easy task to get the required number just when wanted. After January the guns are laid aside, though some ferreting is still going on.

from *Wild Life in a Southern County,* 1879

Shooting a Rabbit

Towards half-past five or six o'clock on a summer afternoon the shadow of a summer-rick will be found to have lengthened sufficiently to shelter anyone who sits behind it from the heat of the sun. For this purpose a margin of shadow is necessary, as just within the edge, though the glare ceases, the heat is but little diminished. The light is cut off with a sharp line; the heat, as if refracted, bends in, so that earlier in the afternoon, when the shade would but just include your feet as you sat on the sward, there would not be the anticipated relief from the oppressive warmth. Ladies sometimes go into the garden to read under a favourite tree, and are surprised that it is not cool there; but the sun, nearly vertical at the time, scarcely casts a shade beyond the boughs. There must be a shadow into which you can retire several yards from the verge, as into a darkened cave, before the desired effect can be enjoyed.

About six the sun perceptibly declines, and can be seen at once without throwing the head back to look up; and then the summer-rick has a conical shadow of some extent. It is, too, the time when the rabbits in the burrows along the adjacent mound begin to think of coming out for their evening feed. A summer-rick of course stands in aftermath [remaining stubble] which is short, and allows of everything being seen in it at a glance. This rick is about twenty yards from the hedge, and the burrow, or the principal part of it, as you sit with your back leaning against the hay, is on the left-hand side. Place the double-barrel on the sward close to the rick, with the muzzle towards the burrow. If the gun were stood up against the rick it would not improbably be considered a suspicious object by the first old rabbit that came out, nor could it be got to the shoulder without several movements. But it can be lifted up from the grass, where it lies quite concealed, sidling it up slowly, brushing the rick, without any great change of attitude, and in the gradual imperceptible manner which is essential to success. Sometimes when the rabbit is in full view, right out in the field, the gun must be raised with the deliberate standstill motion of the hour hand on a clock, which if watched does not apparently move, but looked at again presently has gone on. The least jerk – a sudden motion of the arm – is sure to arouse the rabbit's attention. The effect is as with us when reading intently – if anything passes quickly across the corner of the eye we look up involuntarily. Had it passed gradually it would not have been observed. If possible, therefore, in choosing the spot for an ambush, the burrow should be on the left hand, whether you sit behind a rick, a tree, or in a dry ditch. Otherwise this slow clockwork motion is very difficult; for to shoot to the right is never convenient, and in a constrained position sometimes nearly impossible.

When expecting a rabbit in front or to the left it has occasionally happened that one has approached me almost from behind and on the right, where without turning the body it would be actually impossible to bring the gun to bear. Such a movement must alarm not only the particular rabbit, but any that might be about to come out in front; so that the only course is to let the creature remain and resolutely refuse the temptation to try and take aim. This difficulty of shooting to the right is why gamekeepers and others who do much potting learn to fire from the left shoulder, when they can command both sides. The barrel should be placed near the rick and lifted almost brushing it, so that it may be hidden as much as possible till the moment of pressing the trigger. Rabbits and all animals and birds dislike anything pointed at them. They have too good memories, and it is quite within probability that an old rabbit may be out who, though not then hit, or stung only in the skin, may recollect the flash and the thunderous roar which issued from similar threatening orifices. I used to try when waiting on a mound to get a 'gicks', or cow-parsnip, or a frond of fern or some brome grass, to partly overhang the barrel, so that its presence might not be suspected till the sight was taken.

Now, having placed the gun ready and arranged yourself comfortably, next determine to forget the burrow entirely, and occupy the mind with anything rather than rabbits. They will never come out while watched for, and every impatient peep round the side of the rick simply prolongs the time. Nor is a novel of any use: whether it is the faint rustle of the leaves or the unconscious changes of position while reading, but no rabbit will venture near, no wood-pigeon will pass over while there is a book on the knee. Look at anything – look at the grass. At the tip much of it is not pointed but blunt and brown as if burned; these are the blades recently severed by the scythe. They have pushed up higher but bear the scar of the wound. Bare spots by the furrows are where the mower swept his scythe through ant hills, leaving the earth exposed to the hot sun. Fond as the partridges are of ants' eggs, the largest coveys cannot make much impression upon the immense quantity of these insects. The partridges too frequently are diminished in numbers, but not from lack of particular food. A solitary humble-bee goes by to the ditch; he does not linger over the aftermath. Before it was cut the mowing grass was populous with insects; the aftermath has not nearly so many, though the grasshoppers are more visible, as they can be seen after they alight, which is not the case when the grass is tall. A chaffinch or greenfinch may come out from the hedge and perch on the sloping roof of the summer-rick, probably after the seeds in the plants among the hay. The kestrel hawk occasionally swoops down on to a summer-rick, stays for a second, and glides away again.

If you should chance to be waiting like this near a cattle-shed, perhaps you may see the keen muzzle of a weasel peep out from a sparrow's hole in the thatch of the roof. Yonder across the field is a gateway in the hedge, without either gate or rail, through which every now and then passes a blackbird or a thrush, and lesser birds, scarce distinguishable in the distance, flit across. The note of the grasshopper lark, not unlike a very small and non-sonorous bell continually agitated, sounds somewhere; it rings for several minutes, then stops, and rings again with short intervals. For a while it is difficult to tell whence it comes; the swift iteration of exactly the same note gives no indication of locality. But presently the eye seems guided by some unconscious sympathy with the ear to a low hawthorn bush which grows isolated a little way from the ditch a hundred yards down. The bird is there. Under an elm in the hedge on the right hand a gap was mended very early in the spring by driving in a stake and bending down some bushes. The top of the stake is the perch of a flycatcher; he leaves it every few seconds to catch insects floating past, now one side and now the other of the hedge, but immediately returns. His feeble and rather irritating call is repeated at intervals. From the same hedge comes, too, the almost incessant cry of young birds, able to fly, but not yet to find their own food. The dry scent of hay emanates from the summer-rick; the brown stalks of plants, some hollow hedge-parsley mown by the shore of the ditch, project from the side. Now the shadow of a tree which has been silently approaching from behind has reached the rick, and even extends beyond.

Something suddenly appears in the gateway across the field: a rabbit hops with much deliberation through the opening and stays to nibble among the clover, which always grows where the ground has been trodden but not worn bare by cattle. It would seem as if the wild rabbit and the tame did not feed on the same kind of food: the succulent plants carried home in such quantities for the tame animals often grow thickly near large burrows and to all appearance untouched. When shot in the act of grazing in meadows the wild rabbit has seldom anything but grass in his teeth. No doubt he does vary it, yet the sow-thistle flourishes by his bury. The gateway is far beyond the range of small shot, but if the rabbits are coming out there so they may be here.

Very gently, with no jerk or rapid motion, take off your hat, and looking rather at the outline of the rick than at the hedge, slowly peer round so that at first sight of anything you may stay at once and not expose yourself. There is something brown on the grass, not fifteen yards distant; but it is too low, it does not stand above the short aftermath; it is a rabbit, but too young. Another inch of cautious craning round and there is a rabbit on the shore of the ditch, partly hidden by some hawthorn. He is large enough, but it is chance if he can be got: even if severely hit he has but to tumble and kick in a few feet to the bury. Retire as slowly as you advanced and wait again.

A rabbit is out now close to the bush where the grasshopper lark still sings; and another comes forth there shortly afterwards. The first runs twenty or thirty yards into the meadow; the rabbit across at the distant gateway becomes aware that there is company near, and goes to meet it. Further still, on the right hand, there are two or three brown specks in the grass, which stay a long time in one spot, and then move. Something catches the eye on the mound near at hand: it is a rabbit hopping along the ridge of the bank, now visible and now hidden by the bushes. Lower down, a very young one nibbles at the grass which grows at the edge of the sand thrown out from the bury. The rabbit moving along the top of the mound is well within shot, but he, too, if hit will certainly escape, and it is uncertain if he can be hit hard, for although visible to the eye, there are many twigs and branches interposing which would lessen the force of the charge, or even avert it. He has now disappeared; he has gone out into the field on the other side. There seem rabbits everywhere except where wished: what a pity you did not sit behind the isolated hawthorn yonder or near the distant gateway through which a second rabbit comes.

The long-drawn discordant call of a heron sounds; glancing up he floats over with outstretched wings. They are so broad that he does not seem far, yet he is very likely 200 yards high. He loves to see the shadows lengthening beneath him as he sails, till they reach the hedges on the eastern side of the fields, so that he may find the shallow corner of the pool already dusky when he reaches it. The strained glance drops to the grass again… Ah! there is a rabbit on the left side now, scarce five-and-twenty, certainly less than thirty yards away, and almost on a level with the rick, well out therefore from the ditch and the burrows. The left hand steals to the barrels, the right begins to lift the broad stock, first to the knee, then gradually – with slow clockwork motion – to the waistcoat. Stay, he moves to choose a fresh grazing place – but only two yards. The gun rises, the barrels still droop, but the stock is more than halfway up. Stay again – the rabbit moves, but only turns his back completely, and immediately the gun comes to the shoulder. Stay again – is he full or nearly full grown, or is he too small? Is it a buck, or a doe? If the latter, she should be spared at that season. If full-grown, though a buck, he will be very little good at this time of the year. You must judge by the height of the ears, the width across the flanks, and the general outline, by calling to mind previous experience. On comparison with others that you have shot you think this rabbit is little more than half-grown, not quite three quarters – that is, tender and white, and the best for the summer season. But looking along the barrels the hump of the buck intervenes; if hit there he will be cut all to pieces. Shut the lips and cry gently, 'Tcheck!' Instantly the rabbit rises to his haunches with ears up straight. As instantaneously a quick sight is taken at the poll and the trigger pressed. The second barrel is ready, but do not move or rise, or you will most likely miss with that barrel, disconcerted by jumping up. It is not needed; the rabbit is down kicking on his side, but it is merely a convulsive kick which jerks the already lifeless and limp body without progress. As you stoop to pick him up the kick ceases. There is a tremor in the flanks, a little blood oozes up the hollow of the ear, and it is over. Had he crept as far as the threshold of his bury the full dark eyeball would have been dimmed by the sand thrown on it by his last effort.

If you have the patience to resume your seat and wait, you may very likely obtain another shot presently from the same ambush. The young rabbits, which are the sort you want, have not yet had much experience of danger, and may venture forth again, or at all events another may be got in other parts of the same field. I remember firing eight successive times in the same meadow during one evening, by changing about from summer-rick to summer-rick. Once I crept on hands and knees some sixty or eighty yards, keeping a rick all the time between me and the rabbit and so shot him. In long grass by lying down at full length and dragging my limbs behind me – progressing rather by the arms only than with aid of the knees – I have approached rabbits straight across the open meadow without the least shelter, crawling towards them right, as it were, before their faces. At the least perking-up of ears or sign of alarm I stopped. The top of my head was never above the bennets and sorrel, so that the least lowering of my neck was sufficient to hide me altogether. The very fact of approaching in front was favourable, as rabbits do not seem able to see so well straight before them as in any other direction. Hares are notoriously deficient of vision in that way, and rabbits in some degree share the defect. But such approach, whether with gun or rifle, can only be accomplished by the exercise of extreme patience and unwavering attention upon the animals, so that the faintest suspicion may be allayed by stillness.

After such an amount of trouble you naturally wish to make quite sure of your game, and would rather wait some time till the rabbit turns and offers a sure mark, than see him presently scramble wounded into a burrow. The shoulder is the safest spot; a rabbit will often run with shot in the head, but pellets near the heart are usually deadly; besides which, if the shoulder is disabled, it does not matter how much he kicks, he cannot guide himself, and so cannot escape. But as the shoulder is the very best part for eating– like the wing of the fowl – it is desirable when shooting a young rabbit not to injure the flesh there or cause it to be bloodstained. You must, then, wait till near enough to put plenty of shot in the head, enough to stun at once. When you can see the eyeball distinctly you are sure of killing, and it is the deadliest spot if you can draw a bead on it. For in this kind of shooting the one object should be to kill outright; merely to wound is both cruel and bad economy.

Summer-ricks are not general now, the hay being carted to the yard, and sheltered by the rick-cloth, but large haycocks occasionally remain some time in the fields; or you may hide behind a tree, a hawthorn, or projecting bush. A chance shot may be obtained sometimes by walking very quietly up to a hedge and peering through, but many rabbits are lost when shooting at them through a hedge. If there is one out in the grass on the other side, with a little manoeuvring you may manage to get an aim clear of boughs. But if the rabbit be not killed on the instant he is nearly sure to escape, since it is always slow work and sometimes impossible to force one's way through a thick hedge. By the time you have run round to the gate the rabbit is dying four feet deep in the mound. With a dog it might be different, but dogs cannot well be taken for ambush-shooting; even a dog often fails when a rabbit has so long a start as thirty yards. The most difficult running shot at a rabbit is perhaps when he crosses a gateway on the other side; the spars, though horizontal, somehow deceive the eye, and generally receive most of the shot. Nor is it easy to shoot over a gate if at a short distance from it.

The easiest place to procure a rabbit is where there is a hollow or a disused quarry. Such hollows may be seen in meadows at the foot of wooded slopes. If a hedge bounds or crosses the hollow, if there is a burrow in it, you have only to walk in the evening gently up to the verge, and, taking care that your head is not visible too soon, are sure to get a shot, as the rabbits do not for some time scent or see any one above them. Where they feed in the bottom of an old quarry the same thing may be done. Burrows in such places should not be ferreted too much, nor the rabbits too much disturbed. The owner will then be able to shoot a rabbit almost whenever he wishes; a thing he certainly cannot do elsewhere; for although there may be a hundred in a mound, they may not be out just when he wants them. Some people used to take pleasure in having 'blue' rabbits about their grounds. These were the descendants of black tame animals turned out long previously; their colour toned down by interbreeding with the wild. Some thought that they could distinguish between the wood rabbit and the rabbit of the hill or the field warrens, and would pronounce where you had shot your game; the one having a deeper brown than the other, at least in that locality. But of recent years the pleasant minutiae of sport, not alone concerning rabbits, have rather fallen into disuse and oblivion.

from *Chronicles of the Hedges,* 1948

The First Gun

A beautiful piece of workmanship it was: my new double breechloader is a coarse common thing to compare with it. Long and slender and light as a feather, it came to the shoulder with wonderful ease. Then there was a groove on the barrel at the breech and for some inches up which caught the eye and guided the glance like a trough to the sight at the muzzle and thence to the bird. The stock was shod with brass, and the trigger-guard was of brass, with a kind of flange stretching half-way down to the butt and inserted in the wood. After a few minutes' polishing it shone like gold, and to see the sunlight flash on it was a joy.

You might note the grain of the barrel, for it had not been browned; and it took a good deal of sand to get the rust off. By aid of a little oil and careful wiping after a shower it was easy to keep it bright. Those browned barrels only encourage idleness. The lock was a trifle dull at first, simply from lack of use. A small screwdriver soon had it to pieces, and it speedily clicked again sweet as a flute. If the hammer came back rather far when at full-cock, that was because the lock had been converted from a flint, and you could not expect it to be absolutely perfect. Besides which, as the fall was longer the blow was heavier, and the cap was sure to explode.

By old farmhouses, mostly in exposed places (for which there is a reason), one or more huge walnut trees may be found. The provident folk of those days planted them with the purpose of having their own gunstocks cut out of the wood when the tree was thrown. They could then be sure it was really walnut, and a choice piece of timber thoroughly well seasoned. I like to think of those times, when men settled themselves down, and planted and planned and laid out their gardens and orchards and woods, as if they and their sons and sons' sons, to the twentieth generation, were sure to enjoy the fruit of their labour.

The reason why the walnuts are put in exposed places, on the slope of a rise, with open aspect to the east and north, is because the walnut is a foolish tree that will not learn by experience. If it feels the

23

warmth of a few genial days in early spring, it immediately protrudes its buds; and the next morning a bitter frost cuts down every hope of fruit for that year, leaving the leaf as black as may be. Wherefore the east wind is desirable to keep it as backward as possible.

There was a story that the stock of this gun had been cut out of a walnut tree that was thrown on the place by my great-grandfather, who saw it well seasoned, being a connoisseur of timber, which is, indeed, a sort of instinct in all his descendants. And a vast store of philosophy there is in timber if you study it aright.

After cleaning the gun and trying it at a mark, the next thing was to get a good shot with it. Now there was an elm that stood out from the hedge a little, almost at the top of the meadow, not above five-and-twenty yards from the other hedge that bounded the field. Two mounds could therefore be commanded by any one in ambush behind the elm, and all the angular corner of the mead was within range.

It was not far from the house; but the ground sank into a depression there, and the ridge of it behind shut out everything except just the roof of the tallest hayrick. As one sat on the sward behind the elm, with the back turned on the rick and nothing in front but the tall elms and the oaks in the other hedge, it was quite easy to fancy it the verge of the prairie with the backwoods close by.

The rabbits had scratched the yellow sand right out into the grass—it is always very much brighter in colour where they have just been at work—and the fern, already almost yellow too, shaded the mouths of their buries. Thick bramble bushes grew out from the mound and filled the space between it and the elm: there were a few late flowers on them still, but the rest were hardening into red sour berries. Westwards, the afternoon sun, with all his autumn heat, shone full against the hedge and into the recess, and there was not the shadow of a leaf for shelter on that side.

The gun was on the turf, and the little hoppers kept jumping out of the grass on to the stock: once their king, a grasshopper, alighted on it and rested, his green limbs tipped with red rising above his back. About the distant wood and the hills there was a soft faint haze, which is what Nature finishes her pictures with. Something in the atmosphere which made it almost visible: all the trees seemed to stand in a liquid light – the sunbeams were suspended in the air instead of passing through. The butterflies even were very idle in the slumberous warmth; and the great green dragon-fly rested on a leaf, his tail arched a little downwards, just as he puts it when he wishes to stop suddenly in his flight.

The broad glittering trigger-guard got quite hot in the sun, and the stock was warm when I felt it every now and then. The grain of the walnut-wood showed plainly through the light polish: it was not varnished like the stock of the double-barrel they kept padlocked to the rack over the high mantelpiece indoors. Still you could see the varnish. It was of a rich dark horse-chestnut colour, and yet so bright and clear that if held close you could see your face in it. Behind it the grain of the wood was just perceptible; especially at the grip, where hard hands had worn it away somewhat. The secret of that varnish is lost–like that of the varnish on the priceless old violins.

But you could feel the wood more in my gun: so that it was difficult to keep the hand off it, though the rabbits would not come out; and the shadowless recess grew like a furnace, for it focussed the rays of the sun. The heat on the sunny side of a thick hedge between three and four in the afternoon is almost tropical if you remain still, because the air is motionless: the only relief is to hold your hat loose; or tilt it against your head, the other edge of the brim on the ground. Then the grass-blades rise up level with the forehead. There is a delicious smell in growing grass, and a sweetness comes up from the earth.

Still it got hotter and hotter; and it was not possible to move in the least degree, lest a brown creature sitting on the sand at the mouth of his hole, and hidden himself by the fern, should immediately note it. And Orion was waiting in the rickyard for the sound of the report, and very likely the shepherd too. We knew that men in Africa, watched by lions, had kept still in the sunshine till, reflected from the rock, it literally scorched them, not daring to move; and we knew all about the stoicism of the Red Indians. But Ulysses was ever my pattern and model: that man of infinite patience and resource.

So, though the sun might burn and the air become suffocating in that close corner, and the quivering line of heat across the meadow make the eyes dizzy to watch, yet not a limb must be moved. The black flies came in crowds; but they are not so tormenting if you plunge your face in the grass, though they titillate the back of the hand as they run over it. Under the bramble bush was a bury that did not look much used; and once or twice a great blue fly came out of it, the buzz at first sounding hollow and afar off and becoming clearer as it approached the mouth of the hole. There was the carcass of a dead rabbit inside no doubt.

A humble-bee wandering along – they are restless things – buzzed right under my hat, and became entangled in the grass by my ear. Now we knew by experience in taking their honey that they could sting sharply if irritated, though good-tempered by nature. How he 'burred' and buzzed and droned! – till by-and-by, crawling up the back of my head, he found an open space and sailed away. Then, looking out again, there was a pair of ears in the grass not ten yards distant: a rabbit had come out at last. But the first delight was quickly over: the ears were short and sharply pointed, and almost pinkly transparent.

What would the shepherd say if I brought home one of his hated enemies no bigger than a rat? The young rabbit made waiting still more painful, being far enough from the hedge to get a clear view into the recess if anything attracted his notice. Why the shepherd hated rabbits was because the sheep would not feed where they had worn their runs in the grass. Not the least movement was possible now – not even that little shifting which makes a position just endurable: the heat seemed to increase; the thought of Ulysses could hardly restrain the almost irresistible desire to stir.

When, suddenly, there was a slight rustling among the boughs of an oak in the other hedge, as of wings against twigs: it was a woodpigeon, better game than a rabbit. He would, I knew, first look round before he settled himself to preen his feathers on the branch, and, if everything was still while that keen inspection lasted, would

26

never notice me. This is their habit – and the closer you are underneath them the less chance of their perceiving you: for a pigeon perched rarely looks straight downwards. If flying, it is just the reverse; for then they seem to see under them quicker than in any other direction.

Slowly lifting the long barrel of the gun – it was fortunate the sunlight glancing on the bright barrel was not reflected towards the oak – I got it to bear upon the bird; but then came a doubt. It was all eight-and-twenty yards across the angle of the meadow to the oak – a tremendous long shot under the circumstances. For they would not trust us with the large copper powder-flask, but only with a little pistol-flask (it had belonged to the pair of pistols we tried to find), and we were ordered not to use more than a charge and a half at a time. That was quite enough to kill blackbirds. (The noise of the report was always a check in this way; such a trifle of powder only made a slight puff.)

Shot there was in plenty – a whole tobacco-pipe bowl full, carefully measured out of the old yellow canvas money-bag that did for a shot belt. A starling could be knocked off the chimney with this charge easily, and so could a blackbird roosting in a bush at night. But a woodpigeon nearly thirty yards distant was another matter; for the old folk (and the birdkeepers too) said that their quills were so hard the shot would glance aside unless it came with great force. Very likely the pigeon would escape, and all the rabbits in the buries would be too frightened to come out at all.

A beautiful bird he was on the bough, perched well in view and clearly defined against the sky behind; and my eye travelled along the groove on the breech and up the barrel, and so to the sight and across to him; and the finger, which always would keep time with the eye, pulled at the trigger.

A mere puff of a report, and then a desperate fluttering in the tree and a cloud of white feathers floating above the hedge, and a heavy fall among the bushes. He was down, and Orion's spaniel (that came racing like mad from the rickyard the instant he heard the discharge) had him in a moment. Orion followed quickly. Then the shepherd came up, rather stiff on his legs from rheumatism, and stepped the distance, declaring it was thirty yards good; after which we all walked home in triumph.

from *The Amateur Poacher*, 1879

The Partridge and the Hawk

Just at this season last year a sportsman one day sat down 'on a grassy bank', under a shady oak, and waited, with gun in hand, to pick off a couple of young rabbits, whose dainty white meat chanced to be fancied by an invalid. It was in a meadow of the good old English sort, full of tall moving grass and golden buttercups, and surrounded by a thick hawthorn hedge – moated, too, with a deep though dry ditch – and rendered beautiful by numbers of stately elms and oaks. When young June opens, the various greens of such a woodland meadow are lovely beyond compare. There is the light green of the ash, the sober green of the elm, the sheeny green of the willow, the quivering pale green of the aspen; the dark sombre firs, touched up with the yellow of their spring shoots; the grass as the ground colour, spangled with gold, and blue and red flowers; and over all, resting as it were on the top-most oak branches, the glorious azure sky. Here and there scattered along the hawthorn hedge are specks of white – it is the opening wild roses. 'Fink-fink-fink' – listen, it is a passing bevy of greenfinches; they do not sing, yet there is a pleasant sweetness in the sound as they go gaily by.

Perhaps it was the soft warmth of the summer breeze, or the soothing 'coo, coo' of the doves in the hawthorn, but the rabbits were forgotten, the gun was leant against the bank, and with the great oak for a support, he fell asleep. He woke with a sudden start, and instinctively grasped the gun. Right over his head, hardly a yard above it, had flown a frightened partridge, whose loudly whirring wings and cries had disturbed his slumber. After the partridge came a hawk, close on her. With a furious spurt, so to say, the hawk overtook his prey, and struck her to the ground, not twenty-five yards distant. But in falling somehow the two got separate, the hawk had not had the opportunity to fix his talons firmly in his prey; so that for the moment the two birds as it were looked at each other, about a foot apart. This was time enough for a practised shot. There was a flash and a report, and the hawk was knocked all to pieces, not a pellet striking the game bird, secure at that time of year. The partridge was so stunned with fright as to lie quite still and allow herself to be picked up and handled. Beyond the loss of a few feathers she was uninjured, though the rapid pulsations of the heart told of intense terror. In three minutes the bird flew away in safety, for the time at least – for the spring and early summer is a period of cruel warfare with, and merciless pursuit of, the partridge.

The bird had undoubtedly fallen into the power of the hawk while endeavouring to distract him from her young. Anxious Mrs Partridge, so soon as the brood can follow her, likes to lead them near a tolerably thick hedge, so that upon the appearance of a hawk or crow in the sky she can hurry them into cover out of sight. For the keen eyes of the hawk, as he sails slowly above the fields, see with ease all that goes on even in the depths of the tall moving grass, when not so much as a mouse can hide from him, but the thick hawthorn hedge puzzles him. He cannot see through bough and branches, and if only the brood escape his glance for a few seconds they are safe. Here is a use for hedges, O iconoclasts of utility, who would level all our fair woodlands to drive a steam plough over. Yet when the brood can fly well, they seem to leave the cover a good deal, and to seek the more open 'leazes', those great razing fields of thirty, forty, and even sixty acres, where the grass is never very long. Here they keep out a long way from the hedges, and especially so towards the evening, so that when with winter the hedges grow thin and devoid of leaves, the partridges gather together in the midst of these great fields, where it is often extremely difficult to approach them. This may be from dread of the stealthy thieves that prowl about the hedges seeking what they may devour, such as the sneaking weasels and the bolder stoats, and worse, far worse than either, the rat. Shoot him down when and wherever you see him, all ye keepers, aye, and sportsmen too, this most abominable pest, the rat. Not the water-rat, which is harmless, and whose odd ways are pretty to watch, but the larger house-rat, who has gone abroad into the field. He is easily distinguished, growing, as he often does, to immense size, with a tail as thick as a whip-handle. He will kill anything and everything – young partridges, rabbits, all that he can catch or surprise, and nothing can face his terrible teeth. He will take the very moorhens out of your ornamental water, and even the very fish.

from the article 'The Persecution of St. Partridge',
Field and Farm, 1957

Hare Coursing

Apple-bloom and golden fruit too are gone, and the houses show more now among the bare trees; but as the rim of the ruddy November sun comes forth from the edge of a cloud there appears a buff tint everywhere in the background. When elm and ash are bare the oaks retain their leaves, and these are illumined by the autumn beams. Over-topped by tall elms and hidden by the orchards, the oaks were hardly seen in summer; now they are found to be numerous and give the prevailing hue to the place.

Dickon taps the dashboard as the mare at last tops the hill, and away she speeds along the level plateau for the Downs. Two greyhounds are with us; two more have gone on under charge of a boy. Skirting the hills a mile or two, we presently leave the road and drive over the turf: there is no track, but Dickon knows his way. The rendezvous is a small fir plantation, the young trees in which are but shoulder-high. Below is a plain entirely surrounded by the hills, and partly green with root crops: more than one flock of sheep is down there, and two teams ploughing the stubble. Neither the ploughmen nor the shepherds take the least heed of us, except to watch for the sport. The spare couple are fastened in the trap; the boy jumps up and takes the reins. Dickon puts the slip on the couple that are to run first, and we begin to range.

Just at the foot of the hill the grass is tall and grey; there, too, are the dead dry stalks of many plants that cultivation has driven from the ploughed fields and that find a refuge at the edge. A hare starts from the very verge and makes up the Downs. Dickon slips the hounds, and a faint halloo comes from the shepherds and the ploughmen. It is a beautiful sight to see the hounds bound over the sward; the sinewy back bends like a bow, but a bow that, instead of an arrow, shoots itself; he deep chests drink the air. Is there any moment so joyful in life as the second when the chase begins? As we gaze, before we even step forward, the hare is over the ridge and out of sight. Then we race and tear up the slope; then the boy in the trap flaps the reins and away goes the mare out of sight too.

Dickon is long and rawboned, a powerful fellow, strong of limb, and twice my build; but he sips too often at the brown brandy, and after the first burst I can head him. But he knows the hills and the route the hare will take, so that I have but to keep pace. In five minutes as we cross a ridge we see the game again; the hare is circling back—she passes under us not fifty yards away, as we stand panting on the hill. The youngest hound gains, and runs right over her; she doubles, the older hound picks up the running. By a furze-bush she doubles again; but the young one turns her – the next moment she is in the jaws of the old dog.

Again and again the hounds are slipped, now one couple, now the other: we pant, and can scarcely speak with running, but the wild excitement of the hour and the sweet pure air of the Downs supply fresh strength. The little lad brings the mare anywhere: through the furze, among the flint-pits, jolting over the ruts, she rattles along with sure alacrity. There are five hares in the sack under the straw when at last we get up and slowly drive down to the highway, reaching it some two miles from where we left it. Dickon sends the dogs home by the boy on foot; we drive round and return to the village.

from *The Amateur Poacher*, 1879

Game in the Furrows

There are holes on the hills, not above a yard deep and entering the slope horizontally, which are said to be used by the hares more in a playful mood than from any real desire of shelter. Yet they dislike wet; most wild animals do. Birds, on the contrary, find it answers their purpose, grubs and worms abounding at such times. Though the hare is of a wandering disposition he usually returns to the same form, and, if undisturbed, will use it every day for a length of time, at night perhaps being miles away. If hard pressed by the dogs he will leap a broad brook in fine style, but he usually prefers to cross by a bridge. In the evening, as it grows dusk, if you watch from the elevation of the entrenchment, you may see these creatures steal out into the level cornfield below, first one, then two, presently five or six– looming much larger than they really are in the dusk, and seeming to appear on the scene suddenly. They have a trick of stealing along close to the low mounds which divide arable fields, so that they are unobserved till they turn out into the open ground.

It is not easy to distinguish a hare when crouching in a ploughed field, his colour harmonises so well with the clods; so that an unpractised eye generally fails to note him. An old hand with the gun cannot pass a field without involuntarily glancing along the furrows made by the plough to see if their regular grooves are broken by anything hiding therein. The ploughmen usually take special care with their work near public roads, so that the furrows end on to the base of the highway shall be mathematically straight. They often succeed so well that the furrows look as if traced with a ruler, and exhibit curious effects of vanishing perspective. Along the furrow, just as it is turned, there runs a shimmering light as the eye traces it up. The ploughshare, heavy and drawn with great force, smooths the earth as it cleaves it, giving it for a time a 'face' as it were, the moisture on which reflects the light. If you watch the farmers driving to market, you will see that they glance up the furrows to note the workmanship and look for game; you may tell from a distance if they espy a hare by the check of the rein and the extended hand pointing.

The partridges, too, cower as they hear the noise of wheels or footsteps, but their brown backs, rounded as they stoop, do not deceive the eye that knows full well the irregular shape taken by lumps of earth. Both hares and rabbits may be watched with ease from an elevation, and if you remain quiet will rarely discover your presence while you are above them. They keep a sharp look-out all round, but never think of glancing upwards, unless, of course, some unusual noise attracts attention.

Looking away from the brow of the hill here over the rampart, see, yonder in the narrow hollow a flock is feeding: you can tell even so far off that it is feeding, because the sheep are scattered about, dotted hither and thither over the surface. It is their habit the moment they are driven to run together. Farther away, slowly travelling up a distant down, another flock, packed close, rises towards the ridge, like a thick white mist stealthily ascending the slope.

Just outside the trench, almost within reach, there lies a small white something, half hidden by the grass. It is the skull of a hare, bleached by the winds and the dew and the heat of the summer sun. The skeleton has disappeared, nothing but the bony casing of the head remains, with its dim suggestiveness of life, polished and smooth from the friction of the elements. Holding it in the hand the shadow falls into and darkens the cavities once filled by the wistful eyes which once glanced down from the summit here upon the sweet clover fields beneath. Beasts of prey and wandering dogs have carried away the bones of the skeleton, dropping them far apart; the crows and the ants doubtless had their share of the carcass. Perhaps a wound caused by shot that did not immediately check his speed, or wasting disease depriving him of strength to obtain food, brought him low; maybe an insidious enemy crept on him in his form.

The joy in life of these animals – indeed, of almost all animals and birds in freedom – is very great. You may see it in every motion; in the lissom bound of the hare, the playful leap of the rabbit, the song that the lark and the finch must sing; the soft, loving coo of the dove in the hawthorn; the blackbird ruffling out his feathers on a rail. The sense of living – the consciousness of seeing and feeling – is manifestly intense in them all, and is in itself an exquisite pleasure. Their appetites seem ever fresh: they rush to the banquet spread by Mother Earth with a gusto that Lucullus never knew in the midst of his artistic gluttony; they drink from the stream with dainty sips as though it were richest wine. Watch the birds in the spring; the pairs dance from bough to bough, and know not how to express their wild happiness. The hare rejoices in the swiftness of his limbs: his nostrils sniff the air, his strong sinews spurn the earth; like an arrow from a bow he shoots up the steep hill that we must clamber slowly, halting half-way to breathe. On outspread wings the swallow floats above, then slants downwards with a rapid swoop, and with the impetus of the motion rises easily. Therefore it is that this skull here, lying so light in the palm of the hand, with the bright sunshine falling on it, and a shadowy darkness in the vacant orbits of the eyes, fills us with sadness. 'As leaves on leaves, so men on men decay' – how much more so with these creatures whose generations are so short!

from *Wild Life in a Southern County*, 1879

The Art of Shooting

The sense of genuine pleasure felt while enjoying the sport of shooting is, perhaps, the very reason why many who desire to excel in it fail to achieve more than a moderate degree of proficiency. They do not pause a moment to analyse the connection between cause and effect as illustrated by a fortunate hit, or a disgraceful miss. Anxious as they are to succeed they cannot check the irresistible inclination to fire away: there is a natural impatience of cool reflection in the very moment of action; yet it is by the ability to think amid the mad rage of conflict that the General wins the battle. This instinctive eagerness to multiply shot on shot is a subject deserving of philosophic study. The breechloader has intensified it by affording extreme facilities: you may see this characteristic trait of human nature exhibit itself in full force at the pheasant battue, and in more serious frays it is stated that the difficulty is not to march the soldier to the front, but to prevent him from wasting his ammunition. The finger somehow itches to pull the trigger. Is it a hereditary instinct transmitted from the primeval days when men's whole lives were spent in handling the bow? The sportsman is often seemingly only desirous of repeating the excitement of the explosion as rapidly as possibly, and dreams of nothing further. By sheer dint of such repetition he in time acquires a certain purely manual dexterity but can never advance. It is even doubtful whether a man who wishes to become a really good shot should at first use the breechloader, on account of this temptation to indiscriminate firing. But as the change from one kind of weapon to another – which must at some period be made – is always temporarily detrimental to the skill that has been acquired, it appears best to begin at once with the improved gun. The necessary check is easily provided by resolving to carry only a few cartridges – say half-a-dozen – for the excursion, which will teach the lesson of using them to the greatest advantage.

The pleasure of shooting is indeed so intense as to momentarily obscure the reflective faculties by throwing a sort of glamour over the act. The flash from the muzzle, the sound of the discharge – for we quickly grow to love the sound, and even the smell of the powder – the nervous haste to insert fresh cartridges, the motions of the dogs, the knowledge that friendly competitors are close by, all these tend to create an environment which quite suspends judgement and observation. We pull the trigger, and lo! The bird is down as if the barrel were a magic tube that fulfils the wish almost before it has formed itself. The process that intervenes between the lifting of the gun and the fall of the game is lost to notice: the idea that any interval, or process at all, takes place never occurs. But in despite of this glamour, and excitement, it is certain that an interval does elapse, that a process is gone through, and that upon the manner in which this second of time is utilized depends the success of the sportsman.

Putting upon one side for the present, his hand, eye, nerves, and personality, reducing the conditions to the gun itself and to the game, shooting resolves itself into a mathematical problem; how to project a straight line to a given point? A clear idea may be obtained by imagining for a moment that the barrel, instead of ending abruptly at, say, 28 inches from the breech, is elongated till the muzzle touches the object aimed at. Just for the sake of illustration, in order to get a thorough conception of the line of sight, suppose the barrel thirty yards instead of thirty inches long, so that upon pulling the trigger the cartridge might travel all the way to its destination through the tube instead of the air. Take a breech-loading gun, and first holding it in the position of inserting a cartridge, raise it to a level with the eye (the breech open) and glance through the barrel at a distant mark. Then imagine the cylinder continued for the whole of that distance prolonged till the end touches it, and no one can fail to grasp the idea of the line of sight. You have to act in relation to the gun and to the game in such a manner as if the shot traversed the atmosphere in an absolutely straight line – 'as straight as a gunbarrel'. To cause the shot to do that is evident that the barrel at the second of the discharge must exactly correspond with a line drawn from the game to the eye. In actual fact the shot really rises and falls slightly – if the range is a long one – and this is called the trajectory, but this in no degree impairs the accuracy of the deduction above. Roughly the course of the shot answers to a very low arc of which the line of sight forms the chord, but as both chord and arc are in the same plane, in studying the art of shooting and in practice the straight chord alone has to be considered. I am writing of course of the shot-gun only here.

Now close the breech of the gun, and glance along the barrel in the ordinary manner, aiming say at a tree, and endeavour to get rid of the sense of an intervening space between the muzzle and the mark. Much confusion is often caused in the mind of the sportsman by the attempt to do two things at once – to take a correct aim, and to judge the distance to the object. The truth is that the distance should be judged before the stock of the gun comes to the shoulder – in the second of time which elapses while it is being lifted. When the gun is at once at the shoulder, and the sight so to say lies up the barrel, it is in vain to attempt to measure the space intervening between the eye and the bird. It is impossible in such an endeavour to avoid glancing sideways – it may be but for the tenth of a second, but that is long enough to destroy what I must for convenience call the impulse of the aim.

The very best aim is that which comes with the first rush of the senses – of the nerves, the hand, the eye – towards the game. If that is checked either by thought of correcting – of verifying it – or by the mechanical check of the involuntary sideways motion of the eyeball it is in vain to endeavour to recover it. This moment of instinctive impulse is so precious to the sportsman that I would counsel him to run the risk of firing uselessly at a bird a hundred yards off, than degenerate into an involuntary habit of verifying distance. The eye can only judge distance by the assistance of other objects than that at which the aim is taken, as by trees, bushes, a bunch of grass, a gateway, or a tall thistle, anything to act like the graduated marks on a scale. The absence of these aids is the reason why it is so difficult to guess the number of yards across a piece of water, and perhaps still more difficult to determine with any certainty the height of a bird flying overhead with nothing but the sky – the height of which is an unknown quantity – as a background. So far as the sight is concerned, the eye judges distance by the joint action of the two eyes, binocular vision. In taking aim at an object the shooter only uses one eye. This is the true distribution.

from *Field and Farm*, 1957

Snow Shooting

Sir Walter Scott, who was not only a good shot and a good rider but evidently a good sportsman also, represents two of his country gentlemen in 'Guy Mannering' as laughing very heartily at the idea of going shooting in the snow; and no doubt such is not the kind of weather for making a large bag. Nobody would choose such a time for shooting his best pheasant covers. Snipe and woodcock are only really plentiful in open weather. Partridge shooting is out of the question, except in one peculiar case; and as for tracking hares in the snow, that has long been considered rank poaching, in spite of the authority of Xenophon. But for all that, there are certain kinds of shooting to be got in very hard weather, which, by a certain class of sportsmen at all events, are not to be enjoyed at other times, which, combined with the keen frosty air, and the exhilarating effect of a white landscape upon all well-constituted minds, give a charm of its own to a walk in the snow, though the sportsman must be prepared to be content with a moderate number of shots.

In the inland counties, and especially along the running brooks and small rivers which wind along the midland meadows, you rarely have a chance at wildfowl, except in a very hard frost, which, of course, never lasts many weeks without a deep snow. Even then, and where the shooter has other ground to himself, he must not expect to kill many. These birds, ducks, teal, and sometimes a few widgeon, come to the unfrozen streams to feed, and a few remain there all day. But they are, of course, very wild, and of the few that you may find in a walk of three or four miles still fewer will rise within shot. However, if you know the likely places, you will seldom have a blank day, if no one has disturbed the water before your arrival. As the object of the ducks in coming up these inland brooks is to find unfrozen water, the places to look for them are, of course, those where it is slightly protected from the frost, either by deep overhanging banks, by an old hollow tree, or by a clump of bushes. Whenever there is a sharp bend, and consequently a sharp current which rejects the embraces of the frost, or where a smaller brook or ditch empties itself into the main stream, you have a good chance of finding fowl.

One advantage of the snow is that you can steal upon them very quietly, and the best plan is generally to make a slight detour when you approach such a spot as we have mentioned, and then to walk straight down upon it, not to approach it by the bank. Then as you softly but rapidly get near to some snug corner where a tree bent double with age or a straggling blackthorn bush hangs over the confluence of two little rushy streamlets, your dog at heel, and both he and yourself in a state of nervous expectation, suddenly you hear the welcome splash and quack, and straight up into the air shoot three dark objects, and wheel over your head preparatory to going straight off. Two ducks and a mallard. Down comes one of the ducks upon the frozen snow, and away goes the other with her mate. But your second barrel has done its work too. The mallard is hard hit. He gradually lags behind the duck, and, lowering his flight, comes down again at last in a ditch perhaps a quarter of a mile off. But it is on the other side of the brook. How to get over is the puzzle. The ice won't bear, and to go up to your middle in that sort of weather is no joke. However, you must risk it; and eventually, by means of a lucky jump, break through upon the other side in water not above your calves. Now it is Bruno's turn, for wounded ducks lie very close indeed, and you could not mark the place exactly. Luckily the hedge is a low one, so it does not much matter which side he goes out, and your spaniel hunts the ditch with a full consciousness of the importance of his mission. There is a rustle in the reeds, and out scrambles the bird, this time without any quacking, and tries to make a fly of it, straight in front of you. You fire, and his troubles are over; and your dog brings him up to you with an expression upon his honest and sagacious countenance which gives a new charm to success. Now is not this couple of ducks worth six times the number of partridges or pheasants killed in the ordinary fashion? Have you not had more real sport in bagging them; and does not the very weather itself make you think better of yourself for doing it?

But before you go back to the brook it may be worth while to try round some of these ditches and a bit of boggy ground, which is always kept wet by a spring in the hardest weather. Here, as you hoped, up jump a couple of snipe with that peculiar cry more exciting, perhaps, than the noise made in rising by any other game bird. They spring out of some tufts of sedge and coarse grass, and separate to right and left as usual – not, however, in this case to reunite up aloft, like spirits parted on the earth. You feel sure of the first as you pull the trigger, and as he turns up his white waistcoat in the air you wheel round to do the same for his fellow. But he has got rather too far to be made sure of, and gets away apparently untouched, though your conscience will make itself heard for more than one brief moment, telling you that you ought to have killed him. But never mind, you feel the weight of the ducks in your shooting-jacket pockets, and trudge contentedly back to the brook, which you pursue perhaps for another mile or two. If you are lucky, you pick up perhaps a teal or even another duck before you turn your face homewards about sunset, taking part of your way the course of another little brook, the sides of which are a little more swampy than those you have left. There is no reason why you should not get another shot or two at snipe before you leave the low ground, and say you bag another couple. Here you have got a couple of duck, a leash of snipe, and a teal for your day in the snow. And though over the same ground in open November weather you might have killed six or eight couple of snipe, you would have had no chance at wildfowl; and is not such a day, we ask, as thoroughly delightful in the way of sport as the more ordinary kinds of winter shooting? There are few moments, we think, when a man feels better satisfied with himself than when he sits down to take off his wet boots after a long tramp through the snow, rewarded by the kind of bag we have described.

Another kind of sport to be had in perfection in a deep snow and at no other time is shooting French partridges out of hedgerows. Generally speaking, the only way of killing any number of these ignoble fowl is by driving; but in a heavy snow they cannot run, and if you can get them, as you easily can, to take to the ditch bottom, they will lie till a dog turns them out. With a gun on each side of the hedge, both being steady shots and used to the sport, ten or twelve brace may readily be killed in a day where the birds are at all plentiful. But they puzzle a novice. They burst out of the snow-covered briars with a loud noise, and then fly so clumsily and awkwardly that the very ease of the shot makes you miss it, unless you are used to the style. But a couple of practised shots may do great execution in this way; and nobody can pretend that you have not a perfect right to kill French partridges in any way that you can. They never behave themselves like gentlemen, and deserve no quarter. And a few days' shooting of this kind avenges you for wasted days and spoiled dogs in September more amply even than a good drive. There is a sense of having got the birds under for once, which is highly soothing to one's feelings, as they seem to lie more completely at your mercy than when they are driven over your head. Our own opinion is, too, that shooting even fieldfares under the same conditions is no contemptible amusement. The birds are quite as good to eat as a French partridge in January, and quite as difficult to shoot. The only way to kill any quantity is for two guns to take the two sides of some tall thick blackthorn or whitethorn hedge, well stocked with hips and haws, and slightly sinuous in its course. The birds are unapproachable except in the severest weather, and then, too, unless the hard frozen ground is carpeted with snow so as to smother your footfalls. When that is the case you may really have some good sport at what is commonly called schoolboys' game. Those hedges are the best which run a long way without intersection, like the thick tall fences which skirt the wide pastures of Leicestershire or the 'long grey fields' described by the poet of Lincolnshire [Tennyson]. The two guns should station themselves at one end, and a boy at the other, who, as the two shooters advance, will gradually walk towards them. The fieldfares, who are feeding on the hedge fruit, are loth to quit the hedge, especially as no other is near, and keep flying and chattering backwards and forwards across it and alongside of it, giving you good broadside shots, though you must be very quick, as they top the hedge, and shots which you can take more deliberately, as they fly along in front of you.

When you have done one hedge you go off to another; and you may drive the birds backwards and forwards from hedge to hedge as you may drive partridges from turnip-field of turnip-field. In this way two or three dozen of these birds may be killed in a deep snow; and, either served up afterwards in a pudding or cold, roasted, for breakfast, are very nice eating. But we have forgotten a still better bird than the fieldfare, which can be successfully stalked amidst the snow. Even the wood-pigeon grows less wary in the intense cold, and when no ringing sound of footsteps warns him of the approach of man. They feed at these times in the turnip-fields, and if you can creep quietly up to the hedge you can often get a right and left as soon as you stand up and show yourself. Then, of course, in many parts of the country a hard frost and snow brings many unusual winter visitors, and enables the naturalist to enrich his collection with specimens not otherwise procurable.

And this, perhaps, is the place for a few words on the outcry against killing rare birds. Now, when birds indigenous to this country, and which only the increase of population and clearance of woods and marshes have made scarce among us, are deliberately killed in the breeding season when they are evidently preparing to build, no words are strong enough to condemn such wanton destruction, for there is a possibility that such birds, if protected, might become less scarce, though never again numerous. But these observations apply only to a very small class of birds. There is another class, two of which we saw mentioned the other day – the spotted crake and the solitary snipe – which always have been scarce in this country and never would be otherwise, though not a single one were shot throughout the year. What harm can be done by shooting one of these when the rare chance of doing so occurs? The few that are killed every year, probably not a dozen in the three kingdoms, would not prevent them multiplying if it was their nature to do so; while in the case of birds which do not belong to this country, and which, though a solitary couple might be induced to breed here now and then, would never become permanent members of our fauna, it is absurd to cry out against shooting them. There are people who seem to suppose that, if not shot, they would remain here. That is not the case. The hard weather brings them, and the mild weather takes them away. And whatever other crime there may be in shooting them, it is not the crime of killing down rare British birds which, if spared, might become comparatively common.

from *Pall Mall Gazette*, 30 December 1874

A Plea for Pheasant Shooting

'Pheasant-shooting? Mere slaughter, sir, tame as barn-door fowls! Contemptible! All you have to do is blaze away,' such is a rapid summary of the opinions perpetually repeated of late years as regularly as October comes round, and in most cases, probably, by persons who have never felt a double-barrel grow hot in their hand in their lives.

The fact is that, although perhaps in some few instances the battue is organised a little too much in the sense of not allowing sufficient 'law' to the game, pheasant-shooting is by no means such a simple matter. The bird, though apparently big enough to be hit with ease, is really very deceptive, the long neck, and longer tail, and the feathers of the body, occupy so much space, as it were, that the nucleus and vital part is in a measure concealed, or, rather, the eye does not distinguish the difference. This is seen in the numbers of birds that get their tails blown off, and many a man who thought he was going to make a good bag at his first attempt has been woefully disappointed to see a cloud of feathers floating in the air, and the game half a mile away taking shelter in another copse.

Generally, the sportsman has but a limited space in which to take aim, he is posted, say, in a green lane with the edge of a wood on his right hand, and on his left a low hedge, then a narrow, very narrow strip of open ground, bordered by a thick fir plantation. The bird comes with a rush – like a rocket – you cannot see him approach, he is on you all at once, over your head perhaps, and in your haste lest he get into the firs you pull the trigger and lose him. The line of flight is across the eye in nine cases out of ten, instead of away from it, as a hare would usually run, and this increases the difficulty of a fair hit, even when there is plenty of space.

To strike a bird flying across the sight the barrel has to be moved with it, and the chances are that an inexperienced shot will either not moved his barrel quick enough to keep pace with the bird, and so shoot behind it, or too quick, and so shoot in front. The breech-loader has, if anything, increased a novice's nervousness; he hears a continuous rolling fusillade all round, and smells the sulphurous smoke as it drifts through the underwood, and thinks to himself, 'Those fellows are having a fine time; I shall be behindhand,' and so blazes away, hoping to make up by rapid firing for bad aim. At the short range which is so generally the case in pheasant shooting, the cartridges have no time to burst up – the shot goes all in a lump like a bullet, especially with the new choke-bore guns, consequently, if the aim is not exact there is sure to be a miss. If on the other hand the charge does hit, why then the bird gets it hot; frequently it looks as if the shot literally lifted it up a foot or so higher in the air, only to fall with a heavier thud, a crumpled-up mass of sheeny feathers. Some increase the percentage of misses by firing at every bird without exception, no matter in what position, as it were, it presents itself. Your keen old hand knows very well the particular bird he is sure to kill, and the particular bird he will fail to stop. There is a 'personal equation' in shooting as in making astronomical observations; one observer set to note a transit marks it a second or so before it really happens, and another as much after it has occurred. So, in shooting, one man cannot hit with certainty anything over his head, another misses a wobbling bird, a third cannot make sure of anything passing from left to right, and old hands very often reserve their fire, and refrain from shooting at what they do not feel certain of stopping. In this way many a sportsman has got a reputation as a dead shot; and it is very annoying to his companion, not in the secret, to note that while he misses frequently his friend never pulls trigger without bringing down the game. Then, perhaps, in a lull of the noise, when off your guard for a minute, and yet strung up to something, like nervous pitch, a shy rabbit comes out and you waste your shot on him, or – whew! what an escape – how lucky you did not fire! Out from the dead fern creeps a long reddish creature with a lovely tail; Master Reynard has been roused from his lair. So that a city gentleman who has effected to despise them may chance to find that the barn-door fowls, everything considered, are by no means so despicable as he imagined.

Something of the excitement of battle adds its charm to pheasant-shooting; there are the outposts, the ambuscades, the van, the right and left wings, guns posted at every available corner. The noise of the beaters' approaches, the cry of the frightened birds, the rustle of the stray hare as he slips quickly out of the wood far in advance, the jays and blackbirds go by with a scream and a chuckle, the wood-pigeons are off, their strong wings rattling as they rise – everything raises expectation to the highest pitch. Hush! Now, ready, bang! Another and another shot, the skirmishers are at it; then the main line begins; in five minutes the whole wood is ringing with the roar of powder. Faint shouts come on the breeze, thicker and faster comes the enemy, the birds; down with them, shoot, and spare not. The pulses beat quicker; it is difficult to take aim. 'Steady, sir, steady!' says the keeper, as he hands a fresh gun. Up on the edge of the rising ground yonder, under those noble old beech trees, a party of ladies is standing sheltered from the wind, watching the progress of the fight beneath them. Puffs of grey smoke rise up all round the cover, a cloud seems to hang low over the ash underwood in places where the discharges are most frequent, the echo of the fusillade repeats itself along the hills like thunder. If the sun should shine the scene is not without its beauty also, in the masses of colour exhibited by the dying leaves, brown and yellow, buff, and crimson, while the rooks caw in the sky whirling in fantastic flight – startled from their acorn feast – and the ploughman pauses to listen to the unwonted roar. Say what you like, pheasant-shooting is a ducal sport, as the stag is a royal quarry.

Later on in the year, when the birds get scattered about in distant and detached plantations, and one or two guns spend the day searching for them, it is still less easy to make a bag. To shoot a pheasant in a cover, not as he flies out of the cover, requires considerable skill and self-control. He rises almost straight up from the ground, his object being to clear the ash underwood, and then skims along the top or surface of the wood. If you shoot while he is rising ten to one an ash-pole will intervene and receive the charge; the sapling may be cut in two, but the bird will escape. If you wait till he gets up to the top and begins his onward, horizontal flight, in a second he is out of sight, hidden by the tops of the poles. The right moment to catch him is just as he finishes his scramble up, and just before he begins his real flight. Then for a moment he is comparatively stationary, and also well in view, as the boughs are smaller at the top, and will not stop the shot; then you have him.

Therefore, although, as we said at first, a battue may occasionally be too much organised, and degenerate into slaughter, upon the whole pheasant-shooting is true sport, requiring skill, experience, nerve, and quick decision, and affording plenty of genuine excitement. As pheasants are only kept in any numbers where are extensive woods, and as much as possible are confined to those woods, and as they are so valuable, pecuniarily speaking, as to be carefully fed, the damage they do to farming is really very slight compared with some other game. They provide an outlet for the sporting instinct without injustice to others, and there is therefore little or no ground for the ultra-sentimental outcry often hard against the amusement. The food they consume must amount in value to a considerable sum, and, as the phrase is, 'make it good for trade.' As a bird, whether in life or death, the pheasant will compare favourably with any game – in shape, size, beauty of colour to the eye, and in delicacy of flavour to the taste.

from *Livestock Journal and Fancier's Gazette*, 28 September 1877

Thoughts in the Stubbles

The modern routine of agriculture and the use of machinery are not altogether favourable to the interests of sport. Straw has become so valuable of recent years – sometimes almost unattainable for love or money in particular localities – that everyone tries to get as much of it as possible, and consequently the crop is reaped as near the ground as the sickle, or the machine will go. Time was, and not so long ago either, when the old-fashioned reapers left a goodly show of stubble, shall we say a foot or so high, in which the partridges and leverets found almost as much cover as previously in the crop itself. Time was when the stubble itself was cut afterwards, and was sought for by the dairy farmers and others as litter for their yards in winter, or to form the foundation – to protect from damp – on which hayricks were built. But where can you buy stubble now? Reaping in its old sense is a thing of the past in many districts, and rapidly disappearing in the rest. 'Fagging,' which means chopping off the straw close down, has superseded it where the work is still done by hand; a good deal is now mown also with a scythe, and the machine is used more and more every year. The knives are set as near the earth as safety will permit, and in either case the smooth close-shaven ground bears little resemblance to the autumn fields we used to see. From a practical point of view the change is no doubt quite correct, but not so acceptable to the sportsman. In these shaven fields the partridges find scarcely any cover; they can see the enemy coming, and have nowhere to cower down and hide, as it is their nature to do. When a man enters a gateway he can see every inch of the field, and can also be seen, and the natural result is that his chances of getting near a covey are considerably reduced. The covey once flushed flies farther before settling again, and causes an increased amount of tramping. The choke-bore gun, with its long range, was not invented much too soon to meet those drawbacks. Where the steam-plough is much used by degrees the earth gets levelled; the old furrows are filled up, and the humps and irregularities torn down, and in this way also cover is diminished, and a hare might as well try to hide on an asphalt pavement. Then, before the guns have had time to thoroughly beat the land, the little stubble there is buried by the scarifier; and who in the world can walk across a fallow or any other ground that has been turned inside out by that terrible 'earth-compeller?' The huge lumps and clods defy the effort to stroll across them. Fortunately, there are the turnips still, and the grass.

from *Livestock Journal and Fancier's Gazette*, 31 August 1877

Young Partridges

Resting on the wild thyme under the hawthorn, partly hidden and quite silent, we may see stealing out from the corn into the fallow hard by, first one, then two, then half a dozen or more young partridge chicks. With them is the anxious mother, watching the sky chiefly, lest a hawk be hovering about; nor will she lead them far from the cover of the wheat. She stretches her neck up to listen and look; then, reassured, walks on, her head nodding as she moves. The little ones crowd after, one darting this way, another that, learning their lesson of life how and where to find the most suitable food, how to hide from the enemy, imitation of the parent developing hereditary inclinations.

At the slightest unwonted sound or movement she first stretches her neck up for a hurried glance, then, as the labouring folk say, 'quats' – that is, crouches down and in a second or two runs swiftly to cover, using every little hollow of the ground skilfully for concealment on the way, like a practised skirmisher. The ants' nests, which are so attractive to partridges, are found in great numbers along the edge of the cornfields, being usually made on ground that is seldom disturbed. The low mounds that border the green track are populous with ants, whose nests are scattered thickly on these banks, as also beside the paths and wagon-tracks that traverse the fields and are not torn up by the plough. Any beaten track such as this old path, however green, is generally free from them on its surface: ants avoid placing their nests where they may be trampled upon. This may often be noticed in gardens: there are nests at and under the edge of the paths, but none where people walk. It is these nests in the banks and mounds which draw the partridges so frequently from the middle of the fields to the edges where they can be seen; they will come even to the banks of frequented roads for the eggs of which they are so fond.

from *Wild Life in a Southern County*, 1879

Choosing a Gun

The first thought of the amateur sportsman naturally refers to his gun, and the questions arise: What sort of a gun do I want? Where can I get it? What price shall I pay? In appearance there can be no great difficulty in settling these matters, but in practice it is really by no means easy. Some time since, being on a visit to the Metropolis, I was requested by a friend to get him a gun, and accepted the commission, as M. Emile Ollivier went to war, with a light heart, little dreaming of the troubles that would start up in the attempt to conscientiously carry it out. He wanted a good gun, and was not very scrupulous as to maker or price, provided that the latter was not absolutely extravagant. With such carte blanche as this it seemed plain-sailing, and, indeed, I never gave a second thought to the business till I opened the door of the first respectable gunmaker's shop I came across, which happened to be no great distance from Pall Mall. A very polite gentleman immediately came forward, rubbing his hands as if he were washing them (which is an odd habit with many), and asked if there was anything he could do for me. Well, yes, I wanted a gun. Just so – they had one of the largest stocks in London, and would be most happy to show me specimens of all kinds. But was there any special sort of gun required, as then they could suit me in an instant.

'Hum! Ah! Well, I-I' – feeling rather vague – 'perhaps you would let me see your catalogue...'

'Certainly.' And a handsomely got-up pamphlet, illustrated with woodcuts, was placed in my hands, and I began to study the pages. But this did not suit him; doubtless, with the practice of his profession, he saw at once the uncertain manner of the customer who was feeling his way, and thought to bring it to a point.

'You want a good, useful gun, sir, I presume?'

'That is just it' – shutting the catalogue; quite a relief to have the thing put into shape for one!

'Then you can't do better than take our new patent double-action so-and-so. Here it is' – handing me a decent-looking weapon in thorough polish, which I begin to weigh in my hands, poise it to ascertain the balance, and to try how it comes to the present, and whether I can catch the rib quick enough, when he goes on: 'We can let you have that gun, sir, for ten guineas.'

'Oh, indeed! But that's very cheap, isn't it?' I thoughtlessly observe, putting the gun down.

My friend D. had mentioned a much higher amount as his ultimatum. The next instant I saw in what light my remark would be taken. It would be interpreted in this way: Here we have either a rich amateur, who doesn't care what he gives, or else a fool who knows nothing about it.

'Well, sir, of course it's our very plainest gun' – the weapon is tossed carelessly into the background – 'in fact, we sometimes call it our gamekeeper gun. Now, here is a really fine thing – neatly finished, engraved plates, first choice stock, the very best walnut, price...' He names a sum very close to D's outside.

I handle the weapon in the same manner, and for the life of me cannot meet his eye, for I know that he is reading me, or thinks he is, like a book. With the exception that the gun is a trifle more elaborately got up, I cannot see or feel the slightest difference, and begin secretly to suspect that the price of guns is regulated according to the inexperience of the purchaser – a sort of sliding scale, gauged to ignorance, and rising or falling with its density! He expatiates on the gun and points out all its beauties.

'Shooting carefully registered, sir. Can see it tried, or try it yourself, sir. Our range is barely three-quarters of an hour's ride. If the stock doesn't quite fit your shoulder, you can have another – the same price. You won't find a better gun in all London.'

I can see that it really is a very fair article, but do not detect the extraordinary excellencies so glibly described. I recollect an old proverb about the fool and the money he is said to part with hastily. I resolve to see more variety before making the final plunge; and what the eloquent shopkeeper thinks is my growing admiration for the gun which I continue to handle is really my embarrassment, for as yet I am not hardened, and dislike the idea of leaving the shop without making a purchase after actually touching the goods. But D.'s money – I must lay it out to the best advantage. Desperately I fling the gun into his hands, snatch up the catalogue, mutter incoherently, 'Will look it through... like the look of the thing... will call again,' and find myself walking aimlessly along the pavement outside.

An unpleasant sense of having played a rather small part lingered for some time, and ultimately resolved itself into a determination to make up my mind as to exactly what D. wanted, and on entering the next shop, to ask to see that, and that only. So, turning to the address of another gunmaker, I walked towards it slowly, revolving in my mind the sort of shooting D. usually enjoyed. Visions of green fields, woods just beginning to turn colour, puffs of smoke hanging over the ground, rose up, and blotted out the bustling London scene. The shops glittering with their brightest goods placed in front, the throng of vehicles, the crowds of people, faded away, the pace increased and the stride lengthened as if stepping over the elastic turf, and the roar of the traffic sounded low, like a distant waterfall. From this reverie the rude apostrophes of a hansom-cabman awoke me – I had walked right into the stream of the street, and instead of the awning boughs of the wood found a whip upheld, threatening chastisement for getting in the way. This brought me up from imagination to logic with a jerk, and I began to check off the uses D. could put his gun to on the fingers.

(1) I knew he had a friend in Yorkshire, and shot over his moor every August. His gun, then, must be suited to grouse-shooting, and must be light, because of the heat which often prevails at that time, and renders dragging a heavy gun many miles over the heather-before they pack – a serious drawback to the pleasure of the sport.

(2) He had some partridge-shooting of his own, and was peculiarly fond of it.

(3) He was always invited to at least two battues.

(4) A part of his own shooting was on the hills, where the hares were very wild, where there was no cover, and they had to be knocked over at long distances, and took a hard blow. That would require (a) a choke-bore, which was not suitable either, because in covers the pheasants at short ranges would not unlikely get 'blown,' which would annoy the host; or (b) a heavy, strong gun, which would take a stiff charge without too much recoil. But that, again, clashed with the light gun for shooting in August.

(5) He had latterly taken a fancy to wild-fowl shooting by the coast, for which a very hard-hitting, long-range gun was needed. It would never do if D. could not bring down a duck.

(6) He was notorious as a dead shot on snipe-this told rather in favour of a light gun, old system of boring; for where would a snipe or a woodcock be if it chanced to get 200 pellets into it at twenty yards? You might find the claws and fragments of the bill if you looked with a microscope.

(7) No delicate piece of workmanship would do, because he was careless of his gun, knocked it about anyhow, and occasionally dropped it in a brook. And here was the shop-door; imagine the state of confusion my mind was in when I entered!

This was a very 'big' place: the gentleman who approached had a way of waving his hand – very white and jewelled – and a grand, lofty idea of what a gun should cost. 'Twenty, thirty, forty pounds – some of the £30 were second-hand, of course – we have a few, a very few, second-hand guns' – such was the sweeping answer to my first mild inquiry about prices. Then, seeing at once my vacillating manner, he, too, took me in hand, only in a terribly earnest, ponderous way from which there was no escape. 'You wanted a good general gun – yes, a thoroughly good, well-finished, plain gun (great emphasis on the 'plain'). Of course, you can't get anything new for that money, finished in style. Still, the plain gun will shoot just as well (as if the shooting part was scarcely worth consideration). We make the very best plain-finished article for five-and-twenty guineas in London. By-the-by, where is your shooting, sir?' Thrust home like this, not over-gratified by a manner which seemed to say, 'Listen to an authority,' and desiring to keep incognito, I mutter something about 'abroad.' 'Ah well, then, this article is precisely the thing, because it will carry ball, an immense advantage in any country where you may come across large game.'

'How far will it throw a ball?' I ask, rather curious on that subject, for I was under the impression that a smooth-bore of the usual build is not much to be relied on in that way – far less, indeed, than the matchlocks made by semi-civilized nations. But it seems I was mistaken.

'Why a hundred yards point-blank, and ten times better to shoot with than a rifle.'

'Indeed!'

'Of course, I mean in cover, as you're pretty sure to be. Say a wild boar is suddenly started: well, you pull out your No. 4 shot-cartridge, and push in a ball; you shoot as well again – snap-shooting with a smooth-bore in jungle or bush. There's not a better gun turned out

52

in town than that. It's not the slightest use your looking for anything cheaper – rebounding locks, best stocks, steel damascene barrels; fit for anything from snipe to deer, from dust to buck-shot...'

'But I think...' Another torrent overwhelms me.

'Here's an order for twenty of these guns for Texas, to shoot from horseback at buffalo – ride in among them, you know.'

I look at my watch, find it's much later than I imagine, remark that it is really a difficult thing to pick out a gun, and seize the door-handle.

'When gentlemen don't exactly know what they're looking for it is a hard job to choose a gun' – he smiles, sarcastically, and shuts me out politely.

The observation seems hard, after thinking over guns so intently; yet it must be aggravating to attempt to serve a man who does not know what he wants – yet (one's mood changes quickly) it was his own fault for trying to force, to positively force, that twenty-five-guinea thing on me instead of giving me a chance to choose. I had seen rows on rows of guns stacked round the shop, rank upon rank; in the background a door partly open permitted a glimpse of a second room, also perfectly coated with guns, if such an expression is permissible. Now, I look on ranges of guns like this much the same as on a library. Is there anything so delicious as the first exploration of a great library – alone, unwatched? You shut the heavy door behind you slowly, reverently, lest a noise should jar on the sleepers of the shelves. For as the Seven Sleepers of Ephesus were dead and yet alive, so are the souls of the authors in the care of their ancient leathern binding. You walk gently round the walls, pausing here to read a title, there to draw out a tome and support it for a passing glance-half in your arms, half against the shelf. The passing glance lengthens till the weight becomes too great, and with a sigh you replace it, and move again, peering up at those titles which are foreshortened from the elevation of the shelf, and so roam from folio to octavo, from octavo to quarto, till at last, finding a little work whose value, were it in the mart, would be more than its weight in gold, you bear it to the low leather-covered arm-chair and enjoy it at your ease. But to sip the full pleasure of a library you must be alone, and you must take the books yourself from the shelves. A man to read must read alone. He may make extracts, he may work at books in company; but to read, to absorb, he must be solitary. Something in the same way – except in the necessity for solitude, which does not exist in this case – I like to go through a battery of guns, picking up this one, or that, glancing up one, trying the locks of another, examining the thickness of the breech. Why did not the fellow say, 'There are our guns; walk round, take down what you please, do as you like, and don't hurry. I will go on with some work while you examine them. Call me if you want any explanation. Spend the day there if you like, and come again tomorrow.' It would have been a hundred chances to one that I had found a gun to suit D., for the shop was a famous one, the guns really good, the workmanship unimpeachable, and the stock to select from immense. But let a thing be never so good, one does not care to have it positively thrust on one.

By this time my temper was up, and I determined to go through with the business, and get the precise article likely to please D., if I went to every maker in the Metropolis. I went to very nearly every prominent man – I spent several days at it. I called at shops whose names are household words wherever an English sportsman can be found. Some of them, though bright to look at from the pavement, within were mean, and even lacked cleanliness. The attendants were often incapable of comprehending that a customer may be as good a judge of what he wants as themselves; they have got into a narrow routine of offering the same thing to everybody. No two shops were of the same opinion: at one you were told that the choke was the greatest success in the world; at another, that they only shot well for one season, quickly wearing out; at a third, that such and such a 'grip' or breech-action was perfect; at a fourth, that there never was such a mistake; at a fifth, that hammerless guns were the guns of the future, and elsewhere, that people detested hammerless guns because it seemed like learning to shoot over again. Finally, I visited several of the second-hand shops. They had some remarkably good guns – for the leading second-hand shops do not care to buy a gun unless by a crack maker – but the cheapness was a delusion. A new gun might be got for the same money, or very little more. Their system was like this. Suppose they had a really good gun, but, for aught you could tell, twenty or thirty years old (the breech-action might have been altered), for this they would ask, say £25. The original price of the gun may have been £50, and if viewed only with regard to the original price, of course that would be a great reduction. But for the £25 a new gun could be got from a maker whose goods, if not so famous, were thoroughly reliable, and who guaranteed the shooting. In the one case you bought a gun about whose previous history you knew absolutely nothing beyond the mere fact of the barrels having come at first-hand from a leading maker. But they may have been battered about – re-bored; they may be scored inside by someone loading with flints; twenty things that are quite unascertainable may have combined to injure its original perfection. The cheapness will not stand the test of a moment's thought – that is, if you are in search of excellence. You buy a name and trust to chance. After several days of such work as this, becoming less and less satisfied at every fresh attempt, and physically more fatigued than if I had walked a hundred miles, I gave it up for awhile, and wrote to D. for more precise instructions.

When I came to quietly reflect on these experiences, I found that the effect of carefully studying the subject had been to plunge me into utter confusion. It seemed as difficult to choose a gun as to choose a horse, which is saying a good deal. Most of us take our shooting as we take other things – from our fathers – very likely we use their guns, get into their style of shooting; or if we buy guns, buy them because a friend wants to sell, and so get hold of the gun that suits us by a kind of happy chance. But to begin de novo, to select a gun from the thousand and one exhibited in London, to go conscientiously into the merits and demerits of the endless varieties of locks and breeches, and to come to an impartial decision, is a task the magnitude of which is not easily described. How many others who have been placed in somewhat similar positions must have felt the same ultimate confusion of mind, and perhaps at last, in sheer despair, plunged, and bought the first that came to hand, regretting for years afterwards that they had not bought this or that weapon, which had taken their fancy, but which some gunsmith interested in a patent had declared obsolete!

D. settled the question, so far as he was concerned, by ordering two guns: one bored in the old style for ordinary shooting, and a choked gun of larger bore for the ducks. But all this trouble and investigation gave rise to several not altogether satisfactory reflections. For one thing, there seems a too great desire on the part of gunmakers to achieve a colossal reputation by means of some new patent, which is thrust on the notice of the sportsman and of the public generally at every step and turn. The patent very likely is an admirable thing, and quite fulfils the promise so far as the actual object in view is concerned. But it is immediately declared to supersede everything – no gun is of any use without it: you are compelled to purchase it whether or no, or you are given to understand that you are quite behind the age.

The leading idea of the gunmaker nowadays is to turn out a hundred thousand guns of one particular pattern, like so many bales of cloth; everybody is to shoot with this, their speciality, and everything that has been previously done is totally ignored. The workman in the true sense of the word – the artist in guns – is either extinct, or hidden in an obscure corner. There is no individuality about modern guns. One is exactly like another. That is very well, and necessary for military arms, because an army must be supplied with a single pattern cartridge in order to simplify the difficulty of providing ammunition. They fail even in the matter of ornament. The design – if it can be called design – on one lock-plate is repeated on a thousand others, so with the hammers. There is no originality about a modern gun; as you handle it you are conscious that it is well put together, that the mechanism is perfect, the barrels true, but somehow it feels 'hard'; it conveys the impression of being machine-made. You cannot feel the hand of the maker anywhere, and the failure, the flatness, the formality of the supposed ornament, is depressing. The ancient arquebus makers far surpassed the very best manufacturers of the present day. Their guns are really artistic – works of true art. The stocks of some of the

German wheel-lock guns of the sixteenth and seventeenth centuries are really beautiful specimens of carving and design. Their powder-horns are gems of workmanship – hunting scenes cut out in ivory, the minutest detail rendered with life-like accuracy. They graved their stags and boars from Nature, not from conventional designs; the result is that we admire them now because Nature is constant, and her fashions endure. The conventional 'designs' on our lock-plates, etc., will in a few years be despised; they have no intrinsic beauty. The Arab of the desert, wild, untrammelled, ornaments his matchlock with turquoise. Our machine-made guns, double-barrel, breech-loading, double-grip, rebounding locks, first-choice stocks, laminated steel, or damascus barrels, choke-bore, and so forth, will, it is true, mow down the pheasants at the battue as the scythe cuts down the grass. There is slaughter in every line of them. But is slaughter everything? In my idea it is not, but very far from it. Were I offered the choice of participation in the bloodiest battue ever arranged – such as are reserved for princes – the very best position, and the best-finished and swiftest breech-loader invented, or the freedom of an English forest, to go forth at any time and shoot whatever I chose, untrammelled by any attendants, on condition that I only carried a wheel-lock, I should unhesitatingly select the second alternative.

There would be an abiding pleasure in the very fact of using so beautiful a weapon – just in the very handling of it, to pass the fingers over the intricate and exquisite carving. There would be pleasure in winding up the lock with the spanner; in adjusting the pyrites to strike fire from the notches of the wheel; in priming from a delicate flask graven with stag and hounds. There would be delight in stealing from tree to tree, in creeping from bush to bush, through the bracken, keeping the wind carefully, noiselessly gliding forward – so silently that the woodpecker should not cease tapping in the beech, or the pigeon her hoarse call in the oak, till at last within range of the buck. And then! First, if the ball did not hit the vital spot, if it did not pass through the neck, or break the shoulder, inevitably he would be lost, for the round bullet would not break up like a shell, and smash the creature's flesh and bones into a ghastly jelly, as do the missiles from our nineteenth century express rifles. Secondly, if the wheel did not knock a spark out quickly, if the priming had not been kept dry, and did not ignite instantly, the aim might waver, and all the previous labour be lost. Something like skill would be necessary here. There would be art in the weapon itself, skill in the very loading, skill in the approach, nerve in holding the gun steady while the slow powder caught from the priming and expelled the ball. That would be sport. An imperfect weapon – well, yes, but the imperfect weapon would somehow harmonize with the forest, with the huge old hollow oaks, the beeches full of knot-holes, the mysterious thickets, the tall fern, the silence and solitude. It would make the forest seem a forest – such as existed hundreds of years ago; it would make the chase a real chase, not a foregone conclusion. It would equalize the chances, and give the buck 'law.' In short, it would be real shooting. Or with smaller game – I fancy I could hit a pheasant with a wheel-lock if I went alone, and flushed the bird myself. In that lies all the difference. If your birds are flushed by beaters, you may be on the watch, but that very watching unnerves by straining the nerves, and then the sudden rush and noise flusters you, and even with the best gun of modern construction you often miss. If you spring the bird yourself the noise may startle you, and yet somehow you settle down to your aim and drop him. With a wheel-lock, if I could get a tolerably clear view, I think I could bring him down. If only a brace rewarded a day's roaming under oak and beech, through fern and past thicket, I should be amply satisfied. With the antique weapon the spirit of the wood would enter into one. The chances of failure add zest to the pursuit. For slaughter, however, our modern guns are unsurpassed.

Another point which occurs to one after such an overhauling of guns as I went through, is the price charged for them. There does seem something very arbitrary in the charges demanded, and one cannot help a feeling that they bear no proportion to the real value or cost of production. It may, of course, be said that the wages of workmen are very high – although workmen as a mass have long been complaining that such is not really the case. The rent of premises in fashionable localities is also high, no doubt. For my part, I would quite as soon buy a gun in a village as in a crowded thoroughfare of the Metropolis; indeed rather sooner, since there would probably be a range attached where it could be tried. To be offered a range, as is often the case in London, half an hour out – which, with getting to the station and from the station at the other end, to the place and back, may practically mean half a day – is of little use. If you could pick up the gun in the shop, stroll outside and try it at once, it would be ten times more pleasant and satisfactory.

A good gun is like the good wine of the proverb – if it were made in a village, to that village men would go or send for it. The materials for gun making are, surely, not very expensive – processes for cheapening steel and metal generally are now carried to such an extent, and the market for metals has fallen to an extraordinary extent. Machinery and steam-power to drive it is, no doubt, a very heavy item; but are we so anxious for machinery and machine-made guns? Are you and I anxious that ten thousand other persons should shoot with guns exactly, precisely like ours in every single particular? That is the meaning of machinery. It destroys the individuality of sport. We are all like so many soldiers in an army corps firing Government Martini-Henries. In the sporting ranks one does not want to be a private. I wonder some clever workman does not go and set himself up in some village where rent and premises are low, and where a range could be got close to his door, and deliberately set down to make a name for really first-rate guns, at a moderate price, and with some pretensions to individuality and beauty. There is water-power, which is cheaper than steam, running to waste all over the country now. The old gristmills, which may be found three or four in a single parish sometimes, are half of them falling into decay, because we eat American wheat now, which is ground in the city steam-mills, and a good deal imported ready ground as flour. Here and there one would think sufficient water-power might be obtained in this way. But even if we admit that great manufactories are extremely expensive to maintain, wages high, rent dear, premises in fashionable streets fabulously costly, yet even then there is something in the price of guns not quite the thing. You buy a gun and pay a long price for it: but if you attempt to sell it again you find it is the same as with jewellery, you can get hardly a third of its original cost. The intrinsic value of the gun then is less than half its advertised first cost-price. The second-hand gun offered to you for £20 has probably cost the dealer about £6, or £10 at the most. So that, manage it 'how you will,' you pay a sum quite out of proportion to the intrinsic value. It is all very well to talk about the market, custom of trade, supply and demand, and so forth, though some of the cries of the political economist (notably the Free Trade cry) are now beginning to be questioned. The value of a thing is what it will fetch, no doubt, and yet that is a doctrine which metes out half-justice only. It is justice to the seller, but, argue as sophistically as you like, it is not justice to the purchaser.

I should recommend any gentleman who is going to equip himself as a sportsman to ask himself before he starts the question that occurred to me too late in D.'s case: What kind of shooting am I likely to enjoy? Then, if not wishing to go to more expense than absolutely necessary, let him purchase a gun precisely suited to the game he will meet. As briefly observed before, if the sportsman takes his sport early in the year, and practically in the summer – August is certainly a summer month – he will like a light gun; and as the grouse at that time have not packed, and are not difficult of access, a light gun will answer quite as well as a heavy arm, whose powerful charges are not required, and which simply adds to the fatigue. Much lighter guns are used now than formerly; they do not last so long, but few of us now look forward forty years. A gun of 6½ pounds' weight will be better than anything else for summer work. All sportsmen say it is a toy and so it is, but a very deadly one. The same weapon will equally well do for the first of September (unless the weather has been very bad), and for a few weeks of partridge-shooting. But if the sport comes later in the autumn, a heavier gun with a stronger charge (alluding to guns of the old style of boring) will be found useful. For shooting when the leaves are off, a heavier gun has, perhaps, some advantages.

Battue-shooting puts a great strain upon a gun, from the rapid and continuous firing, and a pheasant often requires a hard knock to grass him successfully. You never know, either, at what range you are likely to meet with him. It may be ten yards, it may be sixty; so that a strong charge, a long range, and considerable power of penetration are desirable, if it is wished to make a good performance. I recommend a powerful gun for pheasant-shooting, because probably in no other sport is a miss so annoying. The bird is large and in popular estimation, therefore ought not to get away. There is generally a party at the house at the time, and shots are sure to be talked about, good or bad, but especially the latter, which some men have a knack of noticing, though they may be apparently out of sight, and bring up against you in the pleasantest way possible: 'I say, you were rather in a fluster, weren't you, this morning? Nerves out of order-eh?' Now, is there anything so aggravating as to be asked about your nerves? It is, perhaps, from the operation of competition that pheasants, as a rule, get very little law allowed them. If you want to shine at this kind of sport, knock the bird over, no matter when you see him – if his tail brushes the muzzle of your gun: every head counts. The fact is, if a pheasant is allowed law, and really treated as game, he is not by any means so easy a bird to kill as may be supposed.

If money is no particular object, of course the sportsman can allow himself a gun for every different kind of sport, although luxury in that respect is apt to bring with it its punishment, by making him but an indifferent shot with either of his weapons. But if anyone wishes to be a really good shot, to be equipped for almost every contingency, and yet not to go to great expense, the very best course to follow is to buy two good guns, one of the old style of boring, and the other nearly or quite choked. The first should be neither heavy nor light – a moderately weighted weapon, upon which thorough reliance may be placed up to fifty yards, and that under favourable circumstances may kill much farther. Choose it with care, pay a fair price for it, and adhere to it. This gun, with a little variation in the charge, will suit almost every kind of shooting, from snipe to pheasant. The choke-bore is the reserve gun, in case of specially long range and great penetration being required. It should, perhaps, be a size larger in the bore than the other. Twelve-bore for the ordinary gun, and ten for the second, will cover most contingencies. With a ten-bore choke, hares running wild on hills without cover, partridge coveys getting up at fifty or sixty yards in the same kind of country, grouse wild as hawks, ducks, plovers, and wild-fowl generally, are pretty well accessible. If not likely to meet with duck, a twelve-bore choke will do equally well. Thus armed, if opportunity offers, you may shoot anywhere in Europe. The cylinder-bore will carry an occasional ball for a boar, a wolf, or fallow-deer, though large shot out of the choke will, perhaps, be more effective – so far, at least, as small deer are concerned. If you can afford it, a spare gun (old-style boring) is a great comfort, in case of an accident to the mechanism.

from *The Hills and the Vale*, 1909

Rook Poachers

The young birds are occasionally stolen from the nests, notwithstanding the difficulty of access. Young labourers will climb the trees, though so large that they can scarcely grasp the trunk, and with few branches, and those small for some height; for elms are often stripped up the trunk to make the timber grow straight and free from the great branches called 'limbs.' Even when the marauder is in the tree he has some difficulty in getting at the nests, which are placed where the boughs diminish in size. Climbing-irons used to be sometimes employed for the purpose. As elm trees are so conspicuous, these thieving practices cannot well be carried on while it is light. So the rook-poachers go up the trees in the dead of night; and as the old rooks would make a tremendous noise and so attract attention, they carry a lantern with them, the light from which silences the birds. So long as they can see a light they will not caw.

The time selected to rob a rookery is generally just before the date fixed for the shooting, because the young birds are of little use for cooking till about ready to fly. The trick, it is believed, has often been played for the mere pleasure of spiting the owner, the very night previous to the rook-shooting party being chosen. These robberies of young rooks are much less frequent than they used to be. One reason why those who possess any property in the country do not like to see a labouring man with a gun is because he will shoot an old rook (and often eat it), if he gets the opportunity, without reference to times or seasons, whether they are building or not.

The young rooks that escape being shot seem to be fed, or partly fed, by the old birds for some time after they can fly well and follow their parents. It is easy to know when there are young rooks in a flock feeding in a field. At the first glance the rooks look scattered about, without any order, each independent of the other. But in a few minutes it will be noticed that here and there are groups of three, which keep close together. These are formed of the parents and the young bird – apparently as big and as black as themselves, which they feed now and then. The young bird, by attending to their motions, learns where to find the best food. As late as July trios like this may sometimes be seen.

Besides the young birds that have the good fortune to pass unscathed through the dangers of rook-shooting day, and escape being knocked over afterwards, some few get off on account of having been born earlier than the majority, thus possessing a stronger power of flight. Some nests are known to be more forward than the others; but although the young birds may be on the point of departing, they are not killed because the noise of the firing would disturb the whole settlement. So that it becomes the rook's interest to incubate a little in advance of the rest.

After a few months they are put into another terrible fright – on the first of September. Guns are going off in all directions, no matter where they turn, so that they find it impossible to feel at ease, and instead of feeding, wheel about in the air, or settle on the trees. The glossy plumage of the rook will sometimes, when seen at a certain angle, reflect the sun's rays in such a manner that instead of looking black the bird appears clothed in shining light: it is as if the feathers were polished like a mirror. In feeding they work in a grave, steady way – a contrast to the restless starlings who so often accompany them. They do not put a sentinel in a tree to give warning of the approach of an enemy. The whole flock is generally on the ground together, and, if half-a-dozen perch awhile on the trees, they soon descend. So far are they from setting a watch, that if you pass up outside the hedge to the leeward, on any side except where the wind would carry the noise of footsteps to them, it is easy to get close – sometimes, if they are feeding near the hedge, within three or four yards. Of course if a rook happens to be in a tree it will not be possible to do so; but they do not set a sentinel for this purpose.

Rooks, in a general way, seem more at their ease in the meadows than in the arable fields. In the latter they are constantly fired at, if only with blank charges, to alarm them from the seed, besides being shouted at and frightened with clappers. The bird-keeper's efforts are, however, of very little avail. If he puts the flock up on one side of the field, they lazily sail to a distant corner, and when he gets there, go back again. They are fully aware that he cannot injure them if they keep a certain distance; but this perpetual driving to and fro makes them suspicious. In the meadows it is rare for them to be shot at, and they are consequently much less timid.

At the same time they can perfectly well distinguish a gun from a walking-stick. If you enter a meadow with a gun under your arm, and find a flock feeding, they immediately cease searching for food and keep a strict watch on your movements; and if you approach, they are off directly. If you carry a walking-stick only, you may pass within thirty yards sometimes, and they take little notice, provided you use the stick in the proper way. But now lift it, and point it at the nearest rook, and in an instant he is up with a 'caw' of alarm – though he knows it is not a gun – and flies just above the surface of the ground till he considers himself safe from possibility of danger. Often the whole flock will move before that gesture.

from *Wild Life in a Southern County*, 1879

The Rabbit Warren

Some few dead leaves of last year, not yet decayed though bleached and brittle, lie here at rest from the winds that swept them over the plain. Silky balls of thistledown come irresolutely rolling over the edge, now this way now that: some rise and float across, some follow the surface and cling awhile to the bennets [grasses] in the hollow. Pale blue harebells, drooping from their slender stems here and there, meditate with bowed heads, as if full of tender recollections.

Now, on hands and knees (the turf is dry and soft), creep up one side of the bowl-like hollow, where the thistles make a parapet on the edge, and from behind it look out upon the ground all broken up into low humps, some covered with nettles, others plainly heaps of sand. It is the site of an immense rabbit-burrow, the relic of an old warren which once occupied half the field. The nettle-covered heaps mark old excavations; where the sand shows, there the miners have been recently at work. At the sound of approaching footsteps those inhabitants that had been abroad hastily rushed into their caves, but now (after waiting awhile, and forgetting that the adjacent hollow might hide the enemy) a dozen or more have come forth within easy gunshot. Though a few like this are always looking in and out all through the day, it is not till the approach of evening that they come out in any number.

This is a favourite spot from whence to get a shot at them, but the aim must be deadly, or the rabbit will escape though never so severely wounded. The holes are so numerous that he has never more than a yard to scramble, and as he goes down into the earth his own weight carries him on. If he can but live ten seconds after the lead strikes him, he will generally escape you. Watching patiently (without firing), after the twilight has deepened into night, presently you are aware of a longer, larger creature than a rabbit stealing out, seeming to travel close to the earth: it is a badger. There are almost always a couple somewhere about the warren. Their residence is easily discovered because of the huge heap of sand thrown out from the rabbit-hole they have chosen; and it is this ease of discovery that has caused the diminution of their numbers by shot or spade.

The ground sounds hollow underneath the foot – perhaps half an acre is literally bored away under the surface; and you have to thread your way in and out a labyrinth of holes, the earth about some of them perceptibly yielding to your weight. There must be wagon-loads of the sand that has been thrown out. Beyond this central populous quarter suburbs of burrows extend in several directions, and there are detached settlements fifty and a hundred yards away. In ferreting this place the greatest care has to be taken that the ferret is lined with a long string, or so fed that he will not lie in; otherwise, if he is not picked up the moment he appears at the mouth of the hole, he will become so excited at the number of rabbits, and so thirsty for blood, that he will refuse to come forth.

To dig for him is hopeless in that catacomb of tunnels; there is nothing for it but to send a man day after day to watch, and if possible to seize him while passing along the upper ground from one bury to another. In time thirst will drive him to wander; there is no water near this dry, sandy, and rather elevated spot, and blood causes great thirst. Then he will roam across the open, and by-and-by reach the hedges, where in the ditch some water is sure to be found in winter, when ferreting is carried on. So that, if a ferret has been lost some time, it is better to look for him round the adjacent hedges than in the warren.

Long after leaving the bury it is as well to look to your footsteps, because of solitary rabbit-holes hidden by the grass growing up round and even over them. If the foot sinks unexpectedly into one of these, a sprained ankle or even a broken bone may result. Most holes have sand round the mouth, and may therefore be seen even in the dusk; but there are others also used which have no sand at the mouth, the grass growing at the very edge. Those that have sand have been excavated from without, from above; those that have not, have been opened from below. The rabbit has pushed his way up from an old bury, so that the sand he dug fell down behind him into the larger hole.

The same thing may be seen in banks, though then the holes worked from within are not so much concealed by grass. These holes are always very much smaller than the others, some so small that one might doubt how a rabbit could force his body through them. The reason why the other tunnels appear so much larger is because the rabbit has no means of shoring up his excavation with planks and timbers, and no 'cage' with which to haul up the sand he has moved; so that he must make the mouth wider than is required for the passage of his body, in order to get the stuff out behind him. He can really creep through a much smaller aperture. At night especially, when walking near a bury situated in the open field, beware of putting your foot into one of these holes, which will cause an awkward fall if nothing worse. Some of the older holes, now almost deserted, are, too, so hidden by nettles and coarse grass as to be equally dangerous.

The hereditary attachment of wild animals for certain places is very noticeable at the warren. Though annually ferreted, shot at six months out of the twelve, and trapped – though weasels and foxes prey on the inhabitants – still they cling to the spot. They may be decimated by the end of January, but by September the burrows are as full as ever.

Weasels and stoats of course come frequently, bent on murder, but often meet their own doom through over-greediness; for some one generally comes along with a gun once during the day, and if there be any commotion among the rabbits, waits till the weasel or stoat appears at the mouth of a hole, and sends a charge of shot at him. These animals get caught, too, in the gins, and altogether would do better to stay in the hedgerows.

from *Wild Life in a Southern County*, 1879

The Gamekeeper's Favourite Gun

The ceiling is low and crossed by one huge square beam of oak, darkened by smoke and age. The keeper's double-barrelled gun is suspended from this beam: there are several other guns in the house, but this, the favourite, alone hangs where it did before he had children – so strong is habit; the rest are yet more out of danger. It has been a noble weapon, though now showing signs of age – the interior of the breech worn larger than the rest of the barrel from constant use; so much so that, before it was converted to a breech-loader, the wad when the ramrod pushed it down would slip the last six inches, so loosely fitting as to barely answer its purpose of retaining the shot; so that when cleaned out, before the smoke fouled it again, he had to load with paper. This in a measure anticipated the 'choke-bore,' and his gun was always famous for its killing power. The varnish is worn from the stock by incessant friction against his coat, showing the real grain of the walnut-wood, and the trigger-guard with the polish of the sleeve shines like silver.

It has been his companion for so many years that it is not strange he should feel an affection for it; no other ever fitted the shoulder so well, or came with such delicate precision to the 'present' position. So accustomed is he to its balance and 'hang' in the hand that he never thinks of aiming; he simply looks at the object, still or moving, throws the gun up from the hollow of his arm, and instantly pulls the trigger, staying not a second to glance along the barrel. It has become almost a portion of his body, answering like a limb to the volition of will without the intervention of reflection. The hammers are chased and elegantly shaped – perfectly matching: when once the screw came loose, and the jar of a shot jerked one off among the dead leaves apparently beyond hope of recovery, he never rested night or day till by continuous search and sifting the artistic piece of metal was found. Nothing destroys the symmetry of a gun so much as hammers which are not pairs; and well he knew that he should never get a smith to replace that delicate piece of workmanship, for this gun came originally from the hands of a famous maker, who got fifty or perhaps even seventy guineas for it years ago. It did not shoot to please the purchaser – guns of the very best character sometimes take use to get into thorough order – and was thrown aside, and so the gun became the keeper's.

These fine old guns often have a romance clinging to them, and sometimes the history is a sad one. Upstairs he still keeps the old copper powder-flask curiously chased and engraved, yet strong enough to bear the weight of the bearer, if by chance he sat down upon it while in his pocket, together with the shot-belt and punch for cutting out the wads from card-board or an old felt hat. These the modern system of loading at the breech has cast aside. Here, also, is the apparatus for filling empty cartridge-cases – a work which in the season occupies him many hours.

Being an artist in his way, he takes a pride in the shine and polish of his master's guns, which are not always here, but come down at intervals to be cleaned and attended to. And woe be to the first kid gloves that touch them afterwards; for a gun, like a sardine, should be kept in fine oil, not thickly encrusting it, but, as it were, rubbed into and oozing from the pores of the metal and wood. Paraffin is an abomination in his eyes (for preserving from rust), and no modern patent oil, he thinks, can compare with a drop of gin for the locks – the spirit never congeals in cold weather, and the hammer comes up with a clear, sharp snick. He has two or three small screwdrivers and gunsmith's implements to take the locks to pieces; for gentlemen are sometimes careless and throw their guns down on the wet grass, and if a single drop of water should by chance penetrate under the plate it will play mischief with the works, if the first speck of rust be not forthwith removed.

from *The Gamekeeper at Home*, 1878

Sleight-of-Hand Poaching

When the pale winter sunshine falls upon the bare branches of an avenue of elms – such as so often ornament parks – they appear lit up with a faint rosy colour, which instantly vanishes on the approach of a shadow. This shimmering mirage in the boughs seems due to the myriads of lesser twigs, which at the extremities have a tinge of red, invisible at a distance till the sunbeams illuminate the trees. Beyond this passing gleam of colour, nothing relieves the blackness of the January landscape, except here and there the bright silvery bark of the birch.

For several seasons now in succession the thrush has sung on the shortest days, as though it were spring; a little later, in the early mornings, the blackbird joins, filling the copse with a chorus at the dawn. But, if the wind turns to east or north, the rooks perch on the oaks in the hedgerows in the middle of the day, puffing out their feathers and seeming to abandon all search for food as if seized with uncontrollable melancholy. Hardy as these birds are, a long frost kills them in numbers, principally by slow starvation. They die during the night, dropping suddenly from their roosting-place on the highest boughs of the great beech-trees, with a thud distinctly heard in the silence of the woods. The leaves of the beech decay so gradually as to lie in heaps beneath for months, filling up the hollows, so that an unwary passer-by may plunge knee-deep in leaves. Rooks when feeding usually cross the field facing the wind, perhaps to prevent the ruffling of their feathers.

Wood-pigeons have apparently much increased in numbers of recent years; they frequent sheltered spots where the bushes diminish the severity of the frost. Sometimes on the hills at a lonely farmhouse, where the bailiff has a long-barrelled ancient fowling-piece, he will lay a train of grain for them, and with a double charge of shot, kill many at a time.

Men have boasted of shooting twenty at once. But with an ordinary gun it is not credible; and the statement, without wilful exaggeration, may arise from confusion in counting, for it is a fact that some of the older uneducated country labourers cannot reckon correctly. It is not unusual in parishes to hear of a cottage woman who has had twenty children. Upon investigation the real number is found to be sixteen or seventeen, yet nothing on earth will convince the mother that she has not given birth to a score. They get hazy in figures when exceeding a dozen.

A pigeon is not easily brought down – the quills are so stiff and strong that the shot, if it comes aslant, will glance off. Many pigeons roost in the oaks of the hedges, choosing by preference one well hung with ivy, and when it is a moonlit night, afford tolerable sport. It requires a gun on each side of the hedge. A stick flung up awakes the birds; they rise with a rush and clatter, and in the wildness of their flight and the dim light are difficult to hit. There is a belief that pigeons are partially deaf. If stalked in the daytime they take little heed of footsteps or slight noises which would alarm other creatures; but, on the other hand, they are quick of eye, and are gone directly anything suspicious appears in sight. You may get quite under them and shoot them on the bough at night. It is not their greater wakefulness, but the noise they make in rising which renders them good protectors of preserves; it alarms other birds and can be heard at some distance.

When a great mound is grubbed up, the men engaged in the work often anticipate making a considerable bag of the rabbits, whose holes riddle it in every direction, thinking to dig them out even of those innermost chambers whence the ferret has sometimes been unable to dislodge them. But this hope is almost always disappointed; and when the grub-axe and spade have laid bare the 'buries' only recently teeming with life, not a rabbit is found. By some instinct they have discovered the approach of destruction, and as soon as the first few yards of the hedge are levelled, secretly depart. After a 'bury' has been ferreted it is some time before another colony takes possession: this is seemingly from the intense antipathy of the rabbit to the smell of the ferret. Even when shot at and pressed by dogs, a rabbit in his hasty rush will often pass a hole which would have afforded instant shelter because it has been recently ferreted.

At this season the labourers are busy with 'beetle' (pronounced 'bitel') – a huge mallet – and iron wedges, splitting the tough elm-butts and logs for firewood. In old times a cottager here and there with a taste for astrology used to construct an almanack by rule of thumb, predicting the weather for the ensuing twelve months from the first twelve days of January. As the wind blew on those days so the prevailing weather of the months might be foretold. The aged men, however, say that in this divination the old style must be adhered to, for the sequence of signs and omens still follows the ancient reckoning, which ought never to have been interfered with.

from *The Gamekeeper at Home*, 1878

The Place of Ambush

In approaching the place selected for an ambush it is essential to take a route that will not disturb the game. The habit of suspicion is so inherent in wild creatures that it is necessary to credit them with a defensive cunning equal to the skill brought against them, to rule every motion as if they were actually observing it. Though the hare may crouch in her form apparently heedless of the passing footsteps, her eyes are on the watch, and the ears, and especially the nostrils absorbing every indication. When she leaves the form she will not go in the direction the footsteps have taken nor will the partridge cowering in the furrow nearest the dangerous neighbourhood. The rabbits in their burrows, though they can neither see nor be seen, are perfectly conscious of what is proceeding in their immediate vicinity, for long experience underground has taught them the meaning of every sound, and vibration of the earth. If anyone walks across the entrance to their holes they remain concealed for a length of time: if a person only crosses the centre of the meadow they are soon out again, but let him come up beside the hedge and their caution is doubled.

To avoid anything unusual is the secret – it holds good also in simply observing the ways of bird or animal: they soon become accustomed to anything regularly repeated. So the shepherd strolls about among his sheep and the hare does not move though he can see her eye, the fogger carries out the hay at dawn to the cattle and the rabbit in the grass sits still almost under his heavy shoes, and the wild wood-pigeon contently perches on the elm over the yard when the milkers are busy. The labourer going home from his work in the evening gets through a gap in the hedge and the rabbits scarcely notice him. The crunching and grinding of the flints under the heavy wagon wheels in the lane alarms nothing. But the slightest deviation from the established course of things produces an instant effect: if the grinding and crunching cease, and the carter looks over the gate every ear is perked up. The place of ambush, therefore, whether a ditch or a tree, must be approached as much as possible by the ordinary footpaths, and not by stealthily gliding along beside the hedges.

Crossing a mound is certain to warn every rabbit near, for the hollow soil tunnelled beneath conveys the least jar, and there is sure to be a brushing noise against the parted bushes, and the rustle of dead leaves under foot. This adds to the poacher's difficulties because for the sake of concealment it is in his interest to keep near cover, and while with the background of a hedge he may be invisible, in the open he would at once be perceived. When it is not possible to get any nearer to the tree by the footpath, or by the well-worn track which the cows make going down to water, walking regularly as if drilled the one behind the other and cutting quite a groove in the turf with their hoofs then, instead of following the hedge, strike straight across the open field for it. Keep away too from the furrows, and avoid the bunches of grass in which there may be a form. The tree must be chosen beforehand, and indeed to previously reconnoitre the ground is the constant habit of the poacher and often exposes him to suspicion when found or seen from a distance rambling away from the beaten path, though a search may not reveal a wire or ferret in his pocket. It should of course stand within range of a place frequented by game, and must not present much difficulty in climbing. For most of our trees are bare of boughs to some height, and are not easily ascended when carrying a gun.

A fine horse-chestnut tree stood by the side of a hedge in some secluded meadow lands. It grew on the 'shore' of a wide deep ditch – the 'shore' is the edge towards the field opposite to the bank – which bounded a great double mound. There were many oaks in the hedge, but the advantage of the chestnut was that like a bastion it permitted a flanking fire along the green curtain wall, and was so situated near the corner that a view could be obtained into three meadows at once. The trunk was smooth – the horses rubbing against it and leaving stray hairs adhering to the bark – but the means of ascent were close at hand. An old hurdle which had been used to stop a gap close by was conveniently lying in the ditch, and had only to be quietly pulled out and 'pitched' against the tree behind the shelter of a hawthorn bush.

Placing one foot on this, the left hand could easily grasp the first bough while the right carefully laid the gun on two other branches. Then a slight effort brought the chest up to the bough, and the foot as it left the hurdle gently kicked it away, so that it might fall noiselessly on the grass. The most curious person would then fail to discern anything unusual, and might pass within ten yards and observe nothing. To get down of course is always easy enough. The boughs of the chestnut formed a convenient seat which even had some resemblance to an easy chair, for while sitting on one, the arm could be passed over another, a posture at once pleasant and secure. Two fields could be commanded without moving – those on either side of the mound: to overlook the third, in the rear, it was necessary to stand up.

Here I settled myself one beautiful September afternoon as the sun began to slope downwards and prepared for some hours of silence. The flies whom the heat had unusually animated immediately attacked me but a single frond – the chestnut spray with its spreading leaves attached to one stalk resembled a frond – snapped from the bough formed a natural fan, and waved them away. In such a position there is at first a little restlessness: but by degrees there comes over the mind something of the intense calm of nature.

There was not a breath of wind – not a motion except that of the shadow of the elms in the hedge imperceptibly approaching over the grass. In the blue above, faint white streaks of cloud hung suspended. The sun, his beams lessened by the intervention of the boughs, could be watched descending slowly. There are no words by which the meaning silence of the sun can be conveyed: to me there is a fascination in the light when alone, isolated among the green things of the earth. Green grass beneath, green leaves around, green hills yonder, the touch of the living tree; these seem to awake a finer sense within the senses that opens itself to receive the ethereal part of the light, which is not seen but felt.

Held in such mesmerism no note is taken of time because there are no emotions to mark its flow like the beat of succeeding waves. A sudden rustle in the branches of the oak but a few yards distant disturbs the stillness, and the hand instinctively tightens on the stock of the gun. It is a wood-pigeon that has alighted – he has perched on a bough of the oak that seems almost overhead. He turns his head with a quick motion in every direction – it is the invariable habit of the wood-pigeon to look all round immediately upon alighting, and the slightest motion or sound is then sufficient to startle him. But once the inspection is complete – and it lasts a few seconds only – he seems to lose half his caution, confident in the power of his eye, and you may then move almost freely.

Birds rarely look perpendicularly downwards – that is, when perched. In flying they do, and perceive danger beneath instantly: but when on a bough they overlook what is vertically below unless some unusual noise alarms them. So the pigeon being above and not having spied anything at the first anxious glance, now settles himself and arranges a feather…

from a fragment of manuscript reproduced in
Field and Farm, 1957

Rabbit Shooting

It is not at all an uncommon thing to hear experienced sportsmen declare that after all there is no shooting to beat rabbit-shooting. Without going so far as this, we may allow that it is equal to either partridge or pheasant shooting. It is a greater test of skill, it is equally exciting, and affords as many incidents. Of course, where pointers or setters can be used, partridge-shooting ranks next to grouse-shooting. But where the birds are walked up according to the general fashion of the present day, we find nothing in the sport to entitle it to precedence over rabbit-shooting. To shoot rabbits really well a man must begin young, the necessary quickness of eye and hand being rarely acquired afterwards; and it will generally be found that a first-rate rabbit shot has begun practice while a schoolboy. Different degrees of skill are no doubt required, according to the nature of the cover where you seek your game. But any man who can kill nine rabbits out of ten deserves to be called a good shot, no matter where they may be found.

'Rabbits,' said a distinguished member of the present Cabinet, 'should be three inches longer: then I could hit them.' And it must be owned that this sentiment will find an echo in the breast of all but the most expert artists. Rabbits lie either in their holes, when the ferret must be called into requisition; or else in woods, hedgerows, or any rough open ground adjoining them; though they are only found here in any numbers after they have been disturbed elsewhere. Dry sandy banks are their favourite places for burrowing. When the holes are close together, and the rabbit merely darts out of one to disappear down another, you have the most difficult shot that the animal can offer; though keepers and others who have been used to it will kill them with astonishing precision, hitting nearly all of them in the head, and seldom allow a wounded one to escape down the hole. Rabbit-shooting in cover requires the same kind of dexterity, though not quite the same degree of rapidity; and to kill any number in succession as they bound across a narrow ride is a feat of arms of which any sportsman might be proud. To shoot them while running at full speed through the underwood, especially in an ash plantation, is perhaps an equally meritorious exploit. But then not very many are killed in this manner; most men preferring to stand still and have the rabbit driven up to them, and then firing either as they cross the ride or as they move more slowly through the brushwood.

The ride, or long narrow path, a number of which are cut through all large woods used either for shooting or fox-hunting, should be from twelve to fifteen feet across, and intersected by others at intervals of about a hundred yards. Thus the wood is divided into sections, and each is beaten in its turn. The guns are placed all round it – eight or nine are quite enough – and then the work begins. If you are lucky enough to be placed opposite a thin place in the wood, you will get shots at the rabbits as they approach you, when they are much more easily killed than when they rush across the open. You keep your eye intently fixed on the grass and low boughs which separate you from the beaters, remaining perfectly motionless, as the least noise on your part will turn a rabbit back; while you must watch, in turn, for the slightest sign of motion on his part if you are to bring him to bag.

His coat is not unlike the colour of the ash-bark, and still more like the dry grass. All this time a regular fusillade is going on all around you, and the beaters are yelling like madmen, 'Rabbit forward! Rabbit back! Rabbit right! Rabbit left!' till you wonder when your turn is to come. Ah! here he comes, listening intently to the sounds behind him as he picks his way beneath the bushes. Now he is quite near enough, and your gun is to your shoulder; but he won't show fairly, constantly keeping some stump or trunk between him and you. At last, however, an opening occurs: he has to pass over a yard of unprotected ground, and this is your chance; you have to shoot through some twigs, but this doesn't matter; you pull the trigger, and you do not miss.

Had he dashed boldly over the ride he would perhaps have saved his life. For in shooting at rabbits as they cross you have two different errors to guard against. The first and most obvious is the danger of shooting behind the rabbit – a chance which with the novice is a certainty; the second is the risk of shooting too high. As the rabbit makes his rush, you have to throw your gun forward, so as just to catch him before he gets into the opposite bushes. It is difficult to do this and to depress the barrel sufficiently at the same moment; so that if you shoot well forward you are apt to shoot too high, and if you shoot low enough you are apt to shoot behind. All this, however, is more easily felt than described; and where there are plenty of rabbits you will have had half a dozen shots in the time it takes to write these words. Stationed on a ride, and taking his chance of rabbits coming towards him and rabbits running across, an average shot who does not pick and choose will scarcely bag more than half of these he fires at. The man who does pick his shots, or the man who is a first-rate performer, will of course kill a much larger proportion. But a fair all-round shot, with no special skill in this particular kind of sport, may be satisfied if he gets a rabbit for every two cartridges expended.

But perhaps the best sport to be had with rabbits in cover is when the underwood is short and thin and the ground underneath well covered with long coarse grass. Two guns, with a beater and a spaniel, may then have capital sport where the rabbits are tolerably thick. The shots will be all difficult ones; and you will have the additional pleasure of affording a treat to your dog, who, in finding and starting a rabbit, then seeing it bowled over, and then picking it up, experiences about the highest delight of which he is capable, probably. In beating cover of this kind never pass by any old hollow roots or stubs without having a stick poked into them; for rabbits when they have been driven about a little are very apt to hide in these cavities. I have known two, and sometimes even three, huddled together in one of them.

Always remember, too, that either to enjoy rabbit-shooting or to excel in it, it is necessary to shoot boldly, and not to be afraid of missing. You will find that you often kill where you hardly expected to do; and this in time gives you confidence. The thing to be done is to shoot where the rabbit will be at the right moment; for three times out of four you can barely see him when you shoot. And the power of calculating his pace and his probable twists and turns, which at first you find impossible, is acquired by imperceptible degrees, till at last it becomes a kind of instinct. But this result can only be attained by constant practice, and by taking every shot as it comes. What would be random shooting at any other kind of game and the worst possible style for a beginner is the best at rabbits, and perhaps the only way by which the art of killing them can be acquired. These remarks, however, apply only to cover-shooting. When you get a clear view of the rabbit in the open ground you cannot take too much time over him or shoot too carefully; and many people think that the best sport is to be had in this manner. Rabbits are always fond of hedges; but after the woods have been beaten two or three days in succession, the hedges will be full of them, and you may look for them also on stubble and gallows, and along any narrow ditch or little water-course which has hollow banks and is well roofed over with grass. Where these run down from a wood, as they often do, towards the meadows, you should beat them downwards; for the rabbits when they jump out are sure to make for the wood, thus giving you a cross-shot in passing. You may sometimes shoot as fast as you can load for ten minutes or quarter of an hour along one of these ditches; and capital sport it is. The rabbits go at their top speed on such occasions, and you must be thoroughly cool and understand your business well to make sure of them. Supposing, however, that you have these qualifications, then you ought to kill every rabbit. This is equally true of hedgerow-shooting; though here you have the additional excitement of getting the rabbit to bolt, since he often prefers running up and down the ditch-bottom or along the top of the bank to facing the perils of the open. The best plan is to place a man in the ditch on each side of him, and then to send the dog in. It is needless to say that after this mode of treatment he flies like an arrow from the bow when he does come out, and your nerves must be all right if your dog is not to return empty-mouthed.

from *St. James's Gazette*, 1882

The Single-Barrel Gun

The single-barrel gun has passed out of modern sport; but I remember mine with regret, and think I shall some day buy another. I still find that the best double-barrel seems top-heavy in comparison; in poising it the barrels have a tendency to droop. Guns, of course, are built to balance and lie level in the hand, so as to almost aim themselves as they come to the shoulder; and those who have always shot with a double-barrel are probably quite satisfied with the gun on that score. To me there seems too much weight in the left hand and towards the end of the gun. Quickness of firing keeps the double-barrel to the front; but suppose a repeater were to be invented, some day, capable of discharging two cartridges in immediate succession? And if two cartridges, why not three? An easy thought, but a very difficult one to realise. Something in the power of the double-barrel – the overwhelming odds it affords the sportsman over bird and animal – pleases. A man feels master of the copse with a double-barrel; and such a sense of power, though only over feeble creatures, is fascinating. Besides, there is the delight of effect; for a clever right and left is sure of applause and makes the gunner feel 'good' in himself. Doubtless, if three barrels could be managed, three barrels would be more saleable than doubles. One gun-maker has a four-barrel gun, quite a light weight too, which would be a tremendous success if the creatures would obligingly run and fly a little slower, so that all four cartridges could be got in. But that they will not do. For the present, the double-barrel is the gun of the time.

Still I mean some day to buy a single-barrel, and wander with it as of old along the hedges, aware that if I am not skilful enough to bring down with the first shot I shall lose my game. It is surprising how confident of that one shot you may get after a while. On the one hand, it is necessary to be extremely keen; on the other, to be sure of your own self-control, not to fire uselessly. The bramble-bushes on the shore of the ditch ahead might cover a hare. Through the dank and dark-green aftermath a rabbit might suddenly come bounding, disturbed from the furrow where he had been feeding. On the sandy paths which the rabbits have made aslant up the mound, and on their terraces, where they sit and look out from under the boughs, acorns have dropped ripe from the tree. Where there are acorns there may be pheasants; they may crouch in the fern and dry grey grass of the hedge thinking you do not see them, or else rush through and take wing on the opposite side. The only chance of a shot is as the bird passes a gap – visible while flying a yard – just time to pull the trigger. But I would rather have that chance than have to fire between the bars of a gate; for the horizontal lines cause an optical illusion, making the object appear in a different position from what it really is in, and half the pellets are sure to be buried in the rails.

Wood-pigeons, when eagerly stuffing their crops with acorns, sometimes forget their usual caution; and, walking slowly, I have often got right underneath one – as unconscious of his presence as he was of mine, till a sudden dashing of wings against boughs and leaves announced his departure. This he always makes on the opposite side of the oak, so as to have the screen of the thick branches between himself and the gunner. The wood-pigeon, starting like this from a tree, usually descends in the first part of his flight, a gentle downward curve followed by an upward rise, and thus comes into view at the lower part of the curve. He still seems within shot, and to afford a good mark; and yet experience has taught me that it is generally in vain to fire. His stout quills protect him at the full range of the gun. Besides, a wasted shot alarms everything within several hundred yards; and in stalking with a single-barrel it needs as much knowledge to choose when not to fire as when you may.

The most exciting work with the single-barrel was woodcock shooting; woodcock being by virtue of rarity a sort of royal game, and a miss at a woodcock a terrible disappointment. They have a trick of skimming along the very summit of a hedge, and looking so easy to kill; but, as they fly, the tops of tall briars here, willow-rods next, or an ash-pole often intervene, and the result is apt to be a bough cut off and nothing more. Snipes, on the contrary, I felt sure of with the single-barrel, and never could hit them so well with a double. Either at starting, before the snipe got into his twist, or waiting till he had finished that uncertain movement, the single-barrel seemed to drop the shot with certainty. This was probably because of its perfect natural balance, so that it moved as if on a pivot. With the single I had nothing to manage but my own arms; with the other I was conscious that I had a gun also. With the single I could kill farther, no matter what it was. The single was quicker at short shots – snap-shots, as at rabbits darting across a narrow lane; and surer at long shots, as at a hare put out a good way ahead by the dog.

For everything but the multiplication of slaughter I liked the single best; I had more of the sense of woodcraft with it. When we consider how helpless a partridge is, for instance, before the fierce blow of shot, it does seem fairer that the gunner should have but one chance at the bird. Partridges at least might be kept for single-barrels: great bags of partridges never seemed to be quite right. Somehow it seems to me that to take so much advantage as the double-barrel confers is not altogether in the spirit of sport. The double-barrel gives no 'law'. At least to those who love the fields, the streams, and woods for their own sake, the single-barrel will fill the bag sufficiently, and will permit them to enjoy something of the zest men knew before the invention of weapons not only of precision but of repetition:

inventions that rendered them too absolute masters of the situation. A single-barrel will soon make a sportsman the keenest of shots. The gun itself can be built to an exquisite perfection – lightness, handiness, workmanship, and performance of the very best. It is said that you can change from a single-barrel shot-gun to a sporting rifle and shoot with the rifle almost at once; while many who have been used to the slap-dash double cannot do anything for some time with a rifle. More than one African explorer has found his single-barrel smooth-bore the most useful of all the pieces in his battery; though, of course, of much larger calibre than required in our fields.

from *The Open Air*, 1885

The Use of Dogs in Shooting

There is a prevailing notion that the use of pointers and setters in partridge-shooting has been almost entirely abandoned of late years, and that no dogs are now employed for this purpose except retrievers. But, although it is quite true that there is no longer the same occasion for their services as formerly, it would be a mistake to suppose that they are not still in general demand. The mere fact that dog trials have become so common of late years ought to be enough to show that dogs have still a part to play in the economy of field sports, and one not confined only to grouse-shooting. For grouse-shooting alone cannot furnish employment for a sufficient number to make it worth anybody's while to go to such an expense in breeding and rearing them as many well-known kennel proprietors habitually incur. Nor can it be done merely for the love of the animal, as that would soon die out if he was of no real use. Fond as a man might be of thoroughbred horses, he would hardly keep a racing stud if there were no races.

And it is incredible that the number of persons who are known as celebrated dog-breeders should continue this pursuit if they had nothing for their dogs to do after the short-lived grouse season was over. Besides, the price of good pointers and setters has never really fallen very much. It is plain, therefore, that they must be used somewhere and by some people; and, in fact, a little reflection will convince us that, although in certain special localities dogs may be rather in the way than otherwise, there must still be a large extent of country where they are almost as necessary as they ever were, or where, at all events, the same kind of sport can be enjoyed with them as our fathers enjoyed before us.

There are some parts of England, notably the eastern counties, where there is very little grass land, and where what there is bears only very scanty crops. But the land is light, and yields abundant crops of turnips; while, being at the same time highly farmed, it furnishes little or no stubble. The soil, being dry, is suitable to birds; and in average seasons, even without being much looked after, they are always abundant. As it is almost entirely a corn country, hedgerows have been gradually removed or reduced to the smallest dimensions; so that really in a very dry season you may see acres and acres of land stretching out over hill and dale, looking just like so much bare wooden flooring.

It is easy to see how in a country of this description dogs came to be disused. When the wheat stubbles were abolished there was literally nothing left to hold partridges except the root crops or the clover. It was found even that if a covey were scattered in the middle of a turnip-field and any odd birds dropped in the stubbles or hedges, they always began to run till they reached another piece of cover, and that it was useless to try to find them one by one in the old-fashioned style. Thus it soon became the universal practice to shoot only in turnips; and from that to having the birds driven into them was a very short and easy step. As it was impossible to get a shot anywhere outside the turnips, keepers and beaters might just as well tramp the stubbles as their masters; and so the present system came in. But in a field so thickly packed with birds as some of these turnip-grounds would be, there was no room for a pointer to display his characteristic qualities. He was puzzled by numbers, and inevitably put up many more birds than he stood. So, of course, he was no longer used, and his place was supplied by the retriever. In other parts of England the example has been followed where it was not so absolutely necessary. But there are many parts in which it cannot be followed without losing half the sport which might otherwise be obtained. There are people who affect to believe that the partridge in a grass country is necessarily an inferior bird to the partridge in a corn country. But be this as it may, if the Norfolk bird is a better one, the Cheshire, Shropshire, or Northamptonshire bird is a very good one. In all these counties, especially in the two former, the partridge-shooting is only second to that of the eastern counties; and in all alike pointers and setters still continue to be used. The small rushy enclosures and wide pasture fields, full of thick tufts of grass, or tussocks, as the country people call them still, furnish capital lying for the partridges when driven from the stubbles or the turnips. But without a good dog you would not find a quarter of them. And over ground of this description you may still see pointers and setters range and stand and back as freely and beautifully as of yore. There are many other parts of England, though perhaps not quite such good partridge countries, of which the same is true: Leicestershire, for instance, and parts of Lincolnshire. But among all places in which to see dogs work to perfection, the first place must be assigned to the Essex marshes.

The Essex marshes lie close down to the water, but are never very wet, and are covered all over with long coarse grass, affording quite as thick cover as turnips, and much drier. Regarded from any rising ground they appear to be quite flat; but when you come upon them you find them very uneven walking, being full of little knolls and hollows, in which the birds lie like stones. After driving five or six coveys from the uplands down to a piece of ground of this description, stretching perhaps over six or seven hundred acres without a hedge or a hill in sight, you have work enough and range enough for pointers; and, indeed, without their assistance you cannot find the birds at all. There the use of dogs in shooting is still illustrated to perfection, and better sport, barring the dullness of the scenery, can hardly be imagined.

Lately, we believe, there has been a great demand for pointers and setters in America, enormous prices being readily given for the best English blood. On what game or in what kind of cover they are used we do not know. But at all events there seems no prospect at present of these beautiful breeds becoming extinct, as has been the case with some of our hounds and also with some of our spaniels. The old Sussex spaniel, for instance, a strong, reddish-brown dog, was an excellent dog to shoot behind; but he is rarely seen now. His place has been taken by the Norfolk spaniel, the clumber, and the cocker the last, however, by far less common than he used to be; and various crosses between these three breeds form the bulk of the spaniels which are now used in shooting. They are very useful in partridge-shooting, and some well-known sportsmen have preferred them to any other kind. They can be trained to work very close, and to pause, though of course not to point, when they are close to game. Retrieving is part of their business, and they will catch a winged bird in turnips with much less noise, bustle, and disturbance than the big black animal who often flushes scores in his efforts to catch one. For hedgerows, the spaniel is invaluable, and the regular retriever useless.

from *Pall Mall Gazette*, 1879

The Hunt

Not all the gallant cavalry of the land fearlessly charging hedge and brook can, however, repel the invasion of a foe mightier than their chief. Frost sometimes comes and checks their gaiety. Snow falls, and levels every furrow, and then Hodge going to his work in the morning can clearly trace the track of one of his most powerful masters, Squire Reynard, who has been abroad in the night, and, likely enough, throttled the traditional grey goose. The farmer watches for the frozen thatch to drip; the gentleman visiting the stable looks up disconsolately at the icicles dependent from the slated eave with the same hope. The sight of a stray seagull wandering inland is gladly welcomed, as the harbinger of drenching clouds sweeping up on soft south-westerly gales from the nearest coast.

The hunt is up once more, and so short are the hours of the day in the dead of the year, that early night often closes round the chase. From out of the gloom and the mist comes the distant note of the horn, with a weird and old-world sound. By-and-by the labourer, trudging homeward, is overtaken by a hunter whose horse's neck droops with weariness. His boots are splashed with mud, his coat torn by the thorns. He is a visitor, vainly trying to find his way home, having come some ten or fifteen miles across country since the morning. The labourer shows the route – the longest way round is the shortest at night – and as they go listens eagerly to the hunter's tale of the run. At the cross roads they part with mutual goodwill towards each other, and a shilling, easily earned, pays that night for the cottager's pipe and glass of ale.

from *Hodge and his Masters*, 1880

Early in March

On the southern side of the hedge, where the dead oak leaves still cumber the trailing ivy, pointed tongues of green are pushing up. Some have widened into black-spotted leaves; some are notched like the many-barbed bone harpoons of savage races. The hardy docks are showing, and the young nettles have risen up.

Slowly the dark and grey hues of winter are yielding to the lively tints of spring. The blackthorn has white buds on its lesser branches, and the warm rays of the sun have drawn forth the buds on one favoured hawthorn in a sheltered nook, so that the green of the coming leaf is visible. The climbing woodbine has a few perfect leaves – that it has no more is a sign of the lateness of the season. Bramble bushes still retain their forlorn, shrivelled foliage; the hardy all but evergreen leaves can stand cold, but when biting winds from the north and east blew for weeks together even these curled at the edge and died.

The remarkable power of the wind upon leaves is sometimes seen in May, when a strong gale, even from the west, will so beat and batter the tender horse-chestnut sprays that they bruise and blacken. The northerly winds and the frost kept back the wild violet and the primrose, so that in places they are hardly to be found. The slow plough traverses the earth, and the white dust rises from the road and drifts into the field. In winter the distant copse seemed black; now it appears of a dull reddish brown from the innumerable catkins and buds. The delicate sprays of the birch are fringed with them, the aspen has a load of brown, there are green catkins on the bare hazel boughs, and the willows have white 'pussy-cats.' The horse-chestnut buds – the hue of dark varnish – have enlarged and stick to the finger if touched; some are so swollen as to nearly burst and let the green appear.

Already it is becoming more difficult to look right through the copse. In winter the light could be seen on the other side; now catkin, bud, and opening leaf have thickened and check the view. The same effect was produced not long since by the rime on the branches in the frosty mornings; while each smallest twig was thus lined with crystal it was not possible to see through. Tangled weeds float down the brook, catching against projecting branches that dip into the stream, or slowly rotating and carried apparently up the current by the eddy and back water behind the bridge. In the pond the frogs have congregated in great numbers; their constant 'croo-croo' is audible at some distance.

The meadows, so long bound by frost and covered with snow, are slowly losing their wan aspect, and assuming a warmer green as the young blades of grass come upwards. Where the plough or harrow has passed over the clods they quickly change from the rich brown of fresh-turned soil to a whiter colour, the dryness of the atmosphere immediately dissipating the moisture in the earth. So, examine what you will, from the clod to the tiniest branch, the hedge, the mound, the fen, the water – everywhere a step forward has been taken. The difference in a particular case may be minute; but it is there, and together these faint indications show how closely spring is approaching.

As the sun rises the chaffinch utters his bold challenge on the tree; the notes are so rapid that they seem to come all at once. Welcome, indeed, is the song of the first finch. Sparrows are busy in the garden – the hens are by far the most numerous now, half a dozen together perch on the bushes. One suddenly darts forth and seizes a black insect as it flies in the sunshine. The bee, too, is abroad, and once now and then a yellow butterfly. From the copse on the warmer days comes occasionally the deep hollow bass of the wood pigeon; but even yet his fellows have scarcely paired. Flocks of wood pigeons were feeding together in the arable field quite recently; they came day after day to the same spot, near a hedgerow full of elms. Every few minutes one fluttered up to the ivy growing round the trunks for berries are now ripe.

The quantity of wild ivy berries this season is immense; some elms for twenty feet or more up the trunks are black with the thick bunches. On the very topmost branch of an elm a magpie has perched; now he looks this way, and then turns that, bowing in the oddest manner, and jerking his long tail up and down. Then two of them flutter across the field –feebly, as if they had barely strength to reach the trees in the opposite hedge. Extending their wings they float slowly, and every now and then the body undulates along its entire length. Rooks are building – they fly and feed now in pairs; the rookery is alive with them. To the steeple the jackdaws have returned and fly round and round; now one holds his wings rigid and slides down at an angle of 60 degrees at a breakneck pace, as if about to dash himself in fragments on the garden beneath.

'It is like summer,' was the general remark on the 6th, 7th, 8th and 9th. For those four successive days there was an almost cloudless sky, a gentle warm breeze, and a bright sun filling the fields with a glow of light. The air, though soft and genial, was dry, and perhaps it was this quality which gave so peculiar a definition to hedge, tree, and hill. A firm, almost hard, outline brought copse and wood into clear relief; the distance across the broadest fields appears sensibly diminished. Such freedom from moisture had a deliciously exhilarating effect on those who breathed so pure an atmosphere.

The winds of March differ, indeed, in a remarkable manner from the gales of the early year, which, even when they blow from a mild quarter, compel one to keep in constant movement because of the aqueous vapour they carry. But the true March wind, though too boisterous to be exactly genial, causes a joyous sense of freshness, as if the very blood in the veins were refined and quickened upon inhaling it. There is a difference in its roar – the note is distinct from the harsh sound of the chilly winter blast. On the lonely highway at night, when other noises are silent, the March breeze rushes through the tall elms in a wild cadence. The white clouds hasten over, illuminated from behind by a moon approaching the full; every now and then a break shows a clear blue sky and a star shining. Now a loud roar resounds along the hedgerow like the deafening boom of the surge; it moderates, dies away, then an elm close by bends and sounds as the blast comes again. In another moment the note is caught up and repeated by a distant tree, and so one after another joins the song till the chorus reaches its highest pitch. Then it sinks again, and so continues with pauses and deep inspirations, for March is like a strong man drawing his breath full and long as he starts to run a race.

The sky, too, like the earth, whose hedges, trees, and meadows are acquiring fresher colours, has now a more lovely aspect. At noon-day, if the clouds be absent, it is a rich azure; after sunset a ruddy glow appears almost all round the horizon, while the thrushes sing in the wood till the twilight declines. At night, when the moon does not rise till late, the heavens are brilliant with stars. In the east Arcturus is up; the Great Bear, the Lesser Bear, and Cassiopeia are ranged about the Pole. Procyon goes before the Dog; the noble constellation of Orion stretches broad across the sky; almost overhead lucent Capella looks down. Aries droops towards the west; the Bull follows with the red Aldebaran, and the Pleiades. Behind these, Castor and Pollux, and next the cloud-like, nebulous Cancer. Largest of all, great Sirius is flaming in the south, quivering with the ebb and flow of his light, sometimes with a faint emerald scintillation like a dewdrop on which a sunbeam glances. The grandeur of our northern sky culminates at about the time of the vernal equinox; from the summit of a hill on a clear evening the scene is of surpassing beauty.

Though every presage speaks of spring, and the sun has reached a sufficient height to shine with considerable heat on a still day, yet snowflakes have still to fall. The present season is at least a fortnight later than last – that is, vegetation has been delayed so much longer. The following diary shows the progress of nature in the neighbourhood of London:

Feb. 1st: the woodbine began to open a leaf or two, much checked by the bitter winds. Next day the marsh tit was sharpening his saw; the note resembles a file on the teeth of a saw.

Feb. 5th: The chaffinch began his call in the morning; his lively 'chink tink', the herald of milder days, was singularly welcome after the long silence of some eight weeks. For great part of that time even the robins were voiceless, so that the chaffinch was hailed with delight.

Feb. 7th: There was a little rain in the morning; the afternoon was mild, with a strong westerly wind. A lark soared up from the moist arable field, singing all the while, to an immense height; the first noticed, a gladsome sight. Two or three more rose and sang also. The misselthrush sang in the copse, and the chaffinches began to battle for their mates.

Feb. 12th: Partridges have paired; so, too, rooks. A lark soaring at half-past five in the evening; twilight.

Feb. 20th: A plough at work again. A beautiful sunset; pale green sky near horizon, above rosy-tinted clouds. Next morning the snow was deep on the ground once more; the long slender boughs of the broom, that naturally point upwards, were so heavily laden that they bowed down and pointed to the earth.

It did not thaw until the 27th March: Frogs congregated in pond; last year (the same pond) on Feb. 18th – just fifteen days later this season.

March 9th: A yellow butterfly, the first noticed; also about a fortnight later.

March 10th: First hawthorn leaf showing green: say half out.

March 14th: Horse-chestnut buds, on warm situations, on the point of bursting. The starlings have begun nest-building after evincing much hesitation.

from *Hodge and his Masters*, 1880

Fishing for Trout by the River Exe

The whortleberry bushes are almost as thick as the heather in places on the steep, rocky hills that overlook the Exe. Feeding on these berries when half ripe is said to make the heath poults thin (they are acid), so that a good crop of whortleberries is not advantageous to the black game. Deep in the hollow the Exe winds and bends, finding a crooked way among the ruddy rocks. Sometimes an almost inaccessible precipice rises on one shore, covered with firs and ferns, which no one can gather; while on the other is a narrow but verdant strip of mead. Coming down in flood from the moors the Exe will not wait to run round its curves, but rushes across the intervening corner, and leaves behind, as it subsides, a mass of stones, flat as slates or scales, destroying the grass. But the fly-fisherman seeks the spot because the water is swift at the angle of the stream and broken by a ledge of rock. He can throw up stream – the line falls soft as silk on the slow eddy below the rock, and the fly is drawn gently towards him across the current.

When a natural fly approaches the surface of running water, and flutters along just above it, it encounters a light air, which flows in the same direction as the stream. Facing this surface breeze, the fly cannot progress straight up the river, but is carried sideways across it. This motion the artificial fly imitates; a trout takes it, and is landed on the stones. He is not half a pound, yet in the sunshine has all the beauty of a larger fish. Spots of cochineal and gold dust, finely mixed together, dot his sides; they are not red nor yellow exactly, as if gold dust were mixed with some bright red. A line is drawn along his glistening greenish side, and across this there are faintly marked lozenges of darker colour, so that in swimming past he would appear barred. There are dark spots on the head between the eyes, the tail at its lower and upper edges is pinkish; his gills are bright scarlet. Proportioned and exquisitely shaped, he looks like a living arrow, formed to shoot through the water. The delicate little creature is finished in every detail, painted to the utmost minutiae, and carries a wonderful store of force, enabling him to easily surmount the rapids.

from 'By the Exe', *The Life of the Fields*, 1884

The Hedgerow

In the mornings of autumn the webs of the spiders hang along the hedge bowed a little with dew, like hammocks of gossamer slung from thorn to thorn. Then the hedge-sparrows, perching on the topmost boughs of the hawthorn, cry 'peep-peep' mournfully; the heavy dew on the grass beneath arranges itself in two rows of drops along the edges of the blades. From the day when the first leaf appears upon the hardy woodbine, in the early year, to the time when the partridge finds the eggs in the ant-hill, and on again till the last harebell dies, there is always something beautiful or interesting in these great hedgerows. Indeed, it is impossible to exhaust them. I have omitted the wild geranium with its tiny red petals scarce seen in the mass of green, the mosses, the ferns, and have scarcely said a word about the living creatures that haunt it. But then one might begin to write a book about a hedgerow when a boy and find it incomplete in old age.

from *Round About a Great Estate*, 1880

Hares Boxing

There is a rough grass growing within the enclosure of the earthwork and here and there upon the hills, which the sheep will not eat, so that it remains in matted masses. In this the hares make their forms; and they must, somehow, have a trick of creeping into their places, since many of the grass-blades often arch over, and if they sprang into the form heedlessly this could not be the case, as their size and weight would crush it down. When startled by a passer-by the hare – unless there is a dog – goes off in a leisurely fashion, doubtless feeling quite safe in the length of his legs, and after getting a hundred yards or so sits upon his haunches and watches the intruder. Their 'runs' or paths are rather broader than a rabbit's, and straighter – the rabbit does not ramble so far from home; he has his paths across the meadow to the hedge on the other side, but no farther. The hare's track may be traced for a great distance crossing the hills; but while the roads are longer they are much fewer in number. The rabbit makes a perfect network of 'runs' and seems always to feed from a regular path; the hare apparently feeds anywhere, without much reference to the 'runs', which he uses simply to get from one place to another in the most direct line, and also, it may be suspected, as a promenade on which to meet the ladies of his acquaintance by moonlight.

It is amusing to see two of these animals drumming each other; they stand on their hind legs (which are very long) like a dog taught to beg, and strike with the fore-pads as if boxing, only the blow is delivered downwards instead of from the shoulder. The clatter of their pads may be heard much farther than would be supposed. Round and round they go like a couple waltzing; now one giving ground and then the other, the fore-legs striking all the while with marvellous rapidity. Presently they pause – it is to recover breath only; and, 'time' being up, to work they go again with renewed energy, dancing round and round, till the observer cannot choose but smile. This trick they will continue till you are weary of watching.

from *Wild Life in a Southern County*, 1879

Poaching as a Profession *(Part I)*

There are three kinds of poachers, the local men, the raiders coming in gangs from a distance, and the 'mouchers' – fellows who do not make precisely a profession of it, but who occasionally loiter along the roads and hedges picking up whatever they can lay hands on. Philologists may trace a resemblance between the present provincial word 'mouching' and Shakespeare's 'mitcher,' who ate blackberries. Of the three probably the largest amount of business is done by the local men, on the principle that the sitting gamester sweeps the board. They therefore deserve first consideration.

It is a popular belief that the village poacher is an idle, hang-dog ne'er-do-well, with a spice of sneaking romance in his disposition –

the Bohemian of the hamlet, whose grain of genius has sprouted under difficulties, and produced weeds instead of wheat. This is a complete fallacy, in our day at least. Poaching is no longer an amusement, a thing to be indulged in because

It's my delight of a shiny night
In the season of the year;

but a hard, prosaic business, a matter of pounds, shillings and pence, requiring a long-headed, shrewd fellow, with a power of silence, capable of a delicacy of touch which almost raises poaching into a fine art. The real man is often a sober and to all appearance industrious individual, working steadily during the day at some handicraft in the village, as blacksmithing, hedge-carpentering – i.e. making posts and rails, etc – cobbling, tinkering, or perhaps in the mill; a somewhat reserved, solitary workman of superior intelligence and frequently advanced views as to the 'rights of labour.' He has no appetite for thrilling adventure; his idea is simply money, and he looks upon his night-work precisely as he does upon his day-labour.

His great object is to avoid suspicion, knowing that success will be proportionate to his skill in cloaking his operations; for in a small community, when a man is 'suspect,' it is comparatively easy to watch him, and a poacher knows that if he is watched he must sooner or later be caught. Secrecy is not so very difficult; for it is only with certain classes that he need practise concealment: his own class will hold their peace. If a man is seen at his work in the day, if he is moderate in his public-house attendance, shows himself at church, and makes friends with the resident policeman (not as a confederate, but to know his beat and movements), he may go on for years without detection.

Perhaps the most promising position for a man who makes a science of it is a village at the edge of a range of downs, generally fringed with large woods on the lower slopes. He has then ground to work alternately, according to the character of the weather and the changes of the moon. If the weather be wet, windy, or dark from the absence of the moon, then the wide open hills are safe; while, on the other hand, the woods are practically inaccessible, for a man must have the eyes of a cat to see to do his work in the impenetrable blackness of the plantations. So that upon a bright night the judicious poacher prefers the woods, because he can see his way, and avoids the hills, because, having no fences to speak of, a watcher may detect him a mile off.

Meadows with double mounds and thick hedges may be worked almost at any time, as one side of the hedge is sure to cast a shadow, and instant cover is afforded by the bushes and ditches. Such meadows are the happy hunting-grounds of the poacher for that reason, especially if not far distant from woods, and consequently overrun with rabbits. For, since the price of rabbits has risen so high, they are very profitable as game, considering that a dozen or two may be captured without noise and without having to traverse much space – perhaps in a single hedge.

The weather most unsuitable is that kind of frost which comes on in the early morning, and is accompanied with some rime on the grass – a duck's frost, just sufficient to check fox-hunting. Every footstep on grass in this condition when the sun comes out burns up as black as if the sole of the boot were of red-hot iron, and the poacher leaves an indelible trail behind him. But as three duck's frosts usually bring rain, a little patience is alone necessary. A real, downright six weeks' frost is, on the contrary, very useful – game lie close. But a deep snow is not welcome; for, although many starved animals may be picked up, yet it quite suspends the operations of the regular hand: he can neither use wire, net, nor ferret.

Windy nights are disliked, particularly by rabbit-catchers, who have to depend a great deal upon their sense of hearing to know when a rabbit is moving in the 'buries', and where he is likely to 'bolt', so as to lay hands on him the instant he is in the net. But with the 'oak's mysterious roar' overhead, the snapping of dead branches, and the moan of the gale as it rushes through the hawthorn, it is difficult to distinguish the low, peculiar thumping sound of a rabbit in his catacomb. The rabbit is not easily dislodged in rain; for this animal avoids getting wet as much as possible: he 'bolts' best when it is dry and still.

A judicious man rarely uses a gun, for the reason that noise is inconvenient, and a gun is an awkward tool to carry concealed about the person even when taken to pieces. There is a certain prejudice in rural places against a labouring man possessing a gun; it is sure to draw suspicion upon him. A professional poacher is pre-eminently a trapper, relying chiefly upon the dexterous employment of the snare. If he does shoot, by preference he chooses a misty day, knowing that the sound of the report travels scarcely half the usual distance through fog; and he beats the meadows rather than the reserves, where the discharge would instantly attract attention, while in the meadows or ploughed fields it may pass unnoticed as fired by a farmer with leave to kill rabbits.

When the acorns are ripe and the pheasants wander great distances from the plantations along the hedgerows is his best time for shooting; no keepers at that period can protect them. He also observes where the partridges which roost on the ground assemble nightly as it grows dark, easily ascertaining the spot by their repeated calls to each other, and sometimes knocks over three or four at a shot.

Occasionally, also, early in the season, before the legitimate sportsman perhaps has stepped into the stubble, and while the coveys are large, he sees a good chance, and with two or even three ounces of shot makes havoc among them. He invariably fires at his game sitting, first, because he cannot lose an opportunity, and, next, because he can kill several at once. He creeps up behind a hedge, much as the sportsman in Rubens' picture in the National Gallery is represented, stooping to get a view, himself unseen, at the brown birds on the ground. With the antique fire-lock such a practice was necessary; but nothing in our day so stamps a man a poacher as this total denial of 'law' to the game.

When the pheasant is shot his next difficulty is with the feathers. The fluffy, downy under-feathers fly in all directions, scattering over the grass, and if left behind would tell an unmistakable tale. They must therefore be collected as far as possible, and hidden in the ditch. The best pockets for carrying game are those made in the tails of the coat, underneath: many poachers' coats are one vast pocket behind the lining.

When there is special danger of being personally overhauled and searched, or when the 'bag' is large, the game is frequently hidden in a rabbit-hole, taking care to fence the hole some distance inside with a stout stick across it, the object of which is that if the keeper or a sportsman should pass that way his dogs, scenting the game, will endeavour to scratch out the earth and get in after it. This the cross stick will prevent, and the keeper will probably thrash his dog for refusing to obey when called off.

A great deal of poaching used to be accomplished by nets, into which both partridges and pheasants were driven. If skilfully alarmed – that is, not too much hurried – these birds will run a long way before rising, and, if their tracks are known, may be netted in considerable numbers. But of recent years, since pheasants especially have become so costly a luxury to keep, the preserves and roosting-places have been more effectually watched, and this plan has become more difficult to put in practice. In fact, the local man thinks twice before he puts his foot inside a preserve, and, if possible, prefers to pick up outside. If a preserve is broken into the birds are at once missed, and there is a hue and cry; but the loss of outsiders is not immediately noticed. But here, as there is much more to be said about poachers and poaching, we had better stop for the day.

from *The Gamekeeper at Home*, 1878

Poaching as a Profession *(Part II)*

The wire is, perhaps, the regular poacher's best implement, and ground game his most profitable source of income. Hares exist in numbers upon the downs, especially near the localities where the great coursing meetings are held, where a dozen may be kicked out of the grass in five minutes. In these districts of course the downs are watched; but hares cannot be kept within bounds, and wander miles and miles at night, limping daintily with their odd gait (when undisturbed) along the lanes leading into the ploughed fields on the lower slopes and plains. The hills – wide and almost pathless, and practically destitute of fences – where the foot leaves no trail on the short grass and elastic turf, are peculiarly favourable to illicit sport.

Though apparently roaming aimlessly, hares have their regular highways or 'runs' and it is the poacher's business to discover which of these narrow paths are most beaten by continuous use. He then sets his wire, as early in the evening as compatible with safety to himself, for hares are abroad with the twilight.

Long practice and delicate skill are essential to successful snaring. First, the loop itself into which the hare is to run his head must be of the exact size. If it be too small he will simply thrust it aside; if too large his body will slip through, and his hind leg will be captured: being crooked, it draws the noose probably. Then if caught by the hind leg, the wretched creature, mad with terror, will shriek his loudest; and a hare shrieks precisely like a human being in distress. The sound, well-understood by the watchers, will at once reveal what is going forward. But there may be no watchers about; and in that case the miserable animal will tug and tug during the night till the wire completely bares the lower bone of the leg, and in the morning, should any one pass, his leaps and bounds and rolls will of course be seen. Sometimes he twists the wire till it snaps, and so escapes – but probably to die a lingering death, since the copper or brass is pretty sure to mortify the flesh. No greater cruelty can be imagined. The poacher, however, is very anxious to avoid it, as it may lead to detection; and if his wire is properly set the animal simply hangs himself, brought up with a sudden jerk which kills him in two seconds, and with less pain than is caused by the sting of the sportsman's cartridge.

Experience is required to set the loop at the right height above the ground. It is measured by placing the clenched fist on the earth, and then putting the extended thumb of the other open hand upon it, stretching it out as in the action of spanning, when the tip of the little finger gives the right height for the lower bend of the loop – that is, as a rule; but clever poachers vary it slightly to suit the conformation of the ground. A hare carries his head much higher than might be thought; and he is very strong, so that the plug which holds the wire must be driven in firmly to withstand his first convulsive struggle. The small upright stick whose cleft suspends the wire across the 'run' must not be put too near the hare's path, or he will see it, and it must be tolerably stiff, or his head will push the wire aside. Just behind a 'tussocky' bunch of grass is a favourite spot to set a noose; the grass partially conceals it.

The poacher revisits his snares very early in the morning, and if he is judicious invariably pulls them up, whether successful or not, because they may be seen in the day. Half the men who are fined by the magistrates have been caught by keepers who, having observed wires, let them remain; but keep a watch and take the offenders red-handed. The professional poacher never leaves his wires set up all day, unless a sudden change of weather and the duck's frost previously mentioned prevent him from approaching them, and then he abandons those particular snares for ever. For this reason he does not set up more than he can easily manage. If he gets three hares a night (wholesale price 2s. 6d. each) he is well repaid. Rabbits are also wired in great numbers. The loop is a trifle smaller, and should be just a span from the ground.

But the ferret is the poacher's chief assistant in rabbiting: it takes two men, one on each side of the 'bury', and a ferret which will not 'lie in' – stay in the hole and feast till overcome with sleep. Ferrets differ remarkably in disposition, and the poacher chooses his with care; otherwise, if the ferret will not come out the keepers are certain to find him the next day hunting on his own account. Part of the secret is to feed him properly, so that he may have sufficient appetite to hunt well and yet be quickly satisfied with a taste of blood. Skill is essential in setting up the nets at the mouth of the holes; but beyond the mere knack, easily acquired, there is little to learn in ferreting.

The greatest difficulty with any kind of game is to get home unobserved with the bag. Keepers are quite aware of this; and in the case of large estates, leaving one or two assistants near the preserves, they patrol the byways and footpaths, while the police watch the cross-roads and lanes which lead to the villages. If a man comes along at an exceptionally early hour with coat pockets violently bulging, there is a prima facie case for searching him. One advantage of wiring or netting over the gun is here very noticeable: anything shot bleeds and stains the pocket – a suspicious sign even when empty; strangulation leaves no traces. Without a knowledge of the policeman's beat and the keeper's post the poacher can do nothing on a large scale. He has, however, no great trouble in ascertaining these things; the labourers who do not themselves poach sympathise warmly and whisper information. There is reason to think that men sometimes get drunk, or sufficiently so to simulate intoxication very successfully, with the express purpose of being out all night with a good excuse, and so discovering the policeman's ambuscade.

Finding a man whom he knows to be usually sober overtaken with drink in a lonely road, where he injures none but himself, the policeman good-naturedly leads him home with a caution only. The receivers of game are many and various. The low beer-shop keepers are known to purchase large quantities. Sometimes a local pork-butcher in a small way buys and transmits it, having facilities for sending hampers, &c, unsuspected. Sometimes the carriers are the channel of communication; and there is no doubt the lower class of game dealers in the provincial towns get a good deal in this way. The London dealer, who receives large consignments at once, has of course no means of distinguishing poached from other game.

The men who purchase the rabbits ferreted by the keepers during the winter in the woods and preserves, and who often buy £100-worth or more in the season, have peculiar opportunities for conveying poached animals, carefully stowed for them in a ditch on their route. This fact having crept out has induced gentlemen to remove these rabbit contracts from local men, and to prefer purchasers from a distance, who must take some time to get acquainted with the district poachers.

The raiders, who come in gangs armed with guns and shoot in the preserves, are usually the scum of manufacturing towns, led or guided by a man expelled through his own bad conduct from the village, and who has a knowledge of the ground. These gangs display no skill; relying on their numbers, arms, and known desperation of character to protect them from arrest, as it does in nine cases out of ten. Keepers and policemen cannot be expected to face such brutes as these

100

fellows; they do sometimes, however, and get shattered with shot.

The 'mouchers' sneak about the hedgerows on Sundays with lurcher dogs, and snap up a rabbit or a hare; they do not do much damage except near great towns, where they are very numerous. Shepherds, also, occasionally mouch – their dogs being sometimes very expert; and ploughmen set wires in the gateways or gaps where they have noticed the track of a hare, but it is only for their own eating, and is not of much consequence in comparison with the work of the real local professional. These regular hands form a class which are probably more numerous now than ever; the reasons are – first, the high value of game and the immense demand for it since poultry has become so dear, and, secondly, the ease of transmission now that railways spread into the most out-lying districts and carry baskets or parcels swiftly out of reach. Poaching, in fact, well followed, is a lucrative business.

from *The Gamekeeper at Home*, 1878

Technique in Game Shooting

The Squire was a good shot. He handled his double-barrel in the manner authorized by the experience of sportsmen. When a covey was flushed, or a hare started from her form, his gun came easily to the shoulder, his left hand supported it slightly in front of the trigger-guard, and, although long practice had rendered aiming in the full sense of the word unnecessary, he did not fire till the sight was on the game. There was a short but appreciable interval between the levelling of the barrel and the flash, a fatal moment of adjustment, and this calm in effort seemed to control success, for he rarely missed. The bird fell without folding her wings; the hare stopped not to sit up but to lie limp and extended.

Perhaps the most eager time in shooting is when you look through the smoke to see what has been effected. Hardly any length of practice will quite efface the sense of expectation: the gunner must look, even if he knows he has killed.

The Squire's anticipation was often fulfilled; yet he did miss, and that many more times in the course of a day than sportsmen in this somewhat boastful age care to acknowledge. There seems a feverish dread lest the certainty of success should be broken by the failure of a single cartridge: a tension and anxiety as if such an incident were intolerable guilt.

The Squire's field education was completed before this fierce gamble of competition began. He did not feel that he had fallen out of the front rank even if now and then both barrels sent their contents whistling wide into the uninjured air. I think he enjoyed the stubble all the more.

This old-fashioned spirit, antecedent to the modern ideas of machine-precision, rather revolted from the patent shooting recently exhibited. Curiosity was excited, but the Squire did not much admire and was entirely devoid of emulation. Yet it quite upset all his philosophy of the gun, and perhaps that was why he did not like it. The delivery of a thousand rifle bullets pattering in succession on glass balls jerked into the air, infallibly shattering these bubbles as they rose overthrew all tradition. The bitterness was in the extreme simplicity of the trick: that no one ever thought of it. Apart, of course, from practice and natural dexterity, it merely consists in extending the left arm to nearly its full reach and holding the barrel close to the muzzle. On the appearance of the game, at once grasp the gun with the left hand, as high up the barrel as possible without inconveniently straining the muscles, and lift the left hand first, so that the muzzle may come up to the 'present' a moment before the right hand brings the butt to the shoulder. All depends on the left hand, which is the centre of this method, and which must be thrust out at the mark much the same as if it grasped a pistol.

To understand the new exercise correctly, try the experiment of holding the gun steady at the 'present' in this way, and, while keeping the left hand still, lower the right, letting the butt drop several inches and then raising it again. While the muzzle thus remains pointed by the left hand, the least motion of the right hand completes the position: the right, indeed, has little to do except to pull the trigger.

102

Thumb and fingers may meet round the barrels, if preferred, for still greater stability of the left hand, as that is somewhat easier to the muscles than when the palm is hollowed but the fingers are only partly closed. Seize the barrels firmly and push the muzzle up against the mark, just as if the muzzle were going to actually touch it. Thus, the left hand aims: in the most literal sense, positively putting the muzzle on the game.

With the double-barrel shotgun no sight is required; the hand need not be bent or one eye shut, or any process of aiming gone through at all. Simply seize the barrels as near the top as convenient to the length of the arm when not unnaturally stretched, raise the barrels the fraction of a moment before the butt, look fixedly at the game, and pull the trigger: the quicker, the better. Once more let it be repeated, all is centred on the left hand: the left hand must at once, with the very first movement, take hold, high up, and must not be slid there presently; the left hand must be lifted earliest; the left hand must be thrust out at and as if it were put on the game; the left hand aims. (Educate the left arm: teach it to correspond instantaneously with the direction of the glance; teach it to be absolutely stable for the three necessary seconds; let the left hand be your top sight; let the mind act through your left wrist. With practice, such snap-shooting is possible, as has been seen in our fields.)

The trick is not in the least difficult, though so opposite to all former ideas, which attached no special value to the left hand except as a support. To attain the greatest stability consistent with ease, the usual position of the left hand is just in front of, or, with some, partly over, the trigger-guard, much about the centre of gravity of the gun. This minimizes the weight: the barrels and the stock are balanced. The new position abolishes the balance altogether – at first it seems peculiar, but soon becomes natural: and thus the most cherished traditions of shooting are put aside.

With a rifle, some little modification of these instructions is necessary. There being but one pellet, it must be delivered with accuracy, and the top sight is of the utmost importance. That a full view of it may be obtained, the thumb and fingers of the left hand must not meet, as is permissible when shooting with the double-barrel. It should be hollowed, the barrel resting on it exactly as in the old position, but must be as near the muzzle as compatible with common sense: the nearer, the better. In every other respect, the new method, with the rifle, is precisely the same as in the gun. The left hand puts the top sight at once on the mark, with such precision and ease that, with practice, a running hare or rabbit could certainly be hit. The quicker the trigger is pressed, the better: here, again, the new method directly traverses tradition. A slow, deliberative rifleman was always considered, and often with good reason, as the most successful; but, with the new position, fire cannot be delivered too quickly – the very instant the top sight is on the mark – thus converting the rifleman into a snapshooter. Instead of searching about for the mark, like an astronomer for some faint star with his telescope, as was usually the case under the old style, in the new, the muzzle, the top sight, is put immediately on it, held there rigid, and the bullet has done its work before an old style rifleman could have got his weapon comfortably settled at his shoulder. The thing is capable of mathematical demonstration.

Anyone, however, may convince himself of the fact by a simple experiment with a walking-stick. Take the crook or knob in the right hand and place that hand upon the table. This represents the butt of the gun pressed to the shoulder, which is the fixed point. Put the thumb and finger of the left hand on the stick, about a third of its length, reckoning from the right. Then you have the gun held in the ordinary position. Now, while retaining the right hand still (as the shoulder would be), move the left hand laterally either way an inch or so. An inch of movement at the left hand causes thrice the deflection at the fore end of the stick. A mere sixteenth of an inch trebles itself there – the angle widens. This initial error in the aim goes on increasing, every yard, till at the mark forty yards away the largest spread of shot fails of effect. On a smaller scale, the same experiment may be carried out with a cedar pencil, and always with the same result: the closer the left hand is placed to the right, the more a slight initial movement increases the error (or widens the angle) at the top, or muzzle.

On the reverse, the opposite effect is produced. While still holding the crook or knob of the stick steady with the right hand, extend the left arm and place the thumb and finger on the stick as near the top as you conveniently can. Then you have the new position. It now requires a large lateral motion of the left hand to produce an error or divergence equal in extent to that which previously resulted from the least movement. The muzzle, or top of the stick, only varies from the straight line to the amount of the actual movement of the left hand; in the former case, a slight error of the hand multiplied itself at the muzzle.

As the arm is not a mechanical rest of iron which can be fixed irrespective of circumstances, but is endowed with feeling, with a beating pulse, muscles that relax or contract in response to the variation of the will, and is therefore uncertain in its action, anything that reduces these vibrations to a minimum must improve the shooting. The object is to get the eye, the top sight of the rifle or the muzzle of the gun, and the game, all three distinctly in a line with each other. When holding the gun, as the walking-stick was first held, say, at a third of its length, the muzzle has to go searching about for the mark. If practice brings up the gun true in general direction, still it has to be adjusted; and, when adjusted, the faintest error of the arm is doubled at the muzzle.

So that the new position is not only correct mathematically, it is best suited to the practical difficulties of shooting. You do not seem to depend on the gun, but simply on the left hand. You stretch out your left hand and, as it were, put it on the mark, and immediately fire.

All this applies, of course, to sporting only: that is, to shooting at short ranges. At the long distance target it would not answer. It applies also only to quick shooting. It is not possible to shoot slowly in the new position, not meaning the number of discharges but the time occupied in aiming. If anyone wishes to make a steady, slow aim, the old position is best. Indeed, it is scarcely possible to aim long – to dwell on the aim – in the new way: the arm extended very nearly to its full length soon begins to quiver a little; and when once the vibration begins it cannot be quite stopped unless it is lowered for a moment. When first raised, the muzzle is at once put on the mark; the arm retains it there, then fire – whether shotgun or rifle.

As most sporting, even with the improved rifles, takes place at short range, the value of the new method appears very high. One caution it is as well to add: and that is, not to try this plan except with a perfectly trustworthy gun. Since breech-loading has become universal, guns burst less frequently, as it is not possible to double charge, and the barrels can be looked through lest any dirt should choke them. But, even now, guns do burst occasionally.

I have no possible grounds upon which to go, but I have long had a faint suspicion that, since breech-loading was adapted to every gun, many guns have been turned out only just thick enough in the metal to bear the expected strain, and without any provision, as it were, against the chance of extra pressure. As the left hand is much exposed in the new position, let no one use it unless quite certain of his gun.

When a lad, I often used to shoot sparrows at a trap, and became very expert at it; and I remember that my success was due to the manner in which I held the gun, grasping it before giving the signal with the left hand where that hand would have to sustain it when at the shoulder. The difference was that not a second was lost in the adjustment of the left hand or support, and it had not to be slid into position. There was nothing to do but to keep the eyes fixed on the ground about six inches in front of the trap, give the signal, fling up the gun, and pull the trigger. This was, in a measure, an approach to the new position. But then all the sparrows started from the same spot. The new position puts the muzzle of the double-barrel at once on the flying game, just as if the top touched the partridge.

from *The Old House at Coate*, 1948

Wild-Fowling

About the middle of October, each year, large quantities of wild-fowl, ranging from wild swans to ducks, that have migrated from cold northern latitudes, visit our shores, and remain with us until the end of March, experiencing during the intervening period a pretty hard time of it. First they are exposed to the attack of the professional puntsmen, with whom wild-fowling is a special occupation from the time the first flights arrive until the main body take their departure in the early spring. Then there is an army of sportsmen gunners, and the shore-shooters, to many of whom the only chance of a day's sport is amongst the unpreserved fens and saltings or along the numerous creeks and rivers in the immediate vicinity of the seashore. Such localities are at all times a more or less sure find for wild-fowl of one sort or another.

Although the 'professionals' and certain amateur puntsmen have been busy for some weeks past, the majority of shore-shooters defer operations until the appearance of the first hard frost. At such times the birds are more scattered about the fens and marshes, electing during the daytime – their period of repose – to seek shelter in the creeks and ditches rather than betake themselves to the open sea at the break of day, as is their usual custom. On the other hand, during periods of prolonged frost or in boisterous weather wild-fowl on the open sea are more than usually alert, and consequently more difficult to approach in a gunning punt; so that the puntsmen fare but badly; whilst the shore-shooter's chances of making good bags are much enhanced.

It is the opinion of most wild-fowlers that in severe winters quite as many wild-fowl visit our shores as formerly; although it is certain that the continuous shooting to which they are exposed, added to an enormous increase of stream and maritime traffic, renders them each succeeding season more and more wary and difficult to approach even under the most favourable conditions. Moreover, the drainage operations carried out in the various Fen districts – formerly sanctuary of countless geese, ducks, widgeon, teal, grebes, dunbirds, curlew, plover, etc. – have done much to diminish the shore-shooter's chance of success. Apart, however from punt-shooting or traversing the various flats and saltings on foot, there remains to the wild-fowler one branch of his sport which has hardly been injured by the keener vigilance of the birds themselves or the reclamation of their feeding grounds. A vast area of marsh-land still borders certain parts of the eastern coast; and to such places the birds repair night after night to seek their food-supplies, returning to sea again with the first break of returning day if the weather be frosty or tempestuous. Just as the twilight is merging into gloom flocks of wild-fowl of every description wend their way inland to their accustomed haunts, hardly deviating a yard from their regular course. Accurate knowledge of their habits in this respect enables the 'flight' shooter to lay his plans accordingly. Having from some convenient coign of vantage observed for two or three evenings the exact direction the birds take, his next step is to find a suitable shelter directly in the line of flight, behind which he can lie concealed and await their arrival.

As a rule the birds when proceeding to or returning from their feeding-grounds, do not fly at a greater altitude than six or seven yards; and if there be a fall of snow, or the atmosphere changes to be hazy, this distance is often much reduced, so that the birds as they speed onward come within easy range of the ambushed gunner. Important as this advantage is, however, it is by no means conclusive. The velocity of flight is well-nigh incredible; and unless the gunner is aware of the birds' approach before they are close upon him, they will have passed over his head and out of range before he will have time to get his gun to his shoulder. The practised 'flight' shooter, however, will seldom be caught napping; his quick ears will have detected the whistling sound caused by the rapidly beating wings when the birds are still a hundred yards or so distant, and the gun will be levelled and the finger ready to press the trigger the instant the first 'skein' of geese or 'team' of ducks comes in sight. The aim must be well ahead of the bird or birds fired at; otherwise the charge will be expended far in rear of the hindermost feathers.

After all there is no certainty of success about 'flighting', as this style of shooting is termed. The birds may have been observed to take exactly the same line of flight night after night for a week together; but the very first night that the flight-shooter determines to put his observations to practical use he may fail to get a single shot. For some apparently unaccountable reason wild-fowl shift their feeding-grounds and the sportsman waits in vain for the birds that never come. This, however, does not often happen; and a good flighting station is usually much sought after, being almost certain to afford sport more or less good for a limited number of nights at all events.

Many sportsmen profess to find a special pleasure in wild-fowl shooting, as compared with any sport with the gun. But it is a pastime that every man is not fit for. To enjoy wild-fowling a man must have a sound constitution, able to resist extreme cold, which is almost inseparable from the sport, whether the gunner be a 'punstman,' 'shore shooter,' or 'flighter.' And in tramping about the Fens and marches even supposing high waterproof boots, there is always the chance of a false step leading to a partial if not total immersion; and this on a hard winter day is not what everybody can stand.

The old-fashioned method of stalking and shooting wild-fowl by means of a horse trained for the purpose, the shooter walking on the side farthest away from the birds and keeping pace with the animal's movements, has become practically extinct: and with it the practice of substituting a dummy horse, consisting of a wooden frame covered with canvas, and sufficiently roomy to admit of two gunners in its interior, their legs doing duty for those of the supposed animal. But a large area of marshy land yet remains on which the sportsman can enjoy his pastime: and to the man who is equal to the fatigue of carrying about a fowling-piece weighing some 8lb or 10lb, and is capable of much walking exercise without distress, there are many worse ways of spending a winter day than after wildfowl.

The practice of snaring wild-fowl by means of artificially constructed decoys has fallen almost entirely into disuse. It is probable that there are not at the present time a dozen decoys in existence throughout the United Kingdom. The increase of railways and the higher cultivation of land has done much to deter wild-fowl from making more than a merely temporary sojourn on the large inland sheets of water that at one time swarmed with them; and the few decoys that still remain are as probably kept up more for the sake of the thing than for any actual gain they may accrue.

from *St James's Gazette*, 1885

Iron-Bound December

From the north a wind came down that seemed black, for it darkened all the scene, as the month began. The sky was dark, the fields dark, the leaves at last blown from the trees left them dark: nothing but gloom and an icy cutting blast under which the earth became as iron. When the wind fell, the frost took a firmer hold. At night by the silent Thames (far 'above bridge') the footpath was clearly defined by the crystals of snow which thinly covered it, ceasing in a sharp line where the wall fell to the river. On the opposite side, the bank was again visible because of the snow and ice accumulated upon it. Presently, while walking by the shore you heard a low grinding, splintering sound, like breaking glass gently, were such a thing possible.

Then a broad white spot appeared floating on the black surface. It was an ice-floe, formed in some back-water or shallow behind an osier-grown eyot [small island]; and it had not yet been over a weir. After it came another and another; and, with irregular intervals between, these floes followed each other in slow procession through the silence and the darkness. Calm, still, black, and repellent, the river flowed on: coming out of night and going into night, and only made visible by the snow-lined shore and its chilly burden.

By day the banks in places seemed inaccessible, from piles of ice lying high above the water and presenting their jagged edges outwards in layers. Further down in the tidal way the floes, having been carried over the weir, were broken up and roughly rounded. The pieces varied from one to three feet in diameter, and seemed mostly sexagonal or octagonal in shape. Sometimes a dozen such pieces had become frozen together – a mosaic of ice. These rotated slowly as they floated – now swept down and now up the river by the current, passing in two broad bands which in places filled more than half the Thames. The two broad bands were caused by vessels moored in the centre of the stream which divided the ice, and also by the arches of the bridges. The roughly rounded floes, too, collected between barges and wherever there was any impediment, and thus at times and in certain places very nearly presented the appearance of a river frozen right across.

As the tide ebbed, many of the floes became stranded on the mud, and were then seen to be fully a foot thick. They had gradually grown to that thickness by the spray thrown up on their surface and there freezing, and by snowy spicules falling from the atmosphere. The water seemed thick – as it were coagulated – even where it was not quite frozen.

This terrible weather forced the birds to face even the danger of a lurking cat in the garden. Those who desire to befriend birds cannot do better than keep cats indoors as much as possible, especially in the morning. A few hours of such restraint can do no harm to a well-fed domestic animal, and enables the blackbird or thrush to get a breakfast. After roosting all night on boughs coated with rime, birds are ravenous as they awake. One morning in the midst of the frost, as I passed a certain house, I was attracted by an unusual chattering of birds in the garden. Looking over the low enclosure the cause was apparent. There was a poultry-yard just within, fenced all round with wire, but open above. Two or three small trees, cherry and apple, grew in the centre; and these were positively black with starlings, blackbirds, thrushes, and sparrows. Two rooks were perched on one of the trees, and besides this assembled crowd, other birds were coming and going and fluttering about.

On the ground some fowls were leisurely picking up a quantity of food that had been thrown to them. The rooks, the starlings, and the rest had gathered at the sight of this food, and were perched not more than five or six feet above it, on the lower branches of the little trees. Below in the midst of the fowls was crouched a black cat, motionless, and with tail and feet tucked under for warmth. The creature was as fat as it could well be. So the beast crouched among the fowls, not even looking upwards at the birds, but in an attitude of contented repose, though really keeping a sharp watch. Neither rook, starling, nor sparrow dared to descend for a crumb. Now, to the food thrown down for a chained dog the small birds will come without much fear.

Such continued frost, however, forced the blackbirds and thrushes to the walls of the house to search under the dead flowers or ferns lying in the narrow patch beneath the window. On the bitterest mornings, when even the fog hung low, the sparrows, usually so brisk, appeared torpid even at ten o'clock. Several at that hour were seen perched at chimney-sides, with their beaks tucked under their wings in the attitude of sleep. Later on they congregated in the copse at one particular spot, bare of underwood but much strewn with leaves. Another spot in an orchard was resorted to by blackbirds and starlings morning after morning, and, indeed, some could be found there all day. It was a slight depression in the ground, with a little rougher grass than grew elsewhere, and nothing so far as the eye could see to attract them; for the sward was as covered with hoar-frost and the soil seemingly as hard as all around. The rest of the orchard was deserted, but upon that particular place, say about two yards square, there were always blackbirds and starlings. In the middle of the road a crow lingered till approached within twenty yards, and even then he slowly winged his way to an adjacent tree. He was so hard pressed for food that he scarce seemed to care to move. Farther along, a flock of rooks were all huddled together on the ground immediately outside a rickyard; so close to each other as almost to touch. The sun was now shining brilliantly, though without the least apparent effect upon the hoar frost.

A rustling sound in the sward by the roadside made me go nearer, when I found a mole working through the grass and dead leaves all white and frozen together. He heaved them up and pushed through them, hidden and yet above the surface of the ground, which was frozen too hard for him to enter. His course zigzagged from side to side, and tracing it backwards I saw an old mole-hill by the side of a ditch; the sign of a subterranean passage there made when the earth was softer.

From that passage he had gone forth on an exploring expedition, vainly endeavouring to find some earth into which he could dig in search of food. I placed my foot between him and the molehill. He instantly turned to rush back, but finding the obstacle tried his very hardest to burrow. He scratched, he tore at the earth; but it was like iron, and he could do nothing but cling tightly to the fibres of grass. When picked up and placed in the road he wagged his short tail and made off at a considerable speed – much faster than such an animal would seem capable of going, but to all appearance without any sense of direction. If touched he turned on his back, squeaked like a tiny pig, and fought with all four feet vigorously. I now put him in a ditch where I saw the earth was softer. He buried himself out of sight in a couple of minutes, and I left him in snugness and safety.

I had gone but a few yards farther when I saw another mole pass along the bank from the mouth of one small hole to a second. He slipped across in an instant. Not long afterwards I observed a third at work in a similar way, above the surface, but hidden under the grass and leaves; and I presently found a fourth, this time quite exposed and running over the frozen turf. It is not often that so many are seen at once above the surface. A mole at work in a frost is supposed to indicate a coming thaw, and often does so; but these could not work, could not throw up molehills, or extend their subterranean passages, and their coming to the surface showed that the frost had gone deeply into the earth. Possibly the sunshine, though it did not thaw the hoar-frost, may have affected them, for they seem very susceptible to change of temperature.

Low down on the sunny side of the same bank a mouse had ventured forth, searching along under the creeping ivy. A thrush stood on the bricked top of a drain under a gateway, with a small snail in his bill. This he lifted and tapped on the brick till I came quite close: he then flew three or four yards to a clod of earth and tapped the snail on that. Again disturbed he went to the bottom of the ditch and tapped it there. In ordinary winters he would have waited till I had gone by and returned to the brick or to a stone; but every clod, and even the bottom of the ditch, was hard enough for the purpose then.

Wood-pigeons this autumn must have missed the acorns, of which they are extremely fond. The acorns were not only few in number, but those that were found were often shrivelled or very small. Returning along the road, a robin came out from the hedge and alighted on the ground not three yards in front of me. As I came near he flew ahead, alighting every two or three yards. This he repeated for fully a furlong. What he meant was fully expressed: 'I am hungry; feed me.' At last, wearied of asking, the poor thing went to the hedge.

The rime was sometimes so thick upon the trees that small birds and even starlings were hidden when they perched, more so than if the branches had been covered with summer foliage. At midday in the bright sunshine the hoary trees encrusted to the tiniest twig stood out against the pale blue sky. One morning there was no rime, but presently a slight wind arose from the north-east, and under its influence rime formed on the trees, and they gradually grew white in daylight under one's very eyes. That side towards the current – it was a very slight current – became hoar first. Every needle on the Scotch firs was coated with the white crystals. The slender birch boughs seemed enlarged – thickened – by the deposit. When at last a thaw began it was so slow that for three days it hung on the balance, and neither froze nor thawed, properly speaking. Gloomy fogs then ensued and would not lift, for there was an absence of wind; and even now, at the moment of writing, by the river-banks there are considerable quantities of snow and ice remaining, and the ponds are covered with ice. The blocks thrown out where the ice is broken for the cattle are still four inches thick, and the earth, which was softer for a day or two, is hard again. It does not seem to matter which way the air drifts – it does not blow – whether north, west, or even south, it freezes all the same.

from *Pall Mall Gazette*, 1878

Wild Fowl Shooting

Drifting in the darkness in a shallow skiff, with the mercury many degrees below the freezing point – with a blustering wind driving icy particles in the sportsman's face and rocking him on tumbling water that occasionally breaks over him in spray – does not sound specially enjoyable to the uninitiated, nor is a combination of these untoward conditions indispensable to the sport of the wild fowl shooter, yet he infinitely prefers them to such weather as we have lately been experiencing. In a persistently open winter his occupation is well nigh gone, and the wild fowl, with all their senses about them, have it very much their own way. They are shy and wary, diving or rising out of sight or shot; for it takes hard weather to tame them and dull the keenness of their instincts. So the wild fowl shooter ought to be an enthusiast, afraid neither of exposure nor of severe work.

Of course he must be blessed with a sound constitution, or his will speedily be a case for the doctors; and enthusiast as he is, he must have coolness as well as nerve, otherwise excitement will spoil his chances and possibly run him into serious risks. He should have what corresponds in sport to 'the five o'clock in the morning' courage of war. For the long-expected opportunity may come to him when he is stiff and sleepy; he must decide on his tactics on the spur of the moment, and take a deadly aim from a rocking gun carriage. Nor independently of the chances of coughs and chest complaints would a prudent life office insure him on such easy terms as his friends whom he has left reposing on their feather beds. For every now and again, whether he is beating the swamps along the shore or retrieving his game on a mud bank, he may stumble on to some quicksand that is laying hold of his legs, and threatening him with the fate of the Master of Ravenswood; while if his ardour makes him forgetful of hydrographic observations, he may find himself fleeing for his life from a tide that flows like the Solway, with the odds in favour of the swift-running waves.

But in spite of all that, there are men with whom the sport becomes a passion, and we cannot say we are surprised at it, for assuming an average English season, with a fair admixture of cold and storms, the wild fowler may always count upon excitement in one form or another. If he does not come across the flight of swans or geese, if ducks and divers are scarce or shy, he may fall back on the humbler species of waders, such as sandpipers, oxbirds, redshanks, or greenshanks. They offer him the charm of infinite variety, and he never knows what he may next bring to bag. He may be floating silently in the doubtful light, when he becomes aware of a black patch on the water, that perhaps has drawn his attention by a tremulous movement of winds. Then there is the slewing and training of the swivel gun, the report and the flash, with the rustle and flapping of the pinions, and the moments of lively and sanguine expectation, as the punt is pushed forward to learn the result.

We must confess, in passing, that there is a certain amount of cruelty inseparable from sea shooting in punts. You fire into the thick of a flock with a ponderous piece of potting ordnance that sends the deadly shower of mitraille skimming and scattering over the surface of the water; and it is inevitable that many a bird must fly away carrying wounds that will gangrene or heal but slowly. For that reason alone, we have a strong dislike to it. Yet it must be owned that there is great satisfaction in groping in the dimness for the bodies of the slain, and plenty of animation in the episodes when you are following up the chase of the cripples. Nor, perhaps, is there any form of shooting in which you see more of the poetry of the sport. You are always being delighted by strange and picturesque effects as you glide along under the heavy shadows of the shores and strain your eyes over the dark expanse of the water. You hail the long, faint streak of dawning light, that slowly reddens and widens on the horizon between sea and cloud in the small hours. And when the moon is shining softly overhead – a state of things which is by no means so detrimental as is generally supposed to the aim and object of the fowler – you admire the fiftful drift of the clouds, and catch the silvery reflection of the moonlight in the waves and on the slopes of the sandbanks.

But, for ourselves, we prefer the shooting on terra firma, if that can in any sense be called solid ground which is much more generally slough or swamp, which is cut up by countless tiny channels and flooded twice in the twenty-four hours.

There is one great advantage in the sport for men of moderate means, with a limited acquaintance among landowners – you pay no shooting rent, and need fee no keepers. All you have to invest in is a railway ticket and your ammunition; to hire a man to carry your bag, perhaps to punt you about a river; and then our shores are before you, such as they are. Without travelling so far as Western Scotland, whose lochs and streams supplied the author of *A Princess of Thule* with some pretty scenes in one of his more recent novels, there are many places on our southern and eastern coasts where you can hardly go very far wrong. All you have to do, though the advice sounds strangely, is to avoid the localities that have the highest reputation, for they are sure to be indefatigably shot over by professionals, and, independently of the birds being scared away and of the nuisance of having to stalk them against jealous competitors, the hazards of some stray pellets from a rival's gun are unpleasantly multiplied. But there is many a lonely creek or tiny bay that has little beyond a local name, and many a stretch of low-lying salt marsh, which the discreet sportsman may very possibly be suffered to monopolise.

He ought to be up and about betimes, for the early hours are usually the best. He has made a hurried toilet by candlelight, and has driven off in the dark to his starting point. There is already a glimmering of light to the eastward as he steps out of his trap and disencumbers himself of his wrappings, pushing forward his preparations the more rapidly that he has been listening to pipings and whistlings in the gloom. Clearly there are flocks of birds on the feed, although as yet he can see nothing of them. If he means to do satisfactory work, and as comfortably as circumstances will admit of, he will have paid special heed to his equipments. Some sort of light mud shoes – shoe-shaped boards to prevent his sinking – may be advisable in certain dangerous localities; but in any case he will wear the boots that are recommended by experience, whether they are meant to save the legs from a wetting or not. He will have a solid double-barrel of 10 or 12 bore, that will carry a heavy charge without too much of a shock, for nothing puts a man more thoroughly off his shooting than a sharp recoil on chronic bruises. As to the size of the shot, that is matter for the sportsman's own discretion: but he will remember that wild fowl take a great deal of killing, and that the pellets have a strong tendency to roll themselves in the down under the feathers. A well-broken dog is invaluable. In the first place, he is a cheery companion among surroundings that are often depressing, and he will not only fetch the game from places where his master could not venture, but he may help him to a shot that would be otherwise unattainable. He should stick close to his master's heel, unless he has orders to leave it, nor should he shrink from any reasonable amount of swimming.

For the walk from the very beginning is sure to be beset with difficulties. Between the sea and half-submerged farm land lies a long extent of flat. Roughly at right angles to its length it is cut up in all directions by deep serpentine trenches, that fill to overflowing with the rise of the tide. Even when emptied by the reflux of the ebb, these are seldom to be pronounced practicable, for the bottoms of soft ooze are treacherous and terribly tenacious. The wild fowl shooter must endeavour to turn them as best he can, often splashing through a covering of shallow water, in lively expectation of floundering into a pool that may take him up to the knees or to the armpits.

In such an event, whatever may become of yourself, you must see to the safety of your gun, and, if possible of your cartridges. There is one point in your favour; there is no need to be in a hurry. On the contrary, you move steadily and stealthily, setting your foot down silently on the slimy spoil, and keeping all your faculties on the alert. You may be in luck or very much the reverse; but we will take it for granted that on this occasion you have chosen your time judiciously, and that a stretch of severe weather has replenished the feeding grounds. As you hear a low confused clamour to your right, you edge away in that direction. Up gets a small flock of redshanks, rather wild, and scattering and dipping awkwardly, as these birds are wont to do. So you first barrel carries a trifle too high; but then your second one rakes them as they rise again, and three of the party are accounted for;

118

at least, that is the number you retrieve. The noise of the shots has alarmed the vicinity, so in the meantime there is nothing more to be done. You then strike inland round the head of the creeks, and push onwards to some well-remembered flats. Already the land is growing visibly, as the ride begins to recede, and you can see the groups of lively sandsnipe running backwards and forwards in the watery mud. In the hope of something better, you deem these little fellows hardly worth your powder, and take advantage of a low embankment to continue your advances without disturbing them. Your quick-eared follower, who is carrying the bag, lays the touch of a heavy hand on your shoulder.

As you lean forward and listen, a noise is borne to your ear that disengages itself from the gentle murmur of the surf. Ducks on the feed, by all that is fortunate! Taking the bearings by the ear as well as you can, you slip gently forward, stooping under cover of the bank, until you reach the break in it that you have taken for a landmark. Then stopping to draw a refreshing breath or two, and calm the slight tremor of your nerves, you gently raise yourself till your eyes are above the level of the barrier, and there is a bunch of a dozen or so ducks, busy among the briny reeds in a little sand-locked lagoon, and not more than some 40 yards away. As you draw yourself to your full height they have taken the alarm simultaneously, and risen as well, beginning with that heavy, lumbering flight that will change to high-pressure pace when they are once fairly in their swing.

Your first discharge takes a couple of them in a line; it would seem you have made a clean miss with your second, and yet your instinct seems to tell you that you were holding straight. Instinctively you keep your eye on the bird as he soars high into the air with his companions, the whole company streaming out in a waving beauty line, and apparently making straight to sea. Suddenly your friend stops and turns over, as if a rifle-ball had overtaken him then and there. Down he drops in a plumb-line, and, unluckily for him, when he recovers himself he runs for hiding on the land, instead of heading for the other element. For the next hour or so you have your walking for your pains, with the exception of a clever miss at some curlews. You had warning of their approach from the distant whistle, and there was no reason for your firing behind them except a simple miscalculation of pace. But in that kind of rough and wild fowling hit-and-miss shooting is excellent work, for it is as hard to judge of distance as of velocity, while many of the birds, as we have said, take a very great deal of killing.

Such a beginning as we have described is a lucky one, although confidence counts for a great deal, and when the sportsman commences in a happy vein he is very apt to go on in it. We may imagine the next episode to be a rencontre with a flock of plover. Had they been more sensible and less inquisitive, when they were flushed by the sound of the shots, they would have taken themselves away to the landward. Instead of that, they must go sweeping to and fro, as if playing wantonly with the danger they were aware of. Now one wing of the flight seems to fold over altogether, and you lose sight of them for a moment as they turn edgewise in the sunshine. Now they close in again in column, and come straight on over your head. At last in your impatience you hazard a long shot, and are surprised to see one of them comes tumbling down. But in place of laying the warning to heart, they are loth to lose sight of their fallen companion; and when they are swooping over the body and piping the coronach of the slain, you take shameless advantage of their feelings to 'brown' them right and left. So, if your luck lasts as it began, you may make a tolerably heavy and a varied bag in the course of a hard day's walking, with the certainty that the long evening will be made luxurious by the mere enjoyment of warmth and shelter.

from *The Times*, 1877

Ploughing on the Sussex Downs

On the Downs, near the coast, flocks of sea-gulls are flying with the rooks and starlings. The white plumage of the gulls makes them visible at a great distance, whether on the pale green of the grass or on the greyish-brown of the arable fields. The grass on the Downs has not grown in the least during the last month. It is still thin, short, and sapless – kept back by the bitter weather – so that the smallest bird is apparent on it; indeed it would hardly hide a mouse. At the beginning of March the furze was coming out in bloom: there were spots of yellow in places. It remains in the same state: no more bloom has appeared. Ploughing and sowing have proceeded fairly well; for the ploughman does not care how bitter the weather is, so long as it is very dry: and in this respect progress has been made. Winter corn varies much: being in some place in good condition; and in others yellow and thin, injured by the continued rains which preceded March.

Along a distant ridge, drawn thin and sharp against the sky (the north wind is an outline draughtsman) four oxen draw the ancient wheeled plough of hamlet make. As the share turns it up, the loosely compacted soil dries and crumbles immediately: it is so dry that the rooks do not care to search the new furrows up there as they would do on the slope or in the valley. There is not sufficient vegetable mould in it to harbour any considerable number of insects or worms: nothing for the rooks. To and fro on that open ridge, with not so much as a low-cropped hedge on the other side of the field to shelter them, ploughman and oxen receive the full force of the Polar wind. It is like ploughing on the Dome of St. Paul's; yet, cold as it is, much preferable to that dusty stone cold which chills the very bones on the granite pavements of London. The ploughman is not nearly so cold as the miserable wretches who sit on the doorsteps or in corners of the houses in the City, huddling their rags around them. Happy for them if they were at plough. Eight oxen are often yoked: this custom of employing oxen endured in Sussex all through the rage for steam-ploughs and machinery generally, which was to do so much and did so little. Eight oxen harnessed to a plough have a pleasant old-world look: and yet more pleasant it is when the sun shines on their coats, which are often as glossy as a well-kept horse's.

from *Field and Farm*, 1957

121

Hedge Miners

Sometimes while walking on the sunny side of the hedge in early spring, it is almost startling to see a little shower, as it were, of earth suddenly pouring down the bank without apparent cause. The dry crumbling particles falling on dead leaves make far more rustling and noise than would seem to accord with their size, for, put together, they would hardly be a handful. They start from under some creeping ivy, and the slope of the bank shoots them out so as to drop in the ditch. Upon standing still a few minutes, there is another rustle somewhat farther along, and again back the other way, and presently a mouse appears descending the bare branches of a maple stole. He runs along the rough bark so quickly that it is impossible to tell what it is he carries in his mouth. It is something white, but before the eye can, as it were, even question the object, the mouse is out of sight under the creeping ivy. In a minute some motion attracts the glance down into the ditch, and yonder, where there is a bridge over it, a mouse has run across the decayed woodwork, forced out at the side by the weight of earth above. There he sits at the end of his bridge, his reddish brown coat, bright in the sunshine, but only for a second – the next he has gone again. It was one of these that sent down the little shower of crumbling particles long only held in position by some fibre or rootlet, upon which he inadvertently stepped; just as an Alpine climber occasionally starts an avalanche by moving a single stone. This handful of earth may perhaps weigh twice as much as the tiny creature which has thus been the ultimate agent of its removal.

Looking closely into the mound it will be seen to be marked everywhere with these busy little feet. Before the parsley and the herb robert have spread abroad, before the ground-ivy has shot up from its trailing stock, before burdock, thistle, and nettle have covered the earth from sight, their traces are easily found. Their roads, no broader than a ribbon, ascend the bank aslant as a highway goes up a hill, often overhung with a penthouse of earth. Under dead brown stalks of fern and splintered tubes of fallen hedge-parsnip, round stones and roots, and sometimes through the hollow of a decayed hawthorn stole, these narrow tracks penetrate everywhere. At present, while the harsh winds stay the buds, and say to the opening leaves, 'Be still', they are easily discovered. By-and-by, when the hedge seems to have enlarged to twice its winter size and thickness by the appearance of the leaves, and the under-growth of plants and grasses, they will be hidden, and the mice themselves will pass out of sight. If they venture from the mound they are lost in the tall grass, and thus in summer, unless purposely watched for, may escape unseen, and unthought-of. Still, they are there, busily at work, the whole day long, the whole summer long, and the whole year long. As one chancing to step on a rootlet sent down a shower of crumbling particles, so all the year round their tiny feet (and teeth) are boring through or wearing away the solid mound. These, the least of creatures, represent in living shape the yet slower and unseen, but ceaseless attrition of non-animate forces.

That handful of crumbling particles will help to stop the flow of water in the ditch below. When heavy rain falls, these slanting roads act like so many minute channels down which the water rushes and carries with it more alluvial material. It enters, too, into the holes they have bored, and goes down into the very bottom of the mound, reaching the lowest roots. Dry winds blow, and entering at these tiny caves, cause their roofs at the mouth to crumble, crack and fall. The inhabitants clear away the obstruction, and the atoms are thrust out into the ditch. Upon the one hand, therefore, their tunnels let air and light into the centre of the mound and to the roots of the trees, causing thereby an increase of substance in the form of wood; and upon the other, they constantly diminish the bulk of the bank by casting out particles of earth and admitting air and frost and water.

The green snake rustling among the violets travels by these winding narrow roads, which open a passage under thorn and plant, and by them enters into his den in the ground. Humble-bees go down into them and build their comb, filling it with darker honey. Both wasp and humble-bee do their part to eat away the mound; they can excavate far more than would be supposed, and if the entrance is not large enough, will soon make it trumpet-shaped. As for the beetles and the creeping creatures, these too, year by year, labour at the same

123

task, the division or separation of one particle from another. That which is close together, firm and solid, resists time and decay; but that which is honeycombed with innumerable apertures, whether visible or not, must perforce slowly decrease. Moles come along working low down the side of the mound, above the water in the ditch, but where the earth is soft and moist. In frosty weather, the slopes of the ditches and mounds are their favourite places, also long-continued drought and sunshine; the effect of frost and sun being somewhat similar in hardening the earth. So much does long-continued drought and sun harden the ground that it becomes almost as difficult for thrushes to find certain kinds of food as in sharp frosts. There are always moles in or near an old mound, and from thence their tunnels are driven out under the sward of the field. The mole's run seems less carefully finished than that of the mouse; the mole merely pushes through, and cares nothing if the earth falls behind him; the mouse likes his gallery open. As the water in the ditch rises during floods the mole's holes let it into the mound, and after frosts fragments of earth fall off, loosened by these excavations behind them. Water-rats do more work than the moles, because they abide at all times, and, like mice, keep their holes clear. It has always been remarked that the place where decay occurs is between wind and water; it is so with a ship's timbers, and it is so with a post sunk into the ground. Now the water-rat works at this level, between wind and water, and so assists each of these, besides carrying out his own object. His holes are frequently made at the exact surface of the water, so that the stream continually enters as it runs by; many of them open into the water underneath the surface. He dives from the bank, you see him passing along the bottom, and suddenly he disappears, having entered one of his tunnels which tends upwards. He thus maintains an ever-open communication between the water and the air, through the earth. This is the reason, perhaps, that he never seems to form any heap outside his tunnels; he appears to drill a clean hole without having any excavated material to dispose of, the fact being that every particle he dislodges is immediately dissolved in the water and swept away.

from *Chronicles of the Hedges*, 1948

An English Homestead

It is easy to pass along a country road without observing half of the farmhouses, so many being situated at a distance from the highway, and others hidden by the thick hedges and the foliage of the trees. This is especially the case in districts chiefly occupied in pasture farming, meadow land being usually found along the banks of rivers, on broad level plains, or in slightly undulating prairie-like country. A splendid belt of meadows often runs at the base of the chalk hills, where the springs break out; and it is here that some of the most beautiful pastoral scenery is to be found. By the side of the highway there are gates at intervals in the close-cropped hedge – kept close-cropped by the strict orders of the road surveyors – giving access to the green fields through which runs a wagon-track, apparently losing itself in the grass.

This track will take the explorer to a farmhouse. It is not altogether pleasant to drive over in a spring trap, as the wheels jolt in the hard ruts, and the springs are shaken in the deep furrows, the vehicle going up and down like a boat upon the waves. Why there should be such furrows in a meadow is a question that naturally arises in the mind. Whether it be mown with the scythe or the mowing-machine, it is of advantage to have the surface of the field as nearly as possible level; and it is therefore most probable that these deep furrows had their origin at a period when a different state of things prevailed, when the farmer strove to grow as much wheat as possible, and devoted every acre that he dared break up to the plough. Many of these fields were ill adapted for the growth of corn, the soil unsuitable and liable to be partially flooded; consequently as soon as the market was opened, and the price of wheat declined, so that rapid fortunes could no longer be made by it, the fields were allowed to return to their natural condition. No trouble was taken to relevel the land, and the furrows remain silent witnesses to the past. They are useful as drains, it is true; but, being so broad, the water only passes off slowly and encourages the rough grass and 'bull-polls' to spring up, which are as uneatable by cattle as the Australian spinifex.

The wagon-track is not altogether creditable to the farmer, who would, one would have thought, have had a good road up to his house at all events. It is very wide, and in damp weather every one who drives along it goes further and further out into the grass to find a firm spot, till as much space is rendered barren as by one of the great hedges, now so abominated. The expense of laying down stone is considerable in some localities where the geological formation does not afford quarries; yet even then there is a plan, simple in itself, but rarely resorted to, by which a great saving in outlay may be effected. Any one who will look at a cart-track will see that there are three parallel marks left by the passage of the cart upon the ground. The two outside ruts are caused by the wheels, and between these is a third beaten in by the hoofs of the horse. The plan consists in placing stone, broken up small, not across the whole width of the track, but in these three ruts only; for it is in these ruts alone that the wear takes place, and, if the ground were firm there, no necessity would exist to go farther into the field. To be thoroughly successful, a trench, say six or eight inches wide, and about as deep, should be cut in the place of each rut, and these trenches macadamised. Grass grows freely in the narrow green strips between the ruts, and the track has something of the appearance of a railroad. It is astonishing how long these metals, as it were, will last, when once well put down; and the track has a neat, effective look. The foot-passenger is as much benefited as the tenant of the field. In wet weather he walks upon the macadamised strip dryshod, and in summer upon either of the grass strips, easily and comfortably, without going out into the mowing-grass to have the pleasure of turf under his feet.

These deep furrows are also awkward to cross with heavy loads of hay or straw, and it requires much skill to build a load able to withstand the severe jolting and lurching. Some of the worst are often filled up with a couple of large faggots in the harvest season. These tracks run by the side of the hedge, and the ditches are crossed by bridges or 'drocks.' The last gate opens into a small field surrounded with a high thick hawthorn hedge, itself a thing of beauty in May and June, first with the May blossom and afterwards with the delicate-tinted dog or wild roses. A spreading ash-tree stands on either side of the gateway, from which on King Charles's day the ploughboys carefully select small branches, those with the leaves evenly arranged, instead of odd numbers, to place in their hats. Tall elm-trees grow close together in the hedge and upon the 'shore' of the ditch, enclosing the place in a high wall of foliage. In the branches are the rooks' nests, built of small twigs apparently thrown together, and yet so firmly intertwined as to stand the swaying of the tree-tops in the rough blasts of winter. In the spring the rook builds a second nest on the floor of the old one, and this continues till five or six successive layers may be traced; and when at last some ruder tempest strews the grass with its ruin, there is enough wood to fill a bushel basket.

The dovecot is fixed in the fork of one of the larger elms, where the trunk divides into huge boughs, each the size of a tree; and in the long rank grass near the hedge the backs of a black Berkshire pig or two may be seen like porpoises rolling in the green sea. Here and there an ancient apple-tree, bent down and bowed to the ground with age, offers a mossy, shady seat upon one of its branches which has returned to the earth from which it sprung. Some wooden posts grown green and lichen-covered, standing at regular intervals, show where the housewife dries her linen.

Right before the very door a great horse-chestnut tree rears itself in all the beauty of its thousands of blossoms, hiding half the house. A small patch of ground in front is railed in with wooden palings to keep out the pigs, and poultry, and dogs – for almost every visitor brings with him one or more dogs – and in this narrow garden grow velvety wall-flowers, cloves, pinks, shrubs of lavender, and a few herbs which are useful for seasoning. The house is built of brick; but the colour is toned down by age, and against the wall a pear-tree is trained upon one side, and upon the other a cherry-tree, so that at certain seasons one may rise in the morning and gather the fresh fruits from the window. The lower windows were once latticed; but the old frames have been replaced with the sash, which, if not so picturesque, affords more light, and most old farmhouses are deficient in the supply of light. The upper windows remain latticed still. The red tiles of the roof are dull with lichen and the beating of the weather; and the chimney, if looked at closely, is full of tiny holes – it is where the leaden pellets from guns fired at the mischievous starlings have struck the bricks. A pair of doves perched upon the roof-tree coo amorously to each other, and a thin streak of blue smoke rises into the still air.

The door is ajar, or wide open. There is no fear here of thieves, or street-boys throwing stones into the hall. Excepting in rain or rough wind, and at night, that front door will be open almost all the summer long. When shut at night it is fastened with a wooden bar passing across the whole width of the door, and fitting into iron staples on each post – a simple contrivance, but very strong and not easily tampered with. Many of the interior doors still open with the old thumb-latch; but the piece of shoe-string to pull and lift it is now relegated to the cottages, and fast disappearing even there before brass-handled locks. This house is not old enough to possess the nail-studded door of solid oak and broad stone-built porch of some farmhouses still occasionally to be found, and which date from the sixteenth century. The porch here simply projects about two feet, and is supported by trellis-work, up which the honeysuckle has been trained. A path of stone slabs leads from the palings up to the threshold, and the hall within is paved with similar flags. The staircase is opposite the doorway, narrow, and guiltless of oilcloth or carpeting; and with reason, for the tips and nails of the heavy boots which tramp up and down it would speedily wear carpets into rags. There is a door at the bottom of the staircase closed at night. By the side of the staircase is a doorway which leads into the dairy – two steps lower than the front of the house.

The sitting-room is on the left of the hall, and the floor is of the same cold stone flags, which in damp weather become wet and slimy. These flags, in fact, act as a barometer, and foretell rain with great accuracy, as it were perspiring with latent moisture at its approach. The chimney was originally constructed for a wood fire upon the hearth, and of enormous size, so that several sides of bacon could be hung up inside to be smoke-dried. The fireplace was very broad, so that huge logs could be thrown at once upon the fire with very little trouble of sawing them short. Since coal has come into general use, and wood grown scarce, the fireplace has been partly built up and an iron grate inserted, which looks out of place in so large a cavity. The curious fire-dogs, upon which the wood was thrown, may still, perhaps be found upstairs in some corner of the lumber-room. On the mantelpiece are still preserved, well polished and bright, the several pieces of the 'jack' or cooking apparatus; and a pair of great brazen candlesticks ornament it at each end. A leaden or latten tobacco-bowl, a brazen pestle and mortar, and half-a-dozen odd figures in china, are also scattered upon it, surmounted by a narrow looking-glass. In one corner stands an old eight-day clock with a single hour hand – minute hands being a modern improvement; but it is silent, and its duties are performed by an American timepiece supported upon a bracket against the wall.

Upstairs, however, upon the landing, a similar ancient piece of clockmaking still ticks solemn and slow with a ponderous melancholy. The centre of the room is occupied with an oaken table, solid and enduring, but inconvenient to sit at; and upon each side of the fireplace is a stiff-backed armchair. A ledge under the window forms a pleasant seat in summer. Before the fireplace is a rug, the favourite resort of the spaniels and cats. The rest of the floor used to be bare; but of late years a square of coconut matting has been laid down. A cumbrous piece of furniture takes up almost half of one side – not known in modern manufactories. It is of oak, rudely polished, and inlaid with brass. At the bottom are great deep drawers, pulled open with brass rings ornamented with dogs' heads. In these drawers are kept cowdrenches – bottles of oils for the wounds which cattle sometimes get from nails or kicks; dog-whips and pruning-knives; a shot-belt and powder-flask; an old horse-pistol; a dozen odd stones or fossils picked up upon the farm and kept as curiosities; twenty or thirty old almanacs, and a file of the county paper for forty years; and a hundred similar odds and ends. Above the drawers comes a desk with a few pigeon-holes; a desk little used, for the farmer is less of a literary turn than almost any other class. The pigeon-holes are stuffed full of old papers, recipes for cattle medicines, and, perhaps, a book of divinity or sermons printed in the days of Charles II, leather-covered, and worm-eaten. Still higher are a pair of cupboards where china, the tea-set, and the sugar and groceries in immediate use are kept. On the top, which is three or four inches under the ceiling, are two or three small brown-paper parcels of grass seeds, and a variety of nondescript articles. Opposite, on the other wall, and close above the chimneypiece, so as to be kept dry, is the gunrack with two double-barrels, a long single-barrel duck gun, and a cavalry sabre, worn once a year by a son of the house who goes out to training in the yeomanry.

There are a few pictures, not of a high class – three or four prints depicting Dick Turpin's ride to York, and a coloured sketch of some steeplechase winner, or a copy of a well-known engraving representing a feat accomplished many years ago at a farm. A flock of sheep were shorn, the wool carded and spun, and a coat made of it, and worn by the flockowner, and all in one day. From this room a door opens into the cellar and pantry, partly underground, and reached by three or four steps.

On the other side of the hall is the parlour, which was originally floored, like the sitting-room, with stone flags, since taken up and replaced by boards. This is carpeted, and contains a comfortable old-fashioned sofa, horse-hair chairs, and upon the side tables may, perhaps, be found a few specimens of valuable old china, made to do duty as flower-vases, and filled with roses. The room has a fresh, sweet smell from the open window and the flowers. It tempts almost irresistibly to repose in the noontide heat of a summer's day.

Upstairs there are two fair-sized bedrooms, furnished with four-post wooden bedsteads. The second flight of stairs, going up to the attic, has also a door at the foot. This house is built upon a simple but effective design, well calculated for the purposes to be served. It resembles two houses placed not end to end, as in a block, but side by side, and each part has a separate roof. Under the front roof, which is somewhat higher than the other, are the living-rooms of the family: sitting-room, parlour, bedroom, and attics, or servants' bedrooms. Under the lower roof are the offices, the cheese-loft, dairy, kitchen, cellar, and wood-house. Numerous doors give easy communication on each floor, so that the house consists of two distinct portions, and the business is kept quite apart from the living-rooms, and yet close to them. This is, perhaps, the most convenient manner in which a dairy farmhouse can be built; and the plan was undoubtedly the result of experience. Of course, in dairy-farming upon a very extended scale, or as a gentlemanly amusement, it would be preferable to have the offices entirely apart, and at some distance from the dwelling-house. These remarks apply to an ordinary farm of moderate size.

Leaving the hall by the door at the side of the staircase, two steps descend into the dairy, which is almost invariably floored with stone flags, even in localities where brick is used for the flooring of the sitting-room. The great object aimed at in the construction of the dairy was coolness, and freedom from dust as much as possible. The stone flags ensure a cool floor; and the windows always open to the north, so that neither the summer sunshine nor the warm southern winds can injuriously affect the produce. It is a long open room, whitewashed, in the centre of which stands the cheese-tub, until lately invariably made of wood, but now frequently of tin, this material taking much less trouble to keep clean. The cheese-tub is large enough for a Roman lady's bath of milk. Against one wall are the whey-leads – shallow, long, and broad vessels of wood, lined with lead, supported two or three feet above the floor, so that buckets can be placed underneath. In these 'leads' the whey is kept, and drawn off by pulling up a wooden plug. Under the 'leads' – as out of the way – are some of the great milk-pans into which the milk is poured. Pussy sometimes dips her nose into these, and whitens her whiskers with cream.

At one end of the room is the cheese-press. The ancient press, with its complicated arrangement of long iron levers weighted at the end something like a steelyard, and drawn up by cords and pulleys, has been taken down and lies discarded in the lumber-room. The pressure in the more modern machine is obtained from a screw. The rennet-vat is perhaps hidden behind the press, and there are piles of the cheese-moulds or vats beside it, into which the curd is placed when fit to be compressed into the proper shape and consistency. All the utensils here are polished, and clean to the last degree; without extreme cleanliness success in cheese or butter making cannot be achieved. The windows are devoid of glass; they are really wind doors, closed when necessary, with a shutter on hinges like a cupboard door. Cats and birds are prevented from entering by means of wire screens – like a coarse netting of wire – and an upright iron bar keeps out more dangerous thieves. There is a copper for scalding milk. When in good order there is scarcely any odour in a dairy, notwithstanding the decidedly strong smell of some of the materials employed: free egress of air and perfect cleanliness takes off all but the faintest astringent flavour. In summer it is often the custom of dairymaids to leave buckets full of water standing under the 'leads' or elsewhere out of the way, or a milk-pan is left with water in it, to purify the atmosphere. Water, it is well known, has a remarkable power of preventing the air from going 'dead' as it were. A model dairy should have a small fountain in some convenient position, with a jet constantly playing. The state of the atmosphere has the most powerful effect upon the contents of the dairy, especially during times of electrical tension.

To the right of the dairy is the brewhouse, now rarely used for the purpose implied in its' name, though the tubs, and coolers, and other 'plant' necessary for the process are still preserved. Here there is a large copper also; and the oven often opens on to the brewhouse. In this place the men have their meals. Next to it is the wood-house, used for the storage of the wood which is required for immediate use, and must therefore be dry; and beyond that the kitchen, where the fire is still upon the hearth, though coal is mixed with the logs and faggots. Along the whole length of this side of the house there is a paved or pitched courtyard enclosed by a low brick wall, with one or two gates opening upon the paths which lead to the rickyards and the stalls. The buttermilk and refuse from the dairy runs by a channel cut in the stone across the court into a vault or well sunk in the ground, from whence it is dipped for the pigs. The vault is closed at the mouth by a heavy wooden lid. There is a well and pump for water here; sometimes with a windlass, when the well is deep. If the water be low or out of condition, it is fetched in yokes from the nearest running stream. The acid or 'eating' power of the buttermilk, &c., may be noted in the stones, which in many places are scooped or hollowed out. A portion of the court is roofed in, and is called the 'skilling'. It is merely covered in without walls, the roof supported upon oaken posts. Under this the buckets are placed to dry after being cleaned, and here the churn may often be seen.

A separate staircase, rising from the dairy, gives access to the cheese-loft. It is an immense apartment, reaching from one end of the house to the other, and as lofty as the roof will permit, for it is not ceiled. The windows are like those of the dairy. Down the centre are long double shelves sustained upon strong upright beams, tier upon tier from the floor as high as the arms can conveniently reach. Upon these shelves the cheese is stored, each lying upon its side; and, as no two cheeses are placed one upon the other until quite ready for eating, a ton or two occupies a considerable space while in process of drying. They are also placed in rows upon the floor, which is made exceptionally strong, and supported upon great beams to bear the weight.

The scales used to be hung from a beam overhead, and consisted of an iron bar, at each end of which a square board was slung with ropes – one board to pile up the cheese on, and the other for the counterpoise of weights. These rude and primitive scales are now generally superseded by modern and more accurate instruments, weighing to a much smaller fraction. Stone half-hundred-weights and stone quarters were in common use not long since. A cheese-loft, when full, is a noble sight of its kind, and represents no little labour and skill. When sold, the cheese is carefully packed in the cart with straw to prevent its being injured. The oil or grease from the cheese gradually works its way into the shelves and floor, and even into the staircase, till the woodwork seems saturated with it.

Rats and mice are the pests of the loft; and so great is their passion for cheese that neither cats, traps, nor poison can wholly repress these invaders, against whom unceasing war is waged. The starlings – who, if the roof be of thatch, as it is in many farmhouses, make their nests in it – occasionally carry their holes right through, and are unmercifully exterminated when they venture within reach, or they would quickly let the rain and the daylight in.

As the dairy and offices face the north, so the front of the house – the portion used for domestic purposes – has a southern aspect, which experience has proved to be healthy. But at the same time, despite its compactness and general convenience, there are many defects in the building – defects chiefly of a sanitary character. It is very doubtful if there are any drains at all. Even though the soil be naturally dry, the ground floor is almost always cold and damp. The stone flags are themselves cold enough, and are often placed upon the bare earth. The threshold is on a level with the ground outside, and sometimes a step lower, and in wet weather the water penetrates to the hall.

There is another disadvantage. If the door be left open, which it usually is, frogs, toads, and creeping things generally, sometimes make their way in, though ruthlessly swept out again; and an occasional snake from the long grass at the very door is an unpleasant, though perfectly harmless visitor. The floor should be raised a foot or so above the level of the earth, and some provision made against the damp by a layer of concrete or something of the kind. If not, even if boards be substituted for the flags, they will soon decay. It often happens that farmhouses upon meadow land are situated on low ground, which in winter is saturated with water which stands in the furrows, and makes the footpaths leading to the house impassable except to water-tight boots. This must, and undoubtedly does affect the health of the inmates, and hence probably the prevalence of rheumatism.

The site upon which the house stands should be so drained as to carry off the water. Some soils contract to an appreciable extent in a continuance of drought, and expand in an equal degree with wet – a fact apparent to anyone who walks across a field where the soil is clay, in a dry time, when the deep, wide cracks cannot be overlooked. Alternate swelling and contraction of the earth under the foundations of a house produce a partial dislocation of the brickwork, and hence it is common enough to see cracks running up the walls. Had the site been properly drained, and the earth consequently always dry, this would not have happened; and it is a matter of consideration for the landlord, who in time may find it necessary to shore up a wall with a buttress. The great difference in the temperature of a drained soil and an undrained one has often been observed, amounting sometimes to as much as twenty degrees – a serious matter where health is concerned. A foolish custom was observed in the building of many old farmhouses, i.e. of carrying beams of wood across the chimney – a practice that has led to disastrous fires. The soot accumulates. These huge cavernous chimneys are rarely swept, and at last catch alight and smoulder for many days; presently fire breaks out in the middle of a room under which the beam passes.

Houses erected in blocks or in towns do not encounter the full force of the storms of winter to the same degree as a solitary farmhouse, standing a quarter or half-a-mile from any other dwelling. This is the reason why the old farmers planted elm-trees and encouraged the growth of thick hawthorn hedges close to the homestead. The north-east and the south-west are the quarters from whence most is to be dreaded: the north-east for the bitter wind which sweeps along and grows colder from the damp, wet meadows it passes over; and the south-west for the driving rain, lasting sometimes for days and weeks together. Trees and hedges break the force of the gales, and in summer shelter from the glaring sun.

The architectural arrangement of the farmhouse just described gives almost perfect privacy. Except visitors, no one comes to the front door or passes unpleasantly close to the windows. Labourers and others all go to the courtyard at the back. The other plans upon which farmsteads are built are far from affording similar privacy. There are some which, in fact, are nothing but an enlarged and somewhat elongated cottage, with the dwelling-rooms at one end and the dairy and offices at the other, and the bedrooms over both. Everybody and everything brought to or taken from the place has to pass before the dwelling-room windows – a most unpleasant arrangement.

Another style is square, with low stone walls whitewashed, and thatched roof of immense height. Against it is a lean-to, the eaves of the roof of which are hardly three feet from the ground. So high-pitched a roof necessitates the employment of a great amount of woodwork, and the upper rooms have sloping ceilings. They may look picturesque from a distance, but are inconvenient and uncouth within, and admirably calculated for burning. A somewhat superior description is built in the shape of a carpenter's 'square'. The dwelling-rooms form, as it were, one house, and the offices, dairy and cheese-loft are added on at right angles. The courtyard is in the triangular space between. For some things this is a convenient arrangement; but there still remains the disagreeableness of the noise, and, at times, strong odours from the courtyard under the windows of the dwelling-house. Nearly all farmsteads have awkwardly low ceilings, which in a town would cause a close atmosphere, but are not so injurious in the open country, with doors constantly ajar. In erecting a modern house this defect would, of course, be avoided. The great thickness of the walls is sometimes a deception; for in pulling down old buildings it is occasionally found that the interior of the wall is nothing but loose broken stones and bricks enclosed or rammed in between two walls. The staircases are generally one of the worst features of the old houses, being between a wall and a partition – narrow, dark, steep, and awkwardly placed, and without windows or handrails. These houses were obviously built for a people living much out of doors.

from *Toilers of the Field*, 1892

The Wild Thyme of the Hills

It is the place of its growth which makes the wild thyme sweet. The labour of the ascent – the panting chest and quickened pulse – increases the pleasure of finding it. Up the long slope, over the turf, up till the strong air, inflating the chest, seems as if it would stretch the very bones: always upwards; but the grey bees win in this race and pass to the front easily. At each step the yoke of artificial life lightens on the shoulder; and at the summit falls away. The heart beats faster, being free; and the mind opens to the opening horizon. So intimately are the body and the mind bound together that, as the one climbs, the other aspires; and, on the ridge, we walk on a level above our old selves left beneath us.

from *Chronicles of the Hedges*, 1948

Hunting on the Estate

The head rides to the hunt, as his ancestors rode to battle, with a hundred horsemen behind him. His colours are like the cockades of olden times. Once now and then even Royalty honours the meet with its presence. Round that ancient house the goodwill of the county gathers; and when any family event – as a marriage – takes place, the hearty congratulations offered come from far beyond the actual property. His pastime is not without its use – all are agreed that hunting really does improve the breed of horses. Certainly it gives a life, a go, a social movement to the country which nothing else imparts.

It is a pleasant land withal – a land of hill and vale, of wood and copse. How well remembered are the copses on the hills, and the steeples, those time-honoured landmarks to wandering riders! The small meadows with double mounds have held captive many a stranger. The river that winds through them enters by-and-by a small but ancient town, with its memories of the fierce Danes, and its present talk of the hunt. About five o'clock on winter afternoons there is a clank of spurs in the courtyard of the old inn, and the bar is crowded with men in breeches and top-boots. As they refresh themselves there is a ceaseless hum of conversation, how so-and-so came a cropper, how another went at the brook in style, or how some poor horse got staked and was mercifully shot. A talk, in short, like that in camp after a battle, of wounds and glory.

from *Hodge and his Masters*, 1880

The Country in November

People who take only a holiday view of the country, who know nothing of its enjoyments except in connection with warm summer days, rich green woods, and such amusements as croquet and picnics, naturally imagine that November in the country must be a dreary season. Even Christmas, when, if the ground is not covered with snow, it ought to be, has attractions intelligible to townspeople; and skating is an accomplishment familiar to them. The country during a hard frost wears a beauty of its own, while town at the same time is proportionably disagreeable. But November! When the country is as foggy, damp, and dreary as London, without any compensating diversions – that is a month in which such persons can see no comfort away from the gas lamps. They are wrong, however, even as regards the weather, which, in the earlier part of November at least, and in a woodland country, is often singularly beautiful.

The elms at such a time are one unbroken mass of light gold contrasting with the dark green of the oak, not yet more than flecked with the rust of autumn. The fiery maple, and the crimson wild cherry mingle in the hedgerows and copses with the holly and the yew.

The fields and meadows have not yet lost all their verdure; and when over the whole landscape the pensive sun of St. Martin is shedding his subdued light, many lovers of natural beauty would hardly exchange the effect for either the tenderer charms of spring, or the meridian glories of the summer. No doubt there is an air of melancholy about a beautiful November day. Its very silence, broken only by an occasional leaf or acorn pattering to the ground, is touching.

If indeed you are in the neighbourhood of a corn rick, you will hear noise enough, for clouds of small birds, sparrows, linnets, yellowhammers, and chaffinches, leaving the bare fields, now begin to congregate where food is to be found, and all along the lanes and footpaths, where stacks are at hand, may be seen flying backwards and forwards in hundreds, chattering, twittering, and quarrelling in the cheerfullest way possible. Elsewhere, however, as we have said, a profound silence is characteristic of this month, and more especially in the woods, except towards evening, when the rooks come home, and the pheasants begin to crow.

By November, too, country society has settled down into its normal shape, and the country season has begun. Between August and Michaelmas the country is to some extent unsettled. Some people are abroad, some are on the moors, some are at the seaside. The partridge shooting is often kept waiting till the beginning of October. But by the first of November everybody is back in his place. The vicar has brought back his wife and daughter from Tenby, or Brighton, or Scarborough, as the case may be. My Lord has returned to the castle, and Sir John to the hall. The full tide of country hospitality sets in. Dinner-parties, and balls, and early breakfasts, and 'lawn meets' are in full bloom; and even in the absence of these sources of excitement there are the quiet country pleasures in which English ladies take delight, and in which it is delightful to see them occupied. The young pheasants have not got so wild but what they will still come up to the breakfast-room window to be fed. Poultry and pigeons claim their share of attention. The lady of the house is very likely a bit of a farmer, and may be seen trudging about her farmyard, and deeply interested in pigs. The clergyman and perhaps the young ladies have a new source of employment in the night school which commences the long evenings – though here let us say at once that this institution interferes grievously with dinner – and the approach of winter invests with additional interest the duty of visiting the poor.

The extent, however, to which English country life is dependent for some of its most characteristic features upon field sports, gives a pre-eminence to November in the country which no other month can dispute with it. In this month hunting and shooting are both in their perfection, the grayling is in his prime, and we must not disallow the pretensions of the pike and the perch to afford good sport to the anglers. There is no reason, of course, why hunting in November should be better than in any of the winter months, except the weather. In November the ground is usually soft without being slushy; but after this come the frosts, and then that indescribable sticky, slippery, clinging mud, which is the legacy of a thaw. In November, moreover, we seldom have heavy floods, making the meadows impassable, or at all events the brooks unjumpable. Men and horses, too, are alike fresh to the work, and the first cry of the hounds in cover on the first day of the season sounds to every true sportsman like a marriage bell proclaiming the fox-hunter's bridal. What is the noblest kind of sport these islands supply is a question which different people will continue to answer differently as long as any sport remains. Mr T. Hughes thinks that nothing can equal your first big trout. Some give the palm to salmon-fishing. Of shooters some will say that even the best sport on the moors is not equal to your first woodcock. Deer-stalking and fox-hunting are the other two candidates for first place. For ourselves we do not undertake to decide. We imagine that a numerical majority would be in favour of fox-hunting, though that proves little, because more people can take part in it. But if we consider that probably every living sportsman who placed some other kind of sport first would place fox-hunting second we shall be able to draw a tolerably just estimate of the rank to which it is entitled. If we take shooting by itself the same may be said of the woodcock, and both of them come in with November. But this is not all.

November shooting altogether is or may be made the most varied of any. On warm still days such as we have described, the partridges, if they have been left undisturbed, will often lie well in the white turnips, and in the mustard, which in seasons like the present is almost up to your shoulder. We believe that the flavour of the partridge deteriorates as the grain left upon the ground grows scarcer. But that doesn't spoil the sport of shooting him, and five or six brace of November birds shot between eleven and four are no contemptible bag. If people would only shoot their pheasant covers in November too, they would enjoy it a great deal more than during a biting black frost in January, when standing still is misery, and when there is no beauty in the woods that you should desire them. The covers if beaten at that time would afford more woodcock than they do later in the season. It isn't dark either quite so soon, and altogether a prettier day's sport might be expected then. The bag might be smaller, because the foliage is thicker, and that is all some people think of. But over and above the reasons here given for making the battue earlier, it is highly desirable that ground game should be thinned before the autumn-sown corn comes above ground. Still no doubt a vast deal of outlying cover, where you pick up the really wild pheasants, is shot through in November; long strips of ground ash, knee-deep in coarse grass, sloping copses of hazel and holly, on the edge of gorse commons, and dipping into misty hollows, intersected by narrow streamlets, alder and osier beds, and here and there a straggling patch of old fern dotted with some dwarf oaks. These are the spots dear to the heart of the true sportsman. Three or four brace of pheasants, a couple of cocks, a few hares and rabbits, and two or three couple of snipe picked up during a beat of this description are better than a hundred head driven up to you and killed in a ride. Perhaps if you have had a frosty night or two, you may pick up a duck as well, and there is always a chance of plover at the back of the common. Now the two prime birds out of all this bag (the snipe and the woodcock), without being peculiar to November, are in that month most numerous all over the interior of England. The walking too is pleasanter, and there is the lingering smell of autumn still in the air, the lingering colours of autumn still on the trees.

But the keeper says after luncheon that a boy told him just now an uncommon lot of snipe had been seen yesterday 'down agin the river,' and as the water is low, and the banks just a little rotten with the white frost, you determine to try. A glass of sherry round, and off you start. Ha! No go; confound that fellow! Close by the favoured spot. 'The patient angler takes his silent stand.'

Well, it is no use, you must go and ask if he has seen anything? Has he seen any snipe? No; so at least he thinks it more politic to say. Has he had any sport? Pretty well; the water is in good order now, and the weeds are getting rotten. He shows you a fine, seven-pound jack, and another about four pound and even while you are talking to him he has another 'run.' The excitement is to him almost as great as if he had a twenty-pound salmon at the end of his line, and, whatever the degree of different between the two, you cannot but allows as you look at him that this also is sport. However the sun is going down, the November twilight is beginning; you have some way to get home, and you leave the troller still at work. 'The hounds meet at Brushworth tomorrow, don't they Walnuts.'

'Yes, sir, and there be a smart few foxes round that side; they knows the taste of our pheasants I'll warrant 'em'!

'Ah, well, we'll bustle 'em about tomorrow, never mind.' Here you are lost in sight of home, and so ends a day's 'rough' shooting in November.

Thus, we see what November can produce in way of sport. Its indoor life we maintain to be equally agreeable. What more soul subduing than the half hour's chat before dressing when the men have come in from hunting and shooting, and join the ladies sitting over the fire without candles? What's nicer than the ball overnight, followed by the late meet next morning, and the dinner party to come afterwards? All these things have a freshness of their own in November, which wears off by degrees afterwards. It is the May of winter. And if we had to write a song on any month in the year from the country point of view, this is the one we should choose.

from *Graphic*, 1871

Notes on the Year

There are few hedges so thick but that in January it is possible to see through them, frost and wind having brought down the leaves. The nettles, however, and coarse grasses, dry brown stems of dead plants, rushes, and moss still in some sense cover the earth of the mound, and among them the rabbits sit out in their forms. Looking for these with gun and spaniel, when the damp mist of the morning has desired, one sign – one promise – of the warm days to come may chance to be found. Though the sky be gloomy, the hedge bare, and the trees gaunt, yet among the bushes a solitary green leaf has already put forth. It is on the stalk of the woodbine which climbs up the hawthorn, and is the first in the new year – in the very darkest and blackest days – to show that life is stirring. As it is the first to show a leaf, so, too, it is one of the latest to yield to the advancing cold, and even then its bright red berries leave a speck of colour; and its bloom, in beauty of form, hue, and fragrance, is not easily surpassed.

While the hedges are so bare the rabbits are unmercifully ferreted, for they will before long begin to breed. On the milder mornings the thrushes are singing sweetly. Clouds of tiny gnats circle in the sheltered places near houses or thatch. In February 'fill-ditch', as the old folk call it, on account of the rains, although nominally in the midst of the winter quarter, there is a distinct step forward. If the clouds break and the wind is still, the beams of the sun on the southern side of the wall become pleasantly genial. In the third week they bring forth the yellow butterfly, fluttering gaily over the furze; while the larks on a sunny day, chasing each other over the ploughed fields, make even the brown clods of earth seem instinct with awakening life. The pairing off of the birds is now apparent in every hedge, and at the same time on the mounds, and under sheltering bushes and trees a deeper green begins to show as the plants push up. The blackthorn is perhaps the first conspicuous flower; but in date it seems to vary much. On the 22nd of February, 1877, there were boughs of blackthorn in full bloom in Surrey, and elder trees in leaf; nearly three weeks before that, at the beginning of the month, there were hawthorn branches in full leaf in a sheltered nook in Kent. A degree further west, on the contrary, the hawthorn did not show a leaf for some time after the blackthorn had bloomed in Surrey. The farmers say that the grass which comes on rapidly in the latter days of February and early days of March, 'many weathers' (in their phrase), often 'goes back' later in the season, and loses its former progress.

Lady-day (old style) forms with Michaelmas the two eras, as it were, of the year. The first marks the departure of the winter birds and the coming of the spring visitors; the second, in reverse order, marks the departure of the summer birds and the appearance of the vanguard of the winter ones. In the ten days or fortnight succeeding Lady-day (old style) – say from the 6th of April to the 20th – great changes take place in the fauna and flora; or, rather, those changes which have long been slowly maturing become visible. The nightingales arrive and sing, and with them the white butterfly appears. The swallow comes, and the wind-anemone blooms in the copse.

Finally, the cuckoo cries and at the same time the pale lilac cuckoo-flower shows in the moist places of the mead. The exact dates, of course, vary with the character of the season and the locality; but, speaking generally, you should begin to keep a keen lookout for these signs of spring about old Lady-day. In the spring of last year, in a warm district, the nightingale sang on the 12th of April, a swallow appeared on the 13th, and the note of the cuckoo was heard on the 15th. No great reliance should be put upon precise dates, because in the first place they vary annually, and in the next an observer can, in astronomical language, only sweep a limited area, and that but imperfectly; so that it is very likely some ploughboy who thinks nothing of it – except to immediately imitate it – hears the cuckoo forty-eight hours before those who have been listening most carefully. So that these dates are not given because they are of any intrinsic value, but simply for illustration.

On the 14th of April (the same spring) the fieldfares and redwings were passing over swiftly in small parties – or, rather, in a long flock scattered by the march – towards the North Sea and their summer home in Norway. The winter birds, and the distinctly spring and summer birds, as it were, crossed each other and were visible together, their times of arrival and departure overlapping. As the sap rises in plants and trees, so a new life seems to flow through the veins of bird and animal. The flood-tide of life rises to its height, and after remaining there some time, gradually ebbs.

Early in August the leaves of the limes begin to fade, and a few shortly afterwards fall: the silver birch had spots of a pale lemon among its foliage this year on August 13th. The brake fern, soon after it has attained its full growth, begins to turn yellow in places. There is a silence in the hedges and copses, and an apparent absence of birds. But about Michaelmas (between the new and old styles) there is a marked change. It is not that anything particular happens upon any precise day, but it is a date around which, just before and after, events seem to group themselves.

Towards the latter part of September the geometrical spiders become conspicuous, spinning their webs on every bush. Some of these attain an enormous size, and, being so large, it is easier to watch their mode of procedure. When a fly becomes entangled, the spider seizes it by the poll, at the back of the head, and holds it for a short time till it dies. Then he rapidly puts a small quantity of web round it; and next carries it to the centre of the web. There, taking the dead fly on his feet – much as a juggler plays with a ball upon his toes –

the spider rolls it round and round, enveloping it in a cocoon of web, and finally hangs up his game head uppermost, and resumes his own position head downwards.

Another spider wraps his prey in a cocoon by spinning himself and the fly together round and round. At the end of September or beginning of October acres of furze may be seen covered with web in the morning, when the dew deposited upon it renders it visible. As the sun dries up the dew the web is no longer seen. On September 21th of last year the rooks were soaring and diving; they continued to do this several days in succession. I should like to say again that I attach no importance to these dates, but give them for illustration: these, too, were taken in a warm district. Rooks usually soar a good deal about the time of the equinox. On September 29th the heaths and furze were white with the spiders' webs alluded to above. September 27th, larks singing joyously. October 2nd, a few grasshoppers still calling in the grass – heard one or two three or four days later. October 4th, the ivy in full flower. October 7th, the thrushes singing again in the morning. October 6th and 7th, pheasants roaming in the hedges for acorns. October 13th, a dragon-fly – large and green – hawking to and fro on the sunny side of hedge. October 15th, the first redwing. During latter part of September and beginning of October, frogs croaking in the ivy. Now, these dates would vary greatly in different localities, but they show, clearer than a mere assertion, that about that time there is a movement in nature.

The croaking of frogs, the singing of larks and thrushes, are distinctly suggestive of spring (the weather, too, was warm and showery, with intervals of bright sunshine); the grasshopper and dragon-fly were characteristic of summer, and there were a few swallows still flying about; the pheasants and the acorns, and the puff-balls, full of minute powder rising in clouds if struck, spoke of autumn; and, finally, the first redwing indicated winter: so that all the seasons were represented together in about the space of a fortnight. I do not know any other period of the year which exhibits so remarkable an assemblage of the representative features of the four quarters: an artist might design an emblematic study upon it, say for a tesselated pavement.

In the early summer the lime trees flower, and are then visited by busy swarms of bees, causing a hum in the air overhead. So, in like manner, on October 16th, I passed under an old oak almost hidden by ivy, and paused to listen to the loud hum made by the insects that came to the ivy blossom. They were principally bees, wasps, large black flies, and tiny gnats. Suddenly a wasp attacked one of the largest of the flies, and the two fell down on a bush, where they brought up on a leaf. The fly was very large, of a square build, and wrestled with its assailant vigorously. But in a few seconds, the wasp, getting the mastery, brought his tail round, and stung the fly twice, thrice, in rapid succession in the abdomen, and then held tight. Almost immediately the fly grew feeble; then the wasp snipped off its proboscis, and next the legs. Then he seized the fly just behind the head, and bit off pieces of the wings; these, the proboscis, and the legs dropped to the ground. The fell purpose of the wasp is not easily described; he stung and snipped and bit and reduced his prey to utter helplessness, without the pause of a second. So eager was he that while cutting the wings to pieces he fell off the leaf, but clung tight to the fly, and, although it was nearly as big as himself, carried it easily to another leaf. There he rolled the fly round, snipped off the head, which dropped, and devoured the internal part; but slipped again and recovered himself on a third leaf, and as it were picked the remaining small portion. What had been a great insect had almost disappeared in a few minutes.

After the arrival of the fieldfares the days seem to rapidly shorten, till towards the end of December the cocks, reversing their usual practice, crow in the evening, hours before midnight. The cockcrow is usually associated with the dawn, and the change of habit just when the nights are longest is interesting.

from *Wild Life in a Southern County*, 1879

THE OLD MANOR-HOUSE

There is an old park wall which follows the highway in all its turns with such fidelity of curve that for some two miles it seems as if the road had been fitted to the wall. Against it hawthorn bushes have grown up at intervals, and in the course of years their trunks have become almost timber. Ivy has risen round some of these, and, connecting them with the wall, gives them at a distance the appearance of green bastions. Large stems of ivy, too, have flattened themselves upon the wall, as if with arched back they were striving like athletes to overthrow it. Mosses, brown in summer, soft green in winter, cover it where there is shadow, and if pulled up take with them some of the substance of the stone or mortar like a crust. A dry, dusty fern may perhaps be found now and then on the low bank at the foot – a fern that would rather be within the park than thus open to the heated south with the wall reflecting the sunshine behind.

On the other side of the road, over the thin hedge, there is a broad plain of corn-fields. Coming from these the labourers have found out, or made, notches in the wall; so that, by putting the iron-plated toes of their boots in, and holding to the ivy, they can scale it and shorten their long trudge home to the village. In the spring the larks, passing from the green corn to the pasture within, fluttering over with gently vibrating wings and singing as they daintily go, sometimes settle on the top. There too the yellow-hammers stay.

In the crevices blue tits build deep inside passages that abruptly turn, and baffle egg-stealers. Partridges come over with a whir, but just clearing the top, gliding on extended wings, which to the eye look like a slight brown crescent. The wagoners who go by know that the great hawthorn bastions are favourite resorts of wood-pigeons and missel-thrushes. The haws are ripe in autumn and the ivy berries in spring, so that the bastions yield a double crop. A mallow, the mauve petals of which even the dust of the road cannot impair, flowers here and there on the dry bank below, and broad moon-daisies among the ripe and almost sapless grass of midsummer.

If any one climbed the wall from the park and looked across at the plain of corn-fields in early spring, everywhere there would be seen brown dots in the air – above the first slender green blades; above the freshly turned dark furrows; above the distant plough, the share of which, polished like a silver mirror by friction with the clods, reflects the sunshine, flashing a heliograph message of plenty from the earth; everywhere brown dots, and each a breathing creature – larks ceaselessly singing, and all unable to set forth their joy. Swift as is the vibration of their throats, they cannot pour the notes fast enough to express their eager welcome. As a shower falls from the sky, so falls the song of the larks. There is no end to them: they are everywhere; over every acre away across the plain to the downs, and up on the highest hill. Every crust of English bread has been sung over at its birth in the green blade by a lark.

If one looked again in June, the clover itself, a treasure of beauty and sweetness, would be out, and the south wind would come over acres of flower – acres of clover, beans, tares, purple trifolium, far-away crimson sainfoin (brightest of all on the hills), scarlet poppies, pink convolvulus, yellow charlock, and green wheat coming into ear. In August, already squares would be cut into the wheat, and the sheaves rising, bound about the middle, hour-glass fashion; some breadths of wheat yellow, some golden-bronze; besides these, white barley and oats, and beans blackening. Turtle-doves would be in the stubble, for they love to be near the sheaves. The hills after or during rain look green and near; on sunny days, a far and faint blue. Sometimes the sunset is caught in the haze on them and lingers, like a purple veil about the ridges. In the dusk hares come heedlessly along; the elder-bushes gleam white with creamy petals through the night.

Sparrows and partridges alike dust themselves in the white dust, an inch deep, of midsummer, in the road between the wall and the corn – a pitiless Sahara road to traverse at noonday in July, when the air is still and you walk in a hollow way, the yellow wheat on one side and the wall on the other. There is shade in the park within, but a furnace of sunlight without – weariness to the eyes and feet from glare and dust. The wall winds with the highway and cannot be escaped. It goes up the slight elevations and down the slopes; it has become settled down and bound with time. But presently there is a steeper dip, and at the bottom, in a narrow valley, a streamlet flows out from the wheat into the park. A spring rises at the foot of the down a mile away, and the channel it has formed winds across the plain. It is narrow and shallow; nothing but a larger furrow, filled in winter by the rains rushing off the fields, and in summer a rill scarce half an inch deep. The wheat hides the channel completely, and as the wind blows, the tall ears bend over it. At the edge of the bank pink convolvulus twines round the stalks and the green-flowered buckwheat gathers several together. The sunlight cannot reach the stream, which runs in shadow, deep down below the wheat-ears, over which butterflies wander. Forget-me-nots flower under the banks; grasses lean on the surface; willow-herbs, tall and stiff, stand up; but out from the tangled and interlaced fibres the water flows as clear as it rose by the hill. There is a culvert under the road, and on the opposite side the wall admits the stream by an arch jealously guarded by bars. In this valley the wall is lower and thicker and less covered at the top with ivy, so that where the road rises over the culvert you can see into the park. The stream goes rounding away through the sward, bending somewhat to the right, where the ground gradually descends. On the left side, at some distance, stands a row of full-grown limes, and through these there is a glimpse of the old manor-house. It is called the old house because the requirements of modern days have rendered it unsuitable for an establishment. A much larger mansion has been erected in another part of the park nearer the village, with a façade visible from the highway. The old manor-house is occupied by the land-steward, or, as he prefers to be called, the deputy-forester, who is also the oldest and largest tenant on the estate. It is he who rules the park. The labourers and keepers call him the 'squire.'

from 'An English Deer Park', *Field and Hedgerow*, 1887

The Window-Seat in the Gun Room

Now the old squire's favourite resort is the window-seat in the gun-room, because thence he can see a section of the highway, which, where it crosses the streamlet, comes within half a mile of the house. There the hollow and the lower wall permit any one at this window to obtain a view of the road on one of the sides of the valley. At this declivity it almost faces the house, and whether the passers-by are going to the market town, or returning to the village, they cannot escape observation. If they come from the town, the steep descent compels them to walk their horses down it; if from the village, they have a hard pull up. So the oaken window-seat in the gun-room is as polished and smooth as an old saddle; for if the squire is indoors, he is certain to be there. He often rests there after half an hour's work on one or other of the guns in the rack; for, though he seldom uses but one, he likes to take the locks to pieces upon a little bench which he has fitted up, and where he has a vice, tools, a cartridge-loading apparatus, and so forth, from which the room acquired its name. With the naked eye, however, as the road is half a mile distant, it is not possible to distinguish persons, except in cases of very pronounced individuality. Nevertheless old 'Ettles,' the keeper, always declared that he could see a hare run up the down from the park, say a mile and a half. This may be true; but in the gun-room there is a field-glass, said to have been used at the siege of Seringapatam, which the squire can bring to bear upon the road in an instant, for from constant use at the same focus there is a rim round the tarnished brass. No time, therefore, need be lost in trials; it can be drawn out to the well-known mark at once. The window itself is large, but there is a casement in it – a lesser window – which can be thrown open with a mere twist of the thumb on the button, and as it swings open it catches itself on a hasp. Then the field-glass examines the distant wayfarer.

When people have dwelt for generations in one place they come to know the history of their immediate world. There was not a wagon that went by without a meaning to the squire. One perhaps brought a load of wool from the downs: it was old Hobbes's, whose affairs he had known these forty years. Another, with wheat, was Lambourne's team: he lost heavily in 1879, the wet year. The family and business concerns of every man of any substance were as well known to the squire as if they had been written in a chronicle. So, too, he knew the family tendency, as it were, of the cottagers. So and So's lads were always tall, another's girls always tidy. If you employed a member of this family, you were sure to be well served; if of another, you were sure to be cheated in some way. Men vary like trees: an ash sapling is always straight, the bough of an oak crooked, a fir full of knots. A man, said the squire, should be straight like a gun. This section of the highway gave him the daily news of the village as the daily papers give us the news of the world. About two hundred yards from the window the row of limes began, each tree as tall and large as an elm, having grown to its full natural size. The last of the row came very near obstructing the squire's line of sight, and it once chanced that some projecting branches by degrees stretched out across his field of view. This circumstance caused him much mental trouble; for, having all his life consistently opposed any thinning out or trimming of trees, he did not care to issue an order which would almost confess a mistake. Besides which, why only these particular branches? – the object would be so apparent. The squire, while conversing with Ettles, twice, as if unconsciously, directed his steps beneath these limes, and, striking the offending boughs with his stick, remarked that they grew extremely fast. But the keeper, usually so keen to take a hint, only answered that the lime was the quickest wood to grow of which he knew. In his heart he enjoyed the squire's difficulty. Finally the squire, legalising his foible by recognising it, fetched a ladder and a hatchet, and chopped off the boughs with his own hands.

It was from the gun-room window that the squire observed the change of the seasons and the flow of time. The larger view he often had on horseback of miles of country did not bring it home to him. The old familiar trees, the sward, the birds, these told him of the advancing or receding sun. As he reclined in the corner of the broad window-seat, his feet up, and drowsy, of a summer afternoon, he heard the languid cawing of an occasional rook, for rooks are idle in the heated hours of the day. He was aware, without conscious observation, of the swift, straight line drawn across the sky by a wood-pigeon. The pigeons were continually to and fro the cornfields outside the wall to the south and the woods to the north, and their shortcut route passed directly over the limes. To the limes the bees went when their pale yellow flowers appeared. Not many butterflies floated over the short sward, which was fed too close for flowers. The butterflies went to the old garden, rising over the high wall as if they knew beforehand of the flowers that were within. Under the sun the short grass dried as it stood, and with the sap went its green. There came a golden tint on that part of the wheat-fields which could be seen over the road.

A few more days – how few they seemed! – and there was a spot of orange on the beech in a little copse near the limes. The bucks were bellowing in the forest: as the leaves turned colour their loves began and the battles for the fair. Again a few days and the snow came, and rendered visible the slope of the ground in the copse between the trunks of the trees: the ground there was at other times indistinct under brambles and withered fern. The squire left the window for his arm-chair by the fire; but if presently, as often happens when frost quickly follows a snow-storm, the sun shone out and a beam fell on the wall, he would get up and look out. Every footstep in the snow contained a shadow cast by the side, and the dazzling white above and the dark within produced a blue tint. Yonder by the limes the rabbits ventured out for a stray bunch of grass not quite covered by the drift, tired, no doubt, of the bitter bark of the ash-rods that they had nibbled in the night. As they scampered, each threw up a white cloud of snow-dust behind him. Yet a few days and the sward grew greener. The pale winter hue, departing as the spring mist came trailing over, caught for a while in the copse, and, lingering there, the ruddy buds and twigs of the limes were refreshed. The larks rose a little way to sing in the moist air. A rook, too, perching on the top of a low tree, attempted other notes than his monotonous caw. So absorbed was he in his song that you might have walked under him unnoticed. He uttered four or five distinct sounds that would have formed a chant, but he paused between each as if uncertain of his throat. Then, as the sun shone, with a long-drawn 'ca-awk' he flew to find his mate, for it would soon be time to repair the nest in the limes. The butterflies came again and the year was completed, yet it seemed but a few days to the squire. Perhaps if he lived for a thousand years, after a while he would wonder at the rapidity with which the centuries slipped by.

from 'An English Deer Park', *Field and Hedgerow*, 1887

The Coomb

By the limes there was a hollow – the little circular copse was on the slope – and jays came to it as they worked from tree to tree across the park. Their screeching often echoed through the open casement of the gun-room. A faint mark on the sward trended towards this hollow; it was a trail made by the squire, one of whose favourite strolls was in this direction. This summer morning, taking his gun, he followed the trail once more.

The grass was longer and coarser under the shadow of the limes, and upborne on the branches were numerous little sticks which had dropped from the rookery above. Sometimes there was an overthrown nest like a sack of twigs turned out on the turf, such as the hedgers rake together after fagoting. Looking up into the trees on a summer's day, not a bird could be seen, till suddenly there was a quick 'jack-jack' above, as a daw started from his hole or from where the great boughs joined the trunk. The squire's path went down the hollow till it deepened into a thinly wooded coomb, through which ran the streamlet coming from the wheat-fields under the road. As the coomb opened, the squire went along a hedge near but not quite to the top.

Years ago the coomb had been quarried for chalk, and the pits were only partly concealed by the bushes: the yellow spikes of wild mignonette flourished on the very hedge, and even half way down the precipices. From the ledge above, the eye could see into these and into the recesses between the brushwood. The squire's son, Mr. Martin, used to come here with his rook-rifle, for he could always get a shot at a rabbit in the hollow. They could not see him approach; and the ball, if it missed, did no damage, being caught as in a bowl. Rifles in England, even when their range is but a hundred yards or so, are not to be used without caution. Someone may be in the hedge nutting, or a labourer may be eating his luncheon in the shelter; it is never possible to tell who may be behind the screen of brambles through which the bullet slips so easily. Into these hollows Martin could shoot with safety.

As for the squire, he did not approve of rifles. He adhered to his double-barrel; and if a buck had to be killed, he depended on his smoothbore to carry a heavy ball forty yards with fair accuracy. The fawns were knocked over with a wire cartridge unless Mr. Martin was in the way – he liked to try a rifle. Even in summer the old squire generally had his double-barrel with him – perhaps he might come across a weasel, or a stoat, or a crow. That was his excuse; but, in fact, without a gun the woods lost half their meaning to him. With it he could stand and watch the buck grazing in the glade, or a troop of fawns – sweet little creatures – so demurely feeding down the grassy slope from the beeches. Already at midsummer the nuts were full formed on the beeches; the green figs, too, he remembered were on the old fig-tree trained against the warm garden wall. The horse-chestnuts showed the little green knobs which would soon enlarge and hang all prickly, like the spiked balls of a holy-water sprinkle, such as was once used in the wars.

Of old the folk, having no books, watched every living thing, from the moss to the oak, from the mouse to the deer; and all that we know now of animals and plants is really founded upon their acute and patient observation. How many years it took even to find out a good salad may be seen from ancient writings, wherein half the plants about the hedges are recommended as salad herbs: dire indeed would be our consternation if we had to eat them. As the beech-nuts appear, and the horse-chestnuts enlarge, and the fig swells, the apples turn red and become visible in the leafy branches of the apple-trees. Like horses, deer are fond of apples, and in former times, when deer-stealing was possible, they were often decoyed with them.

from 'An English Deer Park', *Field and Hedgerow*, 1887

Shooting in the Forest

There is no tree so much of the forest as the beech. On the verge of woods the oaks are far apart, the ashes thin; the verge is like a wilderness and scrubby, so that the forest does not seem to begin till you have penetrated some distance. Under the beeches the forest begins at once. They stand at the edge of the slope, huge round boles rising from the mossy ground, wide fans of branches – a shadow under them, a greeny darkness beyond. There is depth there – depth to be explored, depth to hide in. If there is a path, it is arched over like a tunnel with boughs; you know not whither it goes. The fawns are sweetest in the sunlight, moving down from the shadow; the doe best partly in shadow, partly in sun, when the branch of a tree casts its interlaced work, fine as Algerian silverwork, upon the back; the buck best when he stands among the fern, alert, yet not quite alarmed – for he knows the length of his leap – his horns up, his neck high, his dark eye bent on you, and every sinew strung to spring away.

One spot of sunlight, bright and white, falls through the branches upon his neck, a fatal place, or near it: a guide, that bright white spot, to the deadly bullet, as in old days to the cross-bow bolt. It was needful even then to be careful of the aim, for the herd, as Shakespeare tells us, at once recognised the sound of a cross-bow: the jar of the string, tight-strained to the notch by the goat's-foot lever, the slight whiz of the missile, were enough to startle them and to cause the rest to swerve and pass out of range. Yet the cross-bow was quiet indeed compared with the gun which took its place. The cross-bow was the beginning of shooting proper, as we now understand it; that is, of taking an aim by the bringing of one point into a line with another. With the long-bow aim indeed was taken, but quite differently, for if the arrow were kept waiting with the string drawn, the eye and the hand would not go true together. The quicker the arrow left the bow the moment that it was full drawn, the better the result. On the other hand, the arblast was in no haste, but was adjusted deliberately – so deliberately that it gave rise to a proverb, 'A fool's bolt is soon shot.' This could not apply to the long-bow, with which the arrow was discharged swiftly, while an arblast was slowly brought to the level like a rifle. As it was hard to draw again, that added strength to the saying; but it arose from the deliberation with which a good cross-bowman aimed.

To the long-bow the cross-bow was the express rifle. The express delivers its bullet accurately point-blank – the bullet flies straight to its mark up to a certain distance. So the cross-bow bolt flew point-blank, and thus its application to hunting when the deer were really killed for their venison. The hunter stole through the fern, or crept about the thickets – thickets and fern exactly like those here today – or waited Indian-like in ambush behind an oak as the herd fed that way, and, choosing the finest buck, aimed his bolt so as either to slay at once or to break the fore-leg. Like the hare, if the fore-leg is injured, deer cannot progress; if only the hind-quarter is hit, there is no telling how far they may go. Therefore the cross-bow, as enabling the hunter to choose the exact spot where his bolt should strike, became the weapon of the chase, and by its very perfection began the extermination of the deer. Instead of the hounds and the noisy hunt, any man who could use the cross-bow could kill a buck.

The long-bow, of all weapons, requires the most practice, and practice begun in early youth. Some of the extraordinary feats attributed to the outlaws in the woods and to the archers of the ancient English army are quite possible, but must have necessitated the constant use of a bow from childhood, so that it became second nature. But almost any man who has strength to set a cross-bow, with moderate practice, and any idea at all of shooting, could become a fairly good shot with it. From the cross-bow to a gun was a comparatively easy step, and it was the knowledge of the power of the one that led to the quick introduction of the other. For gunpowder was hardly discovered before hand-guns were thought of, and no discovery ever spread so swiftly. Then the arquebus swept away the old English chase.

from 'An English Deer Park', *Field and Hedgerow*, 1887

The Deer

These deer exist by permission. They are protected with jealous care; or rather they have been protected so long that by custom they have grown semi-consecrated, and it is rare for anyone to think of touching them. The fawns wander, and a man, if he choose, might often knock one over with his axe as he comes home from his work. The deer browse up to the very skirts of the farmhouse below, sometimes even enter the rick-yard, and once now and then, if a gate be left open, walk in and eat the pease in the garden. The bucks are still a little wilder, a little more nervous for their liberty, but there is no difficulty in stalking them to within forty or fifty yards. They have either lost their original delicacy of scent, or else do not respond to it, as the approach of a man does not alarm them, else it would be necessary to study the wind; but you may get thus near them without any thought of the breeze – no nearer; then, bounding twice or thrice, lifting himself each time as high as the fern, the buck turns half towards you to see whether his retreat should or should not be continued.

The fawns have come out from the beeches, because there is more grass on the slope and in the hollow, where trees are few. Under the trees in the forest proper there is little food for them. Deer, indeed, seem fonder of half-open places than of the wood itself. Thickets, with fern at the foot and spaces of sward between, are their favourite haunts. Heavily timbered land and impenetrable underwood are not so much resorted to. The deer here like to get away from the retreats which shelter them, to wander in the half-open grounds on that part of the park free to them, or, if possible, if they see a chance, out into the fields. Once now and then a buck escapes, and is found eight or ten miles away. If the pale were removed how quickly the deer would leave the close forest which in imagination is so associated with them! It is not their ideal. They would rather wander over the hills and along the river valleys. The forest is, indeed, and always would be their cover, and its shadows their defence; but for enjoyment they would of choice seek the sweet herbage, which does not flourish where the roots of trees and underwood absorb all the richness of the soil. The farther the trees are apart the better the forest pleases them. Those great instinctive migrations of wild animals which take place annually in America are not possible in England.

The deer here cannot escape – solitary individuals getting free of course, now and then; they cannot move in a body, and it is not easy to know whether any such desire remains among them. So far as I am aware, there is no mention of such migrations in the most ancient times; but the omission proves nothing, for before the Normans, before the game laws and parks together came into existence, no one who could write thought enough of the deer to notice their motions. The monks were engaged in chronicling the inroads of the pagans, or writing chronologies of the Roman Empire. On analogical grounds it would seem quite possible that in their original state the English deer did move from part to part of the country with the seasons. Almost all the birds, the only really free things in this country now, move, even those that do not quit the island; and why not the deer in the old time when all the woods were open to them? England is not a large country, but there are considerable differences in the climate and the time at which vegetation appears, quite sufficient of themselves to induce animals to move from place to place. We have no narrowing buffalo zone to lament, for our buffalo zone disappeared long ago. These parks and woods are islets of the olden time, dotted here and there in the midst of the most modern agricultural scenery. These deer and their ancestors have been confined within the pale for hundreds of years, and though in a sense free, they are in no sense wild. But the old power remains still. See the buck as he starts away, and jumps at every leap as high as the fern. He would give the hounds a long chase yet.

The fern is fully four feet tall, hiding a boy entirely, and only showing a man's head. The deer do not go through it unless startled;

they prefer to follow a track already made, one of their own trails. It is their natural cover, and when the buckhounds meet near London the buck often takes refuge in one or other of the fern-grown commons of which there are many on the southern side. But fern is inimical to grass, and, while it gives them cover, occupies the place of much more pleasant herbage. As their range is limited, though they have here a forest of some extent as well as the park to roam over, they cannot always obtain enough in winter. In frost, when the grass will not grow, or when snow is on the ground, that which they can find is supplemented with hay. They are, in fact, foddered exactly the same as cattle. In some of the smaller parks they are driven into inclosures and fed altogether. This is not the case here.

Perhaps it was through the foggers, as the labourers are called who fodder cattle and carry out the hay in the morning and evening, that deer poachers of old discovered that they could approach the deer by carrying a bundle of sweet-smelling hay, which overcame the scent of the body and baffled the buck's keen nostrils till the thief was within shot. The foggers, being about so very early in the morning – they are out at the dawn – have found out a good many game secrets in their time. If the deer were outside the forest at any hour it was sure to be when the dew was on the grass, and thus they noticed that with the hay truss on their heads they could walk up quite close occasionally. Foggers know all the game on the places where they work; there is not a hare or a rabbit, a pheasant or a partridge, whose ways are not plain to them. There are no stories now of stags a century old (three would go back to Queen Elizabeth); they have gone, like other traditions of the forest, before steam and breechloader. Deer lore is all but extinct, the terms of venery known but to a few; few, indeed, could correctly name the parts of a buck if one were sent them. The deer are a picture only – a picture that lives and moves and is beautiful to look at, but must not be rudely handled.

Still, they linger while the marten has disappeared, the polecat is practically gone, and the badger becoming rare. It is curious that the badger has lived on through sufferance for three centuries. Nearly three centuries ago, a chronicler observed that the badger would have been rooted out before his time had it not been for the parks. There was no great store of badgers then; there is no great store now. Sketches remain in old country-houses of the chase of the marten; you see the hounds all yelping round the foot of a tree, the marten up in it, and in the middle of the hounds the huntsman in top-boots and breeches. You can but smile at it. To Americans it must forcibly recall the treeing of a 'coon. The deer need keep no watch, there are no wolves to pull them down; and it is quite probable that the absence of any danger of that kind is the reason of their tameness even more than the fact that they are not chased by man. Nothing comes creeping stealthily through the fern, or hunts them through the night. They can slumber in peace. There is no larger beast of prey than a stoat, or a stray cat. But they retain their dislike of dogs, a dislike shared by cattle, as if they too dimly remembered a time when they had been hunted. The list of animals still living within the pale and still wild is short indeed. Besides the deer, which are not wild, there are hares, rabbits, squirrels, two kinds of rat – the land and the water rat – stoat, weasel, mole, and mouse. There are more varieties of mouse than of any other animal: these, the weakest of all, have escaped best, though exposed to so many enemies. A few foxes, and still fewer badgers, complete the list, for there are no other animals here. Modern times are fatal to all creatures of prey, whether furred or feathered; and so even the owls are less numerous, both in actual numbers and in variety of species, than they were even fifty years ago.

from 'An English Deer Park', *Field and Hedgerow*, 1887

The Life of the Forest

But the forest is not vacant. It is indeed full of happy life. Every hollow tree – and there are many hollow trees where none are felled – has its nest of starlings, or titmice, or woodpeckers. Woodpeckers are numerous, and amusing to watch. Wood-pigeons and turtle-doves abound, the former in hundreds nesting here. Rooks, of course, and jackdaws — daws love hollow trees — jays, and some magpies. The magpie is one of the birds which have partly disappeared from the fields of England. There are broad lands where not one is to be seen. Once looking from the road at two in a field, a gentleman who was riding by stopped his horse and asked, quite interested, 'Are those magpies?' I replied that they were. 'I have not seen any since I was a boy till now,' he said. Magpies are still plentiful in some places, as in old parks in Somersetshire, but they have greatly diminished in the majority of instances. There are some here, and many jays. These are handsome birds, and with the green woodpeckers give colour to the trees. Night-jars or fern-owls fly round the outskirts and through the open glades in the summer twilight. These are some of the forest birds. The rest visit the forest or live in it, but are equally common to hedgerow and copse. Woodpeckers, jays, magpies, owls, night-jars, are all distinctly forest and park birds, and are continually with the deer. The lesser birds are the happier that there are fewer hawks and crows. The deer are not torn with the cruel tooth of hound or wolf, nor does the sharp arrow sting them. It is a little piece of olden England without its terror and bloodshed.

The fawns fed away down the slope and presently into one of the broad green open paths or drives, where the underwood on each side is lined with bramble and with trailing white rose, which loves to cling to bushes scarcely higher than itself. Their runners stretch out at the edges of the drive, so that from the underwood the mound of green falls aslant to the sward. This gradual descent from the trees and ash to the bushes of hawthorn, from the hawthorn to the bramble, thence to the rose and the grass, gives to the vista of the broad path a soft, graceful aspect.

After the fawns had disappeared, the squire went on and entered under the beeches from which they had emerged. He had not gone far before he struck and followed a path which wound between the beech trunks and was entirely arched over by their branches. Squirrels raced away at the sound of his footsteps, darting over the ground and up the stems of the trees in an instant. A slight rustling now and then showed that a rabbit had been startled. Pheasants ran too, but noiselessly, and pigeons rose from the boughs above. The wood-pigeons rose indeed, but they were not much frightened, and quickly settled again. So little shot at, they felt safe, and only moved from habit.

He crossed several paths leading in various directions, but went on, gradually descending till the gable end of a farmhouse became visible through the foliage. The old red tiles were but a few yards distant from the boughs of the last beech, and there was nothing between the house and the forest but a shallow trench almost filled with dead brown leaves and edged with fern. Out from that trench, sometimes stealthily slipping between the flattened fern-stalks, came a weasel, and, running through the plantains and fringe-like mayweed or stray pimpernel which covered the neglected ground, made for the straw-rick. Searching about for mice, he was certain to come across a hen's egg in some corner, perhaps in a hay-crib, which the cattle, now being in the meadow, did not use. Or a stronger stoat crept out and attacked anything that he fancied. Very often there was a rabbit sitting in the long grass which grows round under an old hay-rick. He would sit still and let anyone pass who did not know of his presence, but those who were aware used to give the grass a kick if they went that way, when he would carry his white tail swiftly round the corner of the rick. In winter hares came nibbling at everything in the garden, and occasionally in summer, if they fancied an herb: they would have spoiled it altogether if free to stay there without fear of some one suddenly appearing.

Dogs there were in plenty, but all chained, except a few mere puppies which practically lived indoors. It was not safe to have them loose so near the wood, the temptation to wander being so very strong. So that, though there was a continual barking and long, mournful whines for liberty, the wild creatures came in time to understand that there was little danger, and the rabbit actually sat under the hay-rick.

Pheasants mingled with the fowls, and, like the fowls, only ran aside out of the way of people. In early summer there were tiny partridge chicks about, which rushed under the coop. The pheasants sometimes came down to the kitchen door, so greedy were they. With the dogs and ponies, the pheasants and rabbits, the weasels and the stoats, and the ferrets in their hutches, the place seemed really to belong more to the animals than to the tenant.

The forest strayed indoors. Bucks' horns, feathers picked up, strange birds shot and stuffed, fossils from the sand-pits, coins and pottery from the line of the ancient Roman road, all the odds and ends of the forest, were scattered about within. To the yard came the cows, which, with bells about their necks, wandered into the fern, and the swine, which searched and rooted about for acorns and beech-mast in autumn. The men who dug in the sand-pits or for gravel came this way in and out to their labour, and so did those who split up the fallen trunks into logs. Now and then a woodpecker came with a rush up from the meadows, where he had been visiting the hedgerows, and went into the forest with a yell as he entered the trees. The deer fed up to the precincts, and at intervals a buck at the dawn got into the garden. But the flies from the forest teased and terrified the horses, which would have run away with the heavily loaded wagon behind them if not protected with fine netting as if in armour. They did run away sometimes at harrow, tearing across the field like mad things.

You could not keep the birds out of the garden, try how you would. They had most of the sowings up. The blackbirds pecked every apple in the orchard. How the dead leaves in autumn came whirling in thousands through rick-yard and court in showers upon the tiles! Nor was it of much avail to sweep them away; they were there again tomorrow, and until the wind changed. The swallows were now very busy building; there were not many houses for them, and therefore they flocked here. Up from over the meadows came the breeze, drawing into the hollow recesses of the forest behind. It came over the grass and farther away over corn just yellowing, the shadows of the clouds racing with it and instantly lost in the trees. It drew through the pillars of the forest, and away to the hills beyond.

The squire's ale was duly put for him, the particular gossip he liked was ready for him; and having taken both, he looked at his old watch and went on. His path now led for a while just inside the pale, which here divided the forest from the meadows. In the olden time it would have been made of oak, for they built all things then with an eye to endurance; but it was now of fir, pitched, sawn from firs thrown in the copses. For the purpose of keeping the deer in, it was as useful as the pale of oak. Oak is not so plentiful nowadays. The high spars were the especial vaunting-places of the little brown wrens which perched there and sang, in defiance of all that the forest might hold. Rabbits crept under, but the hares waited till evening and went round by the gates. Presently the path turned and the squire passed a pond partly dried up, from the margin of which several pigeons rose up, clattering their wings. They are fond of the neighbourhood of water, and are sure to be there some time during the day. The path went upwards, but the ascent was scarcely perceptible through hazel bushes, which became farther apart and thinner as the elevation increased, and the soil was less rich. Some hawthorn bushes succeeded, and from among these he stepped out into the open park.

Nothing could be seen of the manor-house here. It was hidden by the roll of the ground and the groups of trees. The close sward was already a little brown – the trampling of hoofs as well as the heat causes the brownish hue of fed sward, as if it were bruised. He went out into the park, bearing somewhat to the right and passing many hawthorns, round the trunks of which the grass was cut away in a ring by the hoofs of animals seeking shadow. Far away on a rising knoll a herd of deer were lying under some elms. In front were the downs, a mile or so distant; to the right, meadows and cornfields, towards which he went. There was no house nor any habitation in view; in the early part of the year, the lambing-time, there was a shepherd's hut on wheels in the fields, but it had been drawn away.

According to tradition, there is no forest in England in which a king has not hunted. A king, they say, hunted here in the old days of the cross-bow; but happily the place escaped notice in that artificial era when half the parks and woods were spoiled to make the engraver's ideal landscape of straight vistas, broad in the foreground and narrowing up to nothing. Wide, straight roads – you can call them nothing else – were cut through the finest woods, so that upon looking from a certain window, or standing at a certain spot in the grounds, you might see a church tower at the end of the cutting. In some parks there are half a dozen such horrors shown to you as a great curiosity; some have a monument or pillar at the end. These hideous disfigurements of beautiful scenery should surely be wiped out in our day. The stiff, straight cutting could soon be filled up by planting, and after a time the woods would resume their natural condition. Many common highway roads are really delightful, winding through trees and hedgerows, with glimpses of hills and distant villages. But these planned, straight vistas, radiating from a central spot as if done with ruler and pen, at once destroy the pleasant illusion of primeval forest. You may be dreaming under the oaks of the chase or of Rosalind: the moment you enter such a vista all becomes commonplace. Happily this park escaped, and it is beautiful.

Our English landscape wants no gardening: it cannot be gardened. The least interference kills it. The beauty of English woodland and country is in its detail. There is nothing empty and unclothed. If the clods are left a little while undisturbed in the fields, weeds spring up and wild-flowers bloom upon them. Is the hedge cut and trimmed, lo! the bluebells flower the more and a yet fresher green buds forth upon the twigs. Never was there a garden like the meadow: there is not an inch of the meadow in early summer without a flower. Old walls, as we saw just now, are not left without a fringe; on the top of the hardest brick wall, on the sapless tiles, on slates, stonecrop takes hold and becomes a cushion of yellow bloom. Nature is a miniature painter and handles a delicate brush, the tip of which touches the tiniest spot and leaves something living. The park has indeed its larger lines, its broad open sweep, and gradual slope, to which the eye accustomed to small inclosures requires time to adjust itself. These left to themselves are beautiful; they are the surface of the earth, which is always true to itself and needs no banks nor artificial hollows. The earth is right and the tree is right: trim either and all is wrong. The deer will not fit to them then.

The squire came near enough to the corn-field to see that the wheat-ears were beginning to turn yellow and that the barley had the silky appearance caused by the beard, the delicate lines of which divide the light and reflect it like gossamer. At some distance a man was approaching; he saw him, and sat down on the grass under an oak to await the coming of Ettles the keeper. Ettles had been his rounds and had visited the outlying copses, which are the especial haunts of pheasants. Like the deer, pheasants, if they can, will get away from the main wood. He was now returning, and the squire, well knowing that he would pass this way, had purposely crossed his path to meet him. The dogs ran to the squire and at once made friends with him. Ettles, whose cheek was the colour of the oak-apples in spring, was more respectful: he stood till the squire motioned him to sit down. The dogs rolled on the sward, but, though in the shadow, they could not extend themselves sufficiently nor pant fast enough. Yonder the breeze that came up over the forest on its way to the downs blew through the group of trees on the knoll, cooling the deer as it passed.

from 'An English Deer Park', *Field and Hedgerow*, 1887

About the Hedges

White columns of smoke rise up slowly into the tranquil atmosphere, till they overtop the tallest elms, and the odour of the burning couch is carried across the meadows from the lately-ploughed stubble, where the weeds have been collected in heaps and fired. The heaps are large this year, and there are more of them than usual, for the wet weather and the consequent difficulty of cleaning the land caused a profuse growth of weeds. So much was this the case, that in some fields when the corn was cut the green surface of weeds underneath resembled at a little distance a rough pasture ground. The stubble itself, short and in regular lines, affords less and less cover every year. As the seed is now almost always drilled in, and the plants grow in mathematically straight lines (for the convenience of horse-hoeing), of course when the crop is reaped, if you stand at one side of the field you can see right across between the short stubbs, so that a mouse could hardly find shelter. Then quickly come the noisy steam ploughing engines, after them the couch collectors, and finally the heaps are burnt, and the strong scent of smoke hangs over the ground. Against these interruptions of their haunts and quiet ways what are the partridges to do? Even at night the place is scarcely their own, for every now and then as the breeze comes along, the smouldering fires are fanned into bright flame, enough to alarm the boldest bird. The thing of course has to be done, but it is now done so soon after the reaping that the pleasure of partridge shooting over highly-farmed land has been reduced to a minimum. And when the wind blows hard the difficulty is naturally increased; the birds, with so little cover, get up before you are hardly within shot, and, carried on the gale, are quickly beyond even the choke-bore. But all the land is not highly farmed, and strolling on beside the hedge we pass another broad arable field, where the teams have been dragging the plough, indeed, but have only just opened a few furrows and gone home. Here a flock of sheep are calmly feeding, or rather picking up a little, having been turned in that nothing might be lost.

There is a sense of quietness – of repose; the trees of the copse close by are still, and the dying leaf as it drops falls straight to the ground. A faint haze clings to the distant woods at the foot of the hills; it is afternoon, the best part of an autumn day, and sufficiently warm to make the stile a pleasant resting-place. A dark cloud, whose edges rise curve upon curve, hangs in the sky, fringed with bright white light, for the sun is behind it, and long, narrow streamers of light radiate from the upper part like the pointed rays of an antique crown. Across an interval of blue to the eastward a second massive cloud, white and shining as if beaten out of solid silver, fronts the sun, and reflects the beams passing horizontally through the upper ether downwards on the earth like a mirror.

The sparrows in the stubble rise in a flock and settle down again. Yonder a solitary lark is singing. Then the sun emerges, and the yellow autumn beams flood the pale stubble and the dark red earth of the furrow. On the bushes in the hedge hang the vines of the bryony, bearing thick masses of red berries. The winters of late have been remarkable for the quantity of hedge berries, and, being so open and mild, the birds have found plenty of food, and have not required to resort to them, as they do in hard weather. Last spring, the holly berries, for instance, remained on the bushes almost till the middle of summer. The hawthorn leaves in places have turned pale, and are touched, too, towards the stalk with a deep brown hue. The contrast of the two tints causes an accidental colour resembling that of bronze, which catches the eye at the first glance, but disappears on looking closer. Spots of yellow on the elms glow the more brilliantly from the background of dull green. The drooping foliage of the birch exhibits a paler yellow; the nut-tree bushes shed brown leaves upon the ground. Perhaps the beech leaves are the most beautiful; two or three tints are blended on the topmost boughs. There is a ruddy orange hue, a tawny brown, and a bright green; the sunlight comes and mingles these together. The same leaf will sometimes show two at least of these colours – green shading into brown, or into a ruddy gold. Later on, the oaks, in a monochrome of buff, will rival the beeches. Now and then an acorn drops from the tree overhead, with a smart tap on the hard earth, and rebounds some inches high. Some of these that fall are already dark – almost black – but if opened they will be found bored by a grub. They are not yet ripe as a crop; the rooks are a good guide in that respect, and they have not yet set steadily to work upon this their favourite autumn food. Others that have fallen and been knocked out of the cup are a light yellow at the base and green towards the middle and the point; the yellow part is that which has been covered by the cup.

In the sward there is a small hole from out of which creeps a wasp at intervals; it is a nest, and some few of them are still at work. But their motions are slow and lack vivacity; before long, numbers must die, and already many have succumbed after crawling miserably on the ground which they spurned a short while since, when with a brisk buzz they flew from apple to plum.

In the quiet woodland lane a covey of partridges are running to and fro on the short sward at the side, and near them two or three pheasants are searching for food. The geometrical spiders – some of them look almost as big as a nut – hang their webs spun to a regular pattern on the bushes. The fungi flourish; there is a huge specimen on the elm there, but the flowers are nearly gone. A few steps down the lane, upon looking over a gate into a large arable field where the harrow has broken up the clods, a faint bluish tinge may be noticed on the dull earth in the more distant parts. A second glance shows that it is caused by a great flock of woodpigeons. Some more come down out of the elms and join their companions; there must be a hundred and fifty or two hundred of them. The woodpigeon on the ground at a distance is difficult to distinguish, or rather to define individually – the pale blue tint seems to confuse the eye with a kind of haze. Though the flock take little notice now – knowing themselves to be far out of gunshot – yet they would be quickly on the alert if an attempt were made to approach them.

Already some of the elms are becoming bare – there are gaps in the foliage where the winds have carried away the leaves. On the bramble bushes the blackberries cluster thickly, unseen and ungathered in this wild spot. The happy hearts that go a-blackberrying think little of the past: yet there is a deep, a mournful significance attached to that joyous time. For how many centuries have the blackberries tempted men, women, and children out into the fields, laughing at scratched hands and nettles, and clinging burrs, all merrily endured for the sake of so simple a treasure-trove. Under the relics of the ancient pile-dwellings of Switzerland, disinterred from the peat and other deposits, have been found quantities of blackberry seeds, together with traces of crabs and sloes; so that by the dwellers in those primeval villages in the midst of the lakes the wild fruits of autumn were sought for much as we seek them now; the old instincts are strong in us still.

The fieldfares will soon be here now, and the redwings, coming as they have done for generations about the time of the sowing of the corn. Without an almanack they know the dates; so the old sportsmen used to declare that their pointers and setters were perfectly aware when September was approaching, and showed it by unusual restlessness. By the brook the meadows are green and the grass long still; the flags, too, are green, though numbers of dead leaves float down on the current. There is green again where the root crops are flourishing; but the brown tints are striving hard, and must soon gain the mastery of colour. From the barn comes the clatter of the winnowing machine, and the floor is covered with heaps of grain.

After the sun has gone down and the shadows are deepening, it is lighter in the open stubbles than in the enclosed meadows – the short white stubs seem to reflect what little light there is. The partridges call to each other, and after each call run a few yards swiftly, till they assemble at the well-known spot where they roost. Then comes a hare stealing by without a sound. Suddenly he perceives that he is watched, and goes off at a rapid pace, lost in the brooding shadow across the field. Yonder a row of conical-roofed wheat-ricks stand out boldly against the sky, and above them a planet shines. Down in the meads beside a brook a white mist draws slowly over the grass: but the twilight lingers, and it is long before it is night.

from 'About the Hedges', first published in the *Standard*, and later in *Hodge and his Masters* (1880)

Pheasant Poaching

Pheasant-poachers go to the centre of a copse, in which they know there are plenty of birds, and make pheasant-creeps. The pheasant is a bird which runs a great deal, and prefers to creep through bushes rather than to fly over. They make tracks through the undergrowth in the copse, and it is across these favourite paths that the poachers form artificial creeps. Briars are pulled down and bent over, bushes broken, or cut half through, so that they will bend, boughs dragged down, and a hedge constructed in the middle of the cover. Through this hedge they leave holes, or 'creeps' for the pheasants to run through, and in these holes place wires with loops to draw up, and hold the pheasant. As the pheasant passes under the creep he puts his neck in the noose, and draws it so that he is caught. The wires are muzzled, so that the bird shall not be strangled. If the loop was left to draw up tightly without a check, the pheasant, pulling against the noose, would hang himself, and be soon dead. But as a pheasant sells best alive the poachers do not want this, and so arrange the loop that it shall only draw up to a certain point, sufficient to hold the bird fast, but not to injure it.

They next go round to one end of the copse – the wired 'creeps' being in the centre – and proceed to drive the pheasants towards the wires by tapping two pieces of stick together, or a couple of stones. At this sound the pheasants begin to run away from it along their accustomed paths. Too much noise would cause them to rise, but this peculiar tap, tapping merely makes them run. In pheasant-shooting, when the keepers wish the pheasants to avoid certain exits from the covers, and to direct them towards points where sportsmen are placed, they set men with two sticks to knock together in the same way, and at this noise the birds turn back, and run in the direction required.

Driven before the poacher's tap, tap, the pheasants presently come to the artificial hedge, and creeping without hesitation through the holes left for them, are noosed by the wires. When the poachers come up they put the captured birds alive in a bag, and then go to the other end of the cover and repeat the process, and so catch all in the copse; first, the birds are driven into the wires from one end of the copse and then from the other.

Poachers also look out for the creeps which the pheasants have made for themselves over mounds. They wander a good deal from cover, and especially towards barley and barley-stubble, called barley-harrish in Red Deer Land. To get to the corn they have to pass through hedges, and their tracks are easily found on the mounds. Wires are set in these creeps, and the pheasants are caught as they go out to feed. Sometimes in winter wires for pheasants are set round corn-ricks, to which the birds resort. All poaching is founded on the habits of wild creatures. Partridges in winter also resort to corn-ricks, and are occasionally shot there by poachers. Both pheasants and partridges are fond of ants' eggs. In covers the large wood-ants, which are about half an inch long, make immense nests of leaves and fibres, quite mounds, and to these the young pheasants go and take as many eggs as they can. The ants often bite them severely; the pheasant jumps as the ant

171

bites. Where partridges are bred in great numbers the keepers seek out the nests of the meadow-ant, go round with a cart, and dig up the nests, earth and all, and throw them into the cart, and so carry them home for the young birds to feed on.

from *Red Deer*, 1884

Willow Tide

Though comparatively a sombre Easter, still the catkins of the willow deck its leafless boughs, and give some relief to the dark hedgerow. The use of the palm willow catkins in connection with religious recollections is well known, and the children gladly break off the gaily-decorated twigs and carry them as emblems of spring. In the tree-planted suburbs the weeping willow is the first to clothe its slender pendant boughs with the palest green, which appear before the almond trees open their buds or the rooks have quite settled to their nests.

Willow, indeed, of some kind seems everywhere – in the shrubbery of the cultivated garden, on the riverside lawn, in the hedge, by the still pool all overhung with bushes, by the winding brook and the stately river. The towing-paths of the Thames are bordered with willow bushes, whose tops are swept aside by the tow-rope as the labouring team drag the laden barge against the current. As the pleasure boat passes by the islets the oarsmen pause, and one of the party holds a willow branch to prevent the skiff floating down the stream as they rest. How the water bubbles and gurgles over the projecting roots that stand out from the hollowed bank! Other islets are covered with osier beds, which also line the shore.

The Kennet, that joins the Thames by Reading, flows through a forest of willow between Newbury and that town. But few, perhaps, of those who float idly past in boats ever think of the willow other than as affording a pleasant bordering to the stream. Yet it has valuable uses, and gives employment to hundreds. The tall poles are made into posts and rails; the trunks of the pollard trees when thrown are cut

172

into small timber that serves many minor purposes; the brushwood or tops that are cut every now and then make thatching sticks and faggots; sometimes hedges are made of a kind of willow wicker work for enclosing gardens. It is, however, the plantations of withy or osier that are most important. The willow grows so often in or near to water that in popular opinion the association cannot be too complete. But in the arrangement of an osier-bed water is utilised indeed, but kept in its place, i.e. at the roots, and not over the stoles. The osier should not stand in the water, or rise, as it were, out of a lake – the water should be in the soil underneath, so that the level of the ground is higher than the surface of the adjacent stream.

Before planting, the land has to be dug or ploughed, and cleared, the weeds collected in the same way as on an arable field. The sticks are then set in rows 18 inches apart, each stick (that afterwards becomes a stole) a foot from its neighbours of the same row. At first the weeds require keeping down, but after a while the crop itself kills them a good deal. Several willows spring from each planted stick, and at the end of twelve months the first crop is ready for cutting. Next year the stick or stole will send up still more shoots, and give a larger yield. The sorts generally planted are called black Spanish and Walnut Leaf. The first has darker bark, and is a tough wood; the other has a light yellow bark, and grows smoother and without knots, which is all the better for working up into the manufactured article. Either will grow to nine feet high – the average height is six or seven feet.

The usual time for cutting is about Good Friday – that is, just before the leaf appears. After cutting, the rods are stacked upright in water, in long trenches six inches deep prepared for the purpose, and there they remain till the leaf comes out. The power of growth displayed by the willow is wonderful – a bough has only to be stuck in the earth, or the end of a pole placed in the brook, for the sap to rise and shoots to push forth. When the leaf shows the willows are carried to the 'brakes,' and the work of stripping off the bark commences. A 'brake' somewhat resembles a pair of very blunt scissors permanently fixed open at a certain angle, and rigidly supported at a convenient height from the ground. The operator stands behind it, and selecting a long wand from the heap beside him places it in the 'brake,' and pulls it through, slightly pressing it downwards. As he draws it towards him, the edges of the iron tear the bark and peel it along the whole length of the stick. There is a knack in the operation, of course, but when it is acquired the wand is peeled in a moment by a dexterous turn of the wrist, the bark falls to the ground on the other side of the brake, and the now white stick is thrown to the right, where a pile soon accumulates. The peel is handy for tying up, and when dried makes a capital material for lighting fires. This stripping of the osiers is a most busy time in the neighbourhood of the large plantations – almost like hop-picking – for men, women, and children can all help. It does not require so much strength as skill and patience.

After the peeling the sticks have to be dried by exposure to the sun; they are then sorted into lengths, and sold in bundles. If it is desired to be kept at any time it must be thoroughly dried, or it will 'heat' and rot and become useless. This willow harvest is looked forward to by the cottagers who live along the rivers as an opportunity for earning extra money. The quantity of osier thus treated seems immense, and yet the demand is said to be steady, and as the year advances the price of the willow rises. It is manufactured into all kinds of baskets – on farms, especially arable farms, numbers of baskets are used. Clothes baskets, market baskets, chaff baskets, bassinettes or cradles, &c., are some few of the articles manufactured from it.

Large quantities of willow, too, are worked up unpeeled into hampers of all kinds. The number of hampers used in these days is beyond computation, and as they are constantly wearing out, fresh ones have to be made. This alone causes a demand for the raw material. An advantage of the willow is that it enables the farmer to derive a profit from land that would otherwise be comparatively valueless. Good land, indeed, is hardly fitted for osier – it would grow rank with much pith in the centre, and therefore liable to break. On common land, on the contrary, it grows just right, and not too coarse. Almost any scrap or corner does for willow, and if properly tended it speedily pays for the labour. The digging and preparation of the ground gives employment, and afterwards the weeding, and the work required to clean the channels that conduct water round and through the beds. Then there is the cutting and the peeling, and finally the basket-making; and thus the willow, though so common as to be little regarded, finds work for many hands. Towards the end of the summer those who frequent the rivers, or fish from punts, cannot fail to notice the thousands and thousands of swallows that perch on the osier in the evening. The planting of osiers is sometimes supposed to purify the air of miasma, and to render moist situations more healthy, after the manner of eucalyptus. Willow bark has been used for tanning – it appears astringent. 'To handle the willow' is synonymous with playing at cricket, the best bats being made of selected willow wood. 'Pliant as willow,' is proverbial; a slim girl is said to have a willowy figure. The willow pattern plates are familiar; at one time vast flames in the shape of gigantic willow leaves were imagined to play over the surface of the sun.

From a distance the course of a brook or stream can easily be traced by the willows that grow along the banks; it is the periodical lopping that gives the bushy appearance to the head of the tree. If left to itself, however, one kind reaches a great height and becomes quite a timber tree, with huge branches almost as large as itself. The size of the branches is, in fact, a source of weakness when the tree gets old, for their weight drags it out of the perpendicular and they have a tendency to split. Such tall trees are very ornamental as they hang over the shore of a pool, and the light grey foliage forms a pleasant contrast to the dark firs on the higher ground and shades well with the pale green of the aspen.

In its shadow the fish swim, and the kingfisher often waits and watches on the broad trunk where it curves low over the water before rising upwards. As the glistening ripples roll towards the shore they come within its shadow and suddenly lose their glory. The swelling roots loosen the earth, and the wash of the current and the waves works out a cavity beneath. When the rivers rise and overflow the level lands adjoining, the position of the fields can only be learnt from the lines of willow that protect above the flood. Such meadows are often only divided by dykes or ditches, and have no other trees growing in them, so that the canvas of those artists that have been accustomed to flat countries is usually full of willows. The gay catkins have for centuries been associated with the joyous spring, and yet the willow itself is an emblem of grief and gloom. A famous willow grew over the tomb of the great Napoleon at St. Helena. Byron in Don Juan satirically alluded to the old idea while that reckless hero waited pensively for the apparition of the monk that visited him on several evenings –

'Beneath his window waved (of course) a willow.'

The ancient ballad of 'Willow' tells how the lover lamented his love who deserted him, sitting under a sycamore tree, and asking that his monument should be blazoned with her falseness:

With these words engraven as epitaph meet,
   O willow, willow, willow!
Here lyes one, drank poison for potion most sweet,
   O willow, willow, willow!
   O willow, willow, willow!
Sing, O the greene willow shall be my garland.

from the *Standard*, and *Hodge and his Masters* (1880)

A Country Walk in June

The brook-sparrows were chattering ceaselessly as I walked among the willow-stoles by the brook one morning towards the end of June. On the left hand the deep stream flowed silently round its gentle curves, and on the other through the willows and alders the grassy slope of the Cuckoo-fields was visible. Broad leaves of the marsh marigold, the flower long since gone, covered the ground; light-green horsetails were dotted thickly about; and tall grasses flourished, rising to the knee. Dark shallow pools were so hidden under these grasses and plants that the presence of the black and yet clear water could not be perceived until the foot sank into it.

The sedge-birds kept just in front of me, now busy on a

willow-stole, and concealed in the grasses and moss which grew out of the decaying wood; now among the sedges covering the mudbanks where the brook had silted up; now in the hedge which divided the willows from the meadow. Still the peculiar sparrow-like note, the ringing chirp, came continually from their throats; the warm sultry day delighted them. One clung to the side of a slender flag, which scarcely seemed strong enough to support it, yet did not even bend under its weight; then on again as I came nearer – but only two or three yards – to recommence singing immediately.

Pushing through the brushwood and past the reddish willow-poles, I entered a very thicket of flags, rising to the shoulder. These were not ribbed or bayonet-shaped, but flat, like a long sword. Three or four sprang from a single root, broad and tall, and beside them a stalk, and on it the yellow iris in full flower. The marsh seemed lit up with these bright lamps of colour under the shadowy willows and the dark alders. There were a dozen at least within a few yards close around, and others dimly visible through the branches – three large yellow petals drooping, and on the curve of each brownish mottled markings or lines delicately stippled, beside them a rolled spike-like bloom not yet unfolded: a flower of the waters, crowned with gold, above the green dwellers by the shore.

Here the sedge-birds left me, doubling back to their favourite willow-stoles and sedges. Further on, the ground rose, and on the drier bank the 'gicks' [hogweed] grew shoulder high, towering over the brambles. It was difficult to move through the tangled underwood, so I went out into the Cuckoo-fields. Hilary had drained away much of the water that used to form a far larger marsh about here, and calculated his levellings in a most ingenious manner with a hollow 'gicks.' He took a wooden bowl, and filled it to the brim with water. Then cutting a dry 'gicks' so that it should be open at either end, like a tube, he floated it – the stalk is very light – on the bowl. Looking through this tube he could get his level almost as accurately as with an engineer's instrument, though of course it was more cumbrous to use.

There was a corner here that had not been mown for a long time, and in the autumn the wild carrots took possession of it, almost to the exclusion of grass and other plants. The flower of the wild carrot gathers together as the seeds mature, and forms a framework cup at the top of the stalk, like a bird's-nest. These 'bird's-nests', brown and weather-beaten, endured far into the winter. The brook-sparrows still sang as I passed by again in the evening; they seem the most unwearied of birds, for you may hear them all day, all the evening, and at one o'clock next morning; indeed, at intervals, all night. By night the note is, or appears to be, less sparrow-like, or perhaps the silence of night improves it to the ear. I stayed that evening in a corner of a wheatfield not yet yellow, and watched the shadows of the trees grow longer and broader as the sun declined.

As the breeze rushed over the corn there was a play of various shades of green, the stalks as they bent this and that way taking different hues. But under the hedge it was still; the wind could not come through, though it moved the boughs above. A mass of cloud like flocks of wool, mottled and with small spaces of blue between, drifted slowly eastwards, and its last edge formed an arch over the western horizon, under which the sun shone. The yellow vetchling had climbed up from the ditch and opened its flower, and there were young nuts on the hazel bough. Far away in a copse a wood-pigeon called; nearer the blackbirds were whistling; a willow wren uttered his note high in the elm, and a distant yellow-hammer sang to the sinking sun.

from *Round About a Great Estate*, 1880

Rabbiting

Rabbits are vermin, we own, from the sylvan and agricultural point of view; nor is it without cause that they are denounced at agricultural dinners and proscribed in leases. You may possibly – possibly, we say – persuade a farmer that the rook is his friend, or prevail on him to withdraw his subscription from the parish sparrow club, although he finds it hard to realize that x, standing for any unknown quantity of grubs and insects destroyed, can be greater than a, representing the conspicuous damage done to root crops and grain seeds. But about the rabbit, his tastes and his habits, there can be no mistake. He possesses the ground like dandelion or ragweed, and it is even more difficult to extirpate him. He breeds and multiplies as no other animal except, possibly, the herring or the pulex orientalis. He has an unfailing appetite, and is always seen to be satisfying it; even while he pricks his ears to your distant footfall, and sits up to look out for you, he continues nibbling.

In spring he is busy among the fresh green stalks of the growing crops; in summer he fattens on the ripening grain; in autumn he ravages the root crops; in winter he is industriously barking the trees, and busy as a beaver among the shoots in the young plantations. His teeth being against the property of every man's hand, every man's hand is turned against him; and if he is hunted, shot, snared, netted, and trapped, he leaves behind him a legacy of hatred and bitterness, and stirs up more bad blood that any other brute in the country. Landlord and tenant are always at logger heads over the damage he has done and the amount of compensation that should be awarded for it. He is continually and most justly abused because the young wood is coming on so poorly and there is so little to show for the nurseryman's bill. The crofter turned poacher swears it was a rabbit he tripped over first when he precipitated himself headlong on his downward career. Had it not been for them blessed vermin that were always a-chewing of his cabbages and belonging rightly to no one could tell who, he would never have got into trouble for meddling with the squire's pheasants. So vermin rabbits are, by consent of the general sentiment as well as by solemn statutory enactment.

Vermin they may be, and yet we should miss them more than many a more respectable animal that glories in the name of game, and is tenderly cherished for the slaughter, and can only be slaughtered by special licence. The enjoyment to be got out of every particular sport bears no sort of relation to the dignity of the quarry. For fun, and for excitement too, a good morning's rabbiting may be backed against a ceremonial tiger hunt with elephants and mahouts. In the first place

– and it is no light consideration – you have no sort of arriere pensee when you are out rabbiting.

You go after the pheasants your keepers have reared with something of the feeling with which you break into a bin of ancient wine that time only can replace. There were just five hundred and thirty of them turned out, we will say. Allowance made for wanderers and promiscuous casualties, that should be the precise number of head in your covers. The pile of blood-stained plumage at the close of a good day presents so much of clear deduction, to say nothing of the wounded and the missing birds that the heavy platoon firing has scared away to your neighbour's woods. Each time you see a pheasant hang his legs and fly off crippled you bewail him exceedingly, although, perhaps, not from humanitarian motives.

Then, if you are a pheasant fancier, you must keep your own covers as quiet as a sick-room or a condemned cell. You must not think of giving the merry-tongued spaniels or beagles a run through them of an autumn's afternoon, or you will scarce have a feather to show your friends in the great days of the battue you have been lying back for. The sport is tame, too, take it as you will. We do not say there is not pretty shooting when scared 'rocketers' driven a bout are shooting sharp into the air from the brushwood at the end of the beat. But to say nothing of a half-dozen of your friends blazing away jealously all around you, corners like these are scarce, and brilliant constellations of rocketers expire swiftly in blood and powder, leaving an incurable blank behind them.

Contrast your circumstances, if you must content yourself – so people call it – with the chase of the humble rabbit. We imagine your lot to have fallen to you somewhere on the confines of civilisation, where crops got home in condition are the exception rather than the rule, where an inclement climate conspires against the agriculturalist with the hungry soil, where the tenant is scarcely awakening even yet to a knowledge of his rights, having hitherto been grateful for the most moderate returns, and regarding the rabbit as an inevitable dispensation of Providence. Be it remembered, on the other hand, that his rent was regulated on the conditions in which he had to raise it; that your property yielded you overhead something perhaps like a couple of shillings per acre, and that, consequently, you could kill your rabbits in all comfort of conscience. Your modest mansion stands upon rolling ground, lightly clothed in shreds and patches of pine plantations. The soil is hungry we said, and it is exceedingly thirsty as well; although it must be confessed that the clouds and mists send it down drink in abundance.

It is sand, in fact, and so the rabbits have found out: ten minutes' play with his paws anywhere, and a muscular buck will bury himself well out of sight. Conceive it then to be honeycombed everywhere with holes and bolting-holes; step where you will in your woods, you may feel it vibrate under your shooting-boots. These woods are enclosed by turf banks, often faced with a rough masonry of loose-fitting stones, and these banks are so many strongholds, where the feeble but fruitful folk may burrow and breed in all security.

As you get farther from the house the fir trees become thicker but more stunted – you may detect the cause in a certain saltness and briny freshness in the air. You have only to ascend that ridge in front of you and you will see the ocean gently washing on the beach that starts the long line of sand-hills. If there are rabbits in abundance in the woods, they absolutely swarm among the sand-hills. What a rabbit will feed on, it is hard to say. He will eat anything to be sure, and as much as you please to leave for him; but then, on the other hand, it seems as if he could thrive equally upon next to nothing at all. Family parties in higher condition than those you break up as you go stumbling about among the sand-heaps it would be difficult to find in the best-tended warren in England. Yet the stiff salt bent grass would not seem to be appetizing food, nor can there be much nourishment in those prickly furze bushes they have nibbled into all manner of fantastic shapes.

Inland, in the woods, it is another affair altogether. Thence they make sorties, in troops and herds, upon oats that make dogged efforts to ripen and the struggling turnip fields. Reversing the order of things in parishes where tenant farmers are capitalists and eloquently outspoken, here it is not the game that takes tithe of the crops, but the farmer who thanks Providence for the tithes the vermin have left him.

Whatever it may be for the farmer, we call a country like that a paradise for the sportsman. If you do not respect times and breeding seasons – and how can you when animals will indulge in such anti-Malthusian habits are these rabbits of yours? – you may shoot freely if you will from the 1st of January to the 31st of December. You have an hour or so hanging upon your hands after luncheon. You take down your gun and step out on the gravel before your door. A shrill whistle, and two or three rough nondescript crop-eared terriers come cantering, on three legs apiece, round the corner of the house. One or two more have followed you out of your sitting-room. Possibly some member of the scratch pack may be absent without leave, hunting on his own account. What matters it? They cannot scare our game to spoil your sport, let them drive your covers as they will.

More leisurely than your dogs, your keeper responds to the signal; a capacious game-bag depending from his shoulder. It is no question of settling a beat. You cannot possibly go wrong, turn which way you will. Fifty yards from your door, you plunge into a semi-shrubbery; evergreens in dense clumps scattered among the clean stems of the fir trees. An impetuous rush like a covey of condensed whirlwinds tearing through the rustling, crashing laurel undergrowth; a burst of not unmusical yelping, and a dozen yards in advance of the sounds a swift grey shadow comes shooting across the gravel path.

You yourself shoot, yet the shadow vanishes, and next moment a half-dozen of shaggy friends, each of them possessed with frenzy, come tumbling headlong, open-jawed upon its trail. You might fancy you had missed your aim, but for the instinct that tells you that you had held straight, short as had been your time for shooting. You must have hit, sure enough; only rabbits will carry away a great deal of shot.

A wave of your hand dismisses the excited retriever who has been dancing at your heel, without budging from the site he has been dancing on. A couple of 'spangs' and he has disappeared after the terriers, and in a second or two he is back with you again, the four white-lined legs of the rabbit depending limply from his velvet mouth.

Once in the fir-woods and the shooting is more open. Now you kick up the quarry yourself from among the tufts of long rushy grass that thrive or wither in rank luxuriance where the hollows hold a little moisture. Now your foot goes crushing through the branches of a fallen fir, and the rabbit comes bolting out from where grass matted over boughs has left snug lying for him.

Again you pause, half doubled up under a tree, as the keeper hails 'A rabbit to you, sir.' Anon, the chorus where the dogs are ringing the woods around you comes swaying in your direction; and, your eye guided by your ear, you watch the skirts of the thicket as the burst of yelping draws nearer and nearer. There they are – not one but a brace of them. You have scarcely been out a couple of hours, yet, capacious as is the keeper's bag, you might well have filled it twice over. But Donald, willing as he is, is not the man to overburden himself if he can help it. He has a series of field larders he knows well; established, for the most part, where there is a bare branch under a pent-house of thick boughs that will screen the suspended rabbits from the keen-eyed and sharp-scented hooded crows. Each time he finds himself in the vicinity of one of these he strides to it; off comes the weighty bag with deliberate swing, and forth he draws his formidable 'galley.' A slit in the thigh sinews of the dexter hind leg, the left limb passed through it dexterously, and forthwith there is a festoon of fat rabbits, to be left hanging until he makes his round in the evening with the pony.

We have hardly left ourselves time to prolong our stroll among the sand-hills today; when we think of extending our sport so far, we generally leave the livelier of our pack at home. A couple of ancient terriers somewhat stiff in the joints and not greatly given to obstreperous ranging in the loose sand are quite enough for that sort of work. Possibly we may invite our friends to go with us there on another occasion. As it is we put it to them whether they have not had a pleasant afternoon's sport, and we ask them whether such quick shooting is not more cheery work than potting ponderous hares as they lollop along at their leisure, or sleek pheasants but a trifle nimbler on the wing than Cochin Chinas.

from *Pall Mall Gazette*, 1873

The Horse as a Social Force

'Let us stroll down to the stables' is a suggestion made so commonly when conversation flags, and the 'weather', etc., is exhausted, that no one thinks of analysing the feeling and the meaning of the mere words. Yet, it is a wonderful cure for ennui; when the host issues that invitation it is astonishing how those faces brighten up. Men whose normal expression is thoroughly blasé, whose forty, or five-and-forty, or even fifty years' experience of life has veneered them over with polite indifference, start up, shake off sloth and slumber, light a fresh cigar, and become young again. Each in his turn examines every animal with critical minuteness, and delivers an opinion, which forthwith leads to the ventilating of theories, and the relating of anecdotes; everybody seems in good-humour and full of vivacity. However much interests may differ elsewhere, so long as a horse is in sight there is a pleasant community of feeling. There are more friendships formed in the stable or on horseback than under any other conditions.

In some peculiar way the horse is a humanizing animal, bringing men together in a bond of fellowship. It has often been noticed how on board ship sailors grow attached to the vessel, and speak of her in terms of affection. They may quarrel amongst themselves, may abuse the captain, and hate the voyage itself; but the ship is quite another matter. When the vessel is concerned they will work with a will, altogether, as one man. But this influence is exercised far more powerfully by the horse because he is alive, and replies as it were to kindness, evidently entering into the wishes of his owner, and making efforts in his service apart from whip or spur. Natures of the rudest mould, rough and coarse, apparently incapable of good will, yet love a horse, and in that love there is a redeeming feature.

The great open-air drawing-room of London held in Hyde Park every afternoon in the season is perhaps the most palpable evidence of the social power of the horse. There, and there almost only, all cliques and coteries mix and mingle freely, and no 'shibboleth' is required of those who would enter.

The horse brings them all together, to see and be seen, and places all on the same level. No such gathering would be possible without its aid, apart from the influence of fashion, the desire of display, or any of the lesser motives, apart from all other considerations, the horse as represented by the daily drive or ride gives society a kind of common basis, a something to do, something about which all are agreed. The spectacle itself is a charming one, and thousands who cannot join in the throng nevertheless view it with genuine admiration.

When riding perhaps the 'touch of nature which makes the whole world kin' is still further developed – the exercise, the gentle excitement, the consciousness that so many others are similarly engaged, and similarly enjoying themselves, cannot but produce an effect. To ladies the fashion of riding in the Row must be most beneficial from a purely physical point of view, calculated to confer an increase of health and vigour. The rapid rise of the practice of coaching – driving four-in-hand – must not be omitted in estimating the social power of the horse. It is, perhaps, the most genial of all amusements, and in this respect superior to the somewhat formal up-an-round of the Park drive. The owner of a four-in-hand can take his party right away into the country, adding charming scenery and variety to the pleasure of easy motion, and the never-failing delight of watching the paces of well-chosen animals. Already some gentlemen have begun to drive in this way from town down to their country-seats in preference to the tame, uninteresting railway journey, and it would not be surprising if the idea were followed up extensively. The pastime of coaching is so thoroughly English in character, that it is almost certain to take a firm hold. Again, in social life, what would become of morning calls and shopping itself, without the assistance of the horse?

But it is over the broad, rolling pastures, over the damp fallows, and among the woodlands, that his rule is supreme. When the hounds give tongue, and the hills echo the cry, then the horse is monarch of the hour. Men and women, young and old, resign themselves to his influence. It is not the fox, it is the horse that gives the pleasure. That is the mistake certain misguided opponents of hunting make when they accuse it of encouraging cruelty to animals, as if the fox were the root and bottom of it. No such thing, it is the horse, and he enjoys it intensely, communicating his excitement to the rider. Without hunting where would country society be? Would there be any country society at all? It would not be possible for it to exist without the animal that gives a common bond of union, and creates a general sympathy. Here again through his agency men meet who would otherwise never see each other, at all events certainly not in a social sense. The asperities, the angles of life, are rubbed off in the hunting field. One gets a broader, better view of one's fellow-creatures; the narrowness and prejudice of too much seclusion are forcibly thrust aside. A man who hunts has always ten times as many friends as a man who does not.

We can all of us remember our first ride, long, long ago; whether it was taken under the care of loving arms that held us safely on the back of a gentle creature, or whether it was a fearful neck-or-nothing gallop, stolen courageously on a half-bred pony found loose upon the common. It is the one memory in which all alike can sympathize. And is not to own a horse or horses the ambition of thousands and thousands whose daily avocations one would imagine would entirely blot out by sheer force of monotony the very idea of such a thing – if the instincts implanted in the human heart ever can be blotted out. The poor carter rising with the sun to feed his horses feels a pleasure in watching their coats grow smooth and glossy under his care. His son, the ploughboy, whistles merrily as he jogs on, on the back of Diamond, as the mare plods homewards in the afternoon. He is happy there. Out among the green lanes, under the elms, or far away on the velvet turf of the Downs, how many times has the old, old tale been told, and listened to with blushing delight. As the song says:

> But I liked you better, Marion, riding through the broom.

So from the ploughboy on Diamond to the richest man who looks in at Tattersall's, the interest is the same. Picnics in the summer season take half their charm from the drive to the forest, or the riverbank.

It might almost be said that the more civilized (and, therefore the more social) a people, the more animals they keep in a tame or domesticated state. Savages have scarcely any, and with them every man's hand is against his neighbour. With the taming of animals, and with affection for them, social life increases. To this day our art students study the famous sculptured horses on the frieze of the Parthenon as the fountain of grace and beauty, and spirited action. The life of the Greeks has come down to us, as it were, through their marvellously appreciative sculpture. Our own painters know well the attraction which a group with a horse in it is sure to exercise. Note what a favourite subject is afforded by charging cavalry.

Reprinted in December 2015 by the Richard Jefferies Society in a self-published collection about farming, but not before republished and otherwise unknown to wider circulation.

from *Field and Farm*, 1957

Snipe Shooting at Home

Of all kinds of shooting, that which may be designated 'scratch' is perhaps the most thoroughly agreeable, and of all kinds of scratch-shooting none is more pleasant than going after snipe. There is none of the pomp and ceremony of sport about it – pomp to be quickly followed by satiety if it does not pave the way for disappointment. There is no great gathering of sportsmen impressed with the solemnity of an impending butchery; no gangs of keepers with their satellites in shape of gun-carriers, markers, and pannier-laden ponies. There is no oppressive sense of stern discipline as you march forward in line and in obedience to the word of command, as little the 'lord of your presence' and personal actions as if you were an automaton moving by mechanism. No, the snipe is the very Bohemian of game birds – not that he is game at all technically, although the game laws do give him a certain protection – and where you think you are likely to find him at home you look him up on the spur of the moment and without the smallest ceremony.

The very insignificance of his person gives an exceptional zest to the chase, for, as in most cases you may carry in your pocket as many snipe as you are likely to kill, you need not embarrass yourself with the unwelcome company of some stolid bearer of your game-bag. We do not say that it will always be wise to dispense with attendance and the counsels of local experience. For the snipe, being regarded as beneath the notice of the gentlemen paid to take care of the coverts, has been endowed with an instinct which teaches him to take uncommonly good care of himself. Unless you are a deacon in the craft and familiar with the district you are shooting in, a hint in season may be useful to help you circumvent him. There are other considerations besides that occasionally render companionship advisable. Small as the snipe is, there may be risk in following; and indeed there is more of the dignity and fascination of danger in the sport than in many others which are more pretentious.

The chance of breaking neck or leg among the cliffs in a highland deer forest is practically small; nor is it much more likely that you will be drowned in some deep salmon pool, while leaping from slippery rock to slippery rock, with a fresh run fifteen-pounder on your line. But when out on certain bogs, with no company but your own, you are never sure that you may not be brought to a sudden end, and a sufficiently tragical one. The quaking foothold of black slime may give way below your boots in a widening chasm that threatens to swallow you. Or you may find that you have slid into a slippery-sided 'mosspot,' and are floundering in three fathoms of ice-cold water, with nothing more buoyant to cling to than your breechloader. The tip of a friendly finger in the one instance might give you purchase enough to pull you out of the jaws of death; and you would part with all your property in the other to have a pair of somebody else's gun-barrels thrust into the clutch of your hands. Although the reality of such accidents must be horrible beyond conception, the possibility of them in a very remote contingency is not without a certain pleasure; and then the circumstances that make them conceivable assure some picturesqueness to the scenes you are shooting among.

The snipe, as we said, is the Bohemian of birds of chase,

and there is nothing whatever that is tame in his tastes. He detests civilization, cultivation, and all their works. As corn comes in the snipe goes out; and he has an insurmountable aversion to your finer breeds of high-fed cattle, who turn up their noses at tufts of rushes, and will not fatten except on soil which is tunnelled by drain-pipes.

He gets on fairly well with lower-caste animals with somewhat lacklustre coats, who will lay on coarse flesh on any kind of herbage, and who ruminate complacently up to their knees in fetid pools of stagnant water. But if he must have strange company, he is most at home with beasts of the mountain breed – shaggy-headed, clean-limbed Highland steers; or those long-horned, black-faced wethers who take as much exercise as deer, and run as little to fat. You follow some mountain stream, along banks which have turned to marsh on the rare stretches of level ground; you diverge now and then to the rush-covered bits of swamp left by the back-flow of the last spate from the high grounds; or perhaps to some abounding spring hard by, which flows over upon an oasis of its own making.

You must keep your eyes about you on ground like that, and your fingers very handy to your triggers, or your sharp friend may be turning the corner of some hillock ahead before you have heard the shrill pipe with which he vanishes. But if you should have an eye to spare for the scenery, be sure it will repay you; from the weather-beaten summits of the hills which lock in the valley, to the grass-grown, heather-grown boulders which have slipped down to lie strewn in the bottom of it.

It is true that the best sport is not to be found among the grandest scenery. What is snipe country par excellence shows bleak and grim enough at the first glance, especially if there be a heavy sky lowering overhead, and a chill grey fog driving before you. It reminds you of one of those sombre studies of the flats in the Low Countries, from which certain eccentric Belgian artists are fond of banishing each semblance of bright colour, until the white cap of some old woman breaks the foreground with a cheering gleam of relief.

A stretch of watery moorland is dismal on a dull day, and nothing but very excellent sport can make you regard the prospect through a rosy medium. But should the sun burst out, and come streaming down on the black-browns of the bog and the vivid greens of the weeds on the surface of the water, then you have a transformation from gloom to glory. The lights are the more brilliant for the depths of the shades: the effects are the more telling from the breadth of the contrasts, and lights and effects conspire in their animating influence on the spirits. Then, whether the shooting be good or bad, it is always exciting as far as it goes. It may have been raw and damp as we have imagined it, with here and there a frosty rime lingering upon some shady bank in spite of the damp or the fitful sunshine. It is an early day in January, and there would be no hope of getting near any other game in the open. Not half frosty enough for the grouse to be chilled into sitting; they are packed in flocks and as wild as the wary curlews. The more domestic partridges are just as shy as the grouse, and would be up and off from you while you were yet a field away from them. The very hares find their forms so comfortless that they take their noonday naps with ears on the prick and one eye open. But the snipe, who luxuriates in cold and wet, is entirely indifferent to weather and temperature; he will sit to be shot at just the same as in the summer time.

Yet snipe-shooting is never the dull certainty of dropping young grouse upon the twelfth, or massacring those hapless coveys of black game on the twentieth, who lie like clods in the heather till they flutter up like chickens. Even if you are to the manner brought up, and your hand be in, the snipe at no time makes the easiest of shooting. As he goes rocketing away in his sharp horizontal zigzags in a flight whose space is extraordinarily deceptive, it would appear that the odds were all against the gun.

Although experience may have assured you that to a man with the knack, snipe-shooting is far more simple than it seems, yet to the last you seldom get altogether rid of an impression that you ought properly to have missed, and are lucky to have killed. It is inevitable that many of your shots should come off under decided difficulties. You may be bounding from hag to hag, like the borderer's pony or the Bilhope stag in the 'Lay of the last Minstrel.' The plash of your boots

190

as they come down in the sopping ground flushes the bird before you are ready for him, and you may have to take a snap-shot while struggling to recover the perpendicular. Or he may try 'a dodge' which his instincts teach him, and which proves that a little learning is a very dangerous thing. He may sit quietly till you have passed on and left him perfectly safe if he only knew it. And then he may foolishly get up when your back is turned, with a note which this time sounds like a challenge. Still, taking easy shots with those that are difficult, if snipe be plenty, the probability is that you make a good bag if you are tolerably steady, and it is certain that you will be perpetually on the qui vive.

Even a solitary bird may give a novice a day's amusement. So long as he is let off, he will offer his pursuer chance after chance with the most generous confidence. He is flushed and missed. He is to be seen rising steadily in the air, till he looks but a speck against the heavens; then he goes circling round and round in jerky rings which gradually descend lower and lower, until at last he drops plump as a stone down upon a upon spot that you may mark to a hair's breadth. If your eyes are good and you keep following him up, he will go on with this game of hide and seek as long as your hope and ammunition hold out. Then when you do consign snipes to the bag, the sentiment of au plaisir de vous revoir is usually heartfelt. All game is good in its several ways, but as a rule the more piquant the flavour, the more quickly it palls. The snipe is the solitary exception. Small and tender as he is, no part of him needs keeping. In the afternoon he is plashing among the rank weeds, stagnant water, and cold bog earth. In the evening he is served hot and brown as the toast he reposes on. There is no better thing to bring out the flavour of Bordeaux or Burgundy, and you tire of him as little as you do of olives.

from *Pall Mall Gazette*, 1874

A Shortest Day Scene

Like black fruit, the rooks collect on the tops of the elms about three o'clock on December afternoons. The sun is not down, but so obscured by watery clouds that the light is perceptibly failing. Thick and heavy, the rooks line the curving tops of the trees, distinct against the sky, so close together that an arrow driven with sufficient force would transfix a score. There seems too much weight for the slender twigs: for not one of all these hundreds has chosen a large branch; they all crowd the summit of the trees. There is still plenty of light for them to search for food; but early in the winter afternoon rooks appear to lose vitality; and to draw into themselves, as it were. They 'caw' very little; they perch silently, or silently fly off and return.

Across the thin watery clouds a beam of pale white light shoots upwards from the west, and another accompanies it – fragments of the radiating crown of sunset. The rooks' day is not much more than seven hours long – from a little before eight till three; the remainder of the twenty-four hours they pass in stillness and somnolence, almost semi-hibernation. Their hardihood is very great. Sometimes a grey frost-mist gathers and thickens with the approaching night: so that by four o'clock the roosting birds are barely visible from the ground below. In this bitter freezing vapour they perch some fourteen hours. A rime forms on the branches, and a cloud of white particles is shaken from the boughs as they spread their wings in the morning. Sometimes the atmosphere deposits a coating of pure ice; a kind of ice-rain falls, encasing the smallest twig as if it were enclosed in glass.

The rooks endure this too. The blackbird seeks the thickest bushes; finches and small birds find yew-trees; even the wood-pigeons, strong birds as they are – roost, if they can, in ivy-grown trees. The rook roosts as high as his nest is built – exposed to frost and vapour, snow, and biting wind.

from *Chronicles of the Hedges*, 1948

Partridges in 1880

The last week in June is usually considered to be the critical time for partridges as far as the hatching season is concerned. Probably two-thirds of all the wild birds bred in the country leave the shell between the longest day and the first of July. And since any which make their appearance much later are hardly fit for powder till the end of September, the prospects of the ordinary sportsman are mainly dependent on the weather that precedes the dog days.

The recent spring has been upon the whole decidedly favourable to the birds. A certain number of eggs would, no doubt, be destroyed by the frosts which seem now as characteristic of May as ever they were of December. But it is only in very exceptional years that we have no drawback to the breeding season. The great points are that the weather should be moderate while the old birds are sitting, so that no rain should get into the nests, and that sufficient showers should fall about hatching time to keep the ground free from those cracks and fissures which in over dry seasons entomb a great number of the chicks. These two conditions we have had, and so far everything looks well.

On the other hand, it is to be feared that in many parts of England so clean a sweep of the partridges was made by the floods of last year that the supply will still be below the average, and if we have many more violent rain-storms, and they are at all general in their incidence, much harm may still be done to the young coveys. However, we may fairly hope that a large majority now will get safely through the perils of infancy; and where there were enough left for breeding, as was the case on the higher grounds, there will probably be fair sport next September. In those districts which suffered more severely it may still be necessary to give the birds a second year of grace if the stock is to be got up again to its former numbers.

Wild partridges require much more looking after now than they did formerly. They are in much greater danger from the mowing machine than they used to be from the scythe, and on carefully preserved estates it is part of the keeper's duty to see that men walk in front of the machine to take care that no birds are decapitated. Where this precaution is neglected, numbers are killed every year, and the worst of it is that the finer and forwarder the spring, the more likely the birds are to make their nests in the meadow grass. Old sportsmen are often heard to say that they like any kind of weather in May which is likely to drive the birds to the uplands and the hedgerows. Nowadays, however, in some of the best partridge countries the uplands and hedgerows afford but little shelter. Under all circumstances, however, the season of 1880 promises to be fairly good. Had last year been a little less disastrous, the current one would, in all probability, have been much above the average. As it is, however, the most we ought to allow ourselves to expect is that partridge-shooters may find game enough to indemnify them to some extent for the blank of 1879. But they will have to be careful of it, for it may be long ere they have another of those golden seasons when you 'can't kill too many birds.' One comfort is that, as the fore part of the season has been good, there ought not to be a great many 'squeakers,' which too often go to swell the bags of the unskilful and unscrupulous.

A young brood of partridges with the old bird is always a very interesting sight: the little ones are so delicate and so pretty in their movements, and the old hen is so motherly – more so, perhaps, than any other wild bird. In a little while you will come upon them suddenly as you get over the stile into the wheat-field, where they are lying by the footpath, half in and half out of the thick green corn. The hen-bird will rise a little way from the ground with a shrill cry, and drop down again in the cover a few yards off, while the little ones all scuttle after her, perhaps making an effort to fly too; or you will see them all running across some dry road, making their way from the warm sunny bank where they have been dusting, through the opposite hedge into their nearest feeding ground. At such times you hardly like to think of the hour when they shall have come to birds' estate and you will go forth armed for their destruction.

from *St James's Gazette*, 1880

An Oak Leaf in December

I saw a brown and dry oak leaf caught in the bushes in December. A sunbeam lit on it and it glowed among the dark branches. Immediately my thought responded and my mind too, received the light. Touching the brown leaf, brittle to the fingers, I gathered the ray from it. In a cold and cheerless upper room the afternoon and sinking sun cast a beam upon the wall. I sat a little while where it reached me, and it sank into me. I saw the sun level on to the fir-tree tops. There was a low sound from them as the air passed; it seemed as if I was looking to the sun. In the morning I can in the winter just see the sun arise; if it is cloudy or not, my first glance is there. I pause on the staircase because the window faces the south and the sunshine falls through it. The thought of the sunshine, even in winter, is beauty.

from *Chronicles of the Hedges*, 1948

November Days

The morning mist lingers over gorse and heath, and on the upper surfaces of the long dank grass blades, bowed by their own weight, are white beads of dew. Wherever the eye seeks an object to dwell on, there the cloud-like mist seems to thicken as though to hide it. The bushes and thickets are swathed in the vapour; yonder, in the hollow, it clusters about the oaks and hangs upon the hedge looming in the distance. There is no sky – a motionless, colourless something spreads above; it is, of course, the same mist, but looking upwards it apparently recedes and becomes indefinite. The glance finds no point to rest on – as with the edges and dark nuclei of clouds – it is a mere opaque expanse. But the air is dry, the moisture does not deposit itself, it remains suspended, and waits but the wind to rise and depart. The stillness is utter: not a bird calls or insect buzzes by. In passing beneath the oaks the very leaves have forgotten to fall, and now rustle to the ground. Only those already on the sward, touched by the frost, crumble under the footstep. When green they would have yielded to the weight, but now stiffened they resist it and are crushed, breaking in pieces. A creaking and metallic rattle, as of chains, comes across the arable field – a steady gaze reveals the dim outline of a team of horses slowly dragging the plough, their shapes indistinctly seen against the hedge. A bent figure follows, and by-and-by another distinct creak and rattle, and yet a third in another direction, show that there are more teams at work, plodding to and fro. Watching their shadowy forms, suddenly the eye catches a change in the light somewhere.

Over the meadow yonder the mist is illuminated; it is not sunshine, but a white light, only visible by contrast with the darker mist around. It lasts a few moments, and then moves, and appears a second time by the copse. Though hidden here, the disk of the sun must be partly visible there, and as the white light does not remain long in one place, it is evident that there is motion now in the vast mass of vapour. Looking upwards there is the faintest suspicion of the palest blue, dull and dimmed by mist, so faint that its position cannot be fixed, and the next instant it is gone again. But the teams at plough are growing momentarily distinct – a breath of air touches the cheek, then a leaf breaks away from the bough and starts forth as if bent on a journey, but loses the impetus and sinks to the ground.

Soon afterwards the beams of the sun light up a distant oak that glows in the hedge – a rich deep buff – and it stands out, clear, distinct, and beautiful, the chosen and selected one, the first to receive the ray. Rapidly the mist vanishes - disappearing rather than floating away; a circle of blue sky opens overhead, and, finally, travelling slowly, comes the sunshine over the furrows. There is a perceptible sense of warmth – the colours that start into life add to the feeling. The bare birch has no leaf to reflect it, but its white bark shines, and beyond it two great elms, the one a pale green and the other a pale yellow, stand side by side. The brake fern is dead and withered; the tip of each frond curled over downwards by the frost, but it forms a brown background to the dull green furze which is alight here and there with scattered blossom, by contrast so brilliantly yellow as to seem like flame. Polished holly leaves glisten, and a bunch of tawny fungus rears itself above the grass.

November Days

On the sheltered sunny bank lie the maple leaves fallen from the bushes, which form a bulwark against the north wind; they have simply dropped upon the ivy which almost covers the bank. Standing here with the oaks overhead and the thick bushes on the northern side it is quite warm and genial; so much so that it is hard to realise that winter is at hand. But even in the shortest days, could we only get rid of the clouds and wind, we should find the sunshine sufficiently powerful to make the noontide pleasant. It is not that the sun is weak or low down, nor because of the sharp frosts, that winter with us is dreary and chill. The real cause is the prevalence of cloud, through which only a dull light can penetrate, and of moisture-laden winds. If our winter sun had fair play we should find the climate very different. Even as it is, now and then comes a break in the masses of vapour streaming across the sky, and if you are only sheltered from the wind (or stand at a southern window), the temperature immediately rises. For this reason the temperatures registered by thermometers are often far from being a correct record of the real weather we have had.

A bitter frost early in the morning sends the mercury below zero, but perhaps, by eleven o'clock the day is warm, the sky being clear and the wind still. The last register instituted – that of the duration of sunshine, if taken in connection with the state of the wind – is the best record of the temperature that we have actually felt. These thoughts naturally arise under the oaks here as the bright sunlight streams down from a sky the more deeply blue from contrast with the brown, and buff, and yellow leaves of the trees. Hark! There comes a joyous music over the fields – first one dog's note, then two, then three, and then a chorus; it is the hounds opening up a strong scent. It rises and falls – now it is coming nearer, in a moment we shall see them break through the hedge on the ridge – surely that was a shout! Just in the very moment of expectation the loud tongues cease; we wait, listening breathlessly, but presently a straggling cry or two shows that the pack has turned and are spread wide trying to recover. By degrees the sounds die away; let us then stroll onwards.

A thick border of dark green firs bounds the copse – the brown leaves that have fallen from the oaks have lodged on the foliage of the firs and are there supported. In the sheltered corner some of the bracken has partly escaped the frost, one frond has two colours. On one side of the rib it is green and on the other yellow. The grass is strewn with the leaves of the aspen, which have turned quite black. Under the great elms there seems a sudden increase of light – it is caused by the leaves which still remain on the branches; they are all of the palest yellow, and, as you pass under, give the impression of the tree having been lit up – illuminated with its own colour. From the bushes hang the red berries of the night shade, and the fruit on the briars glistens in the sun. Inside the copse stand innumerable thistles shoulder high, dead and gaunt; and a grey border running round the field at the bottom of the hedge shows where the tall, strong weeds of summer have withered up. A bird flutters round the topmost boughs of the elm yonder and disappears with a flash of blue – it is a jay. Here the grass of the meadow has an undertone of grey; then an arable field succeeds, where six strong horses are drawing the heavy drill, and great bags of the precious seed are lying on the furrows.

Another meadow, where note a broken bough of elder, the leaves on which have turned black, while still on its living branches they are green, and then a clump of beeches. The trunks are full of knot-holes, after a dead bough has fallen off and the stump has rotted away, the bark curls over the orifice and seemingly heals the wound more smoothly and completely than with other trees. But the mischief is proceeding all the same, despite that flattering appearance; outwardly the bark looks smooth and healthy, but probe the hole and the rottenness is working inwards.

A sudden gap in the clump attracts the glance, and there – with one great beech trunk on this side and another on that – is a view opening down on the distant valley far below. The wood beneath looks dwarfed, and the uneven tops of the trees, some green, some tinted, are apparently so close together as to hide aught else, and the shadows of the clouds move over it as over a sea. A haze upon the horizon brings plain and sky together there; on one side, in the far distance a huge block, a rude vastness stands out dusky and dimly defined – it is a spur of the rolling hills. Out in the plain, many a mile away, the sharp, needle-like point of a steeple rises white above the trees, which there shade and mingle into a dark mass – so brilliantly white as to seem hardly real. Sweeping the view round, there is a strange and total absence of houses or signs of habitation, other than the steeple, and now that, too, is gone. It has utterly vanished – where, but a few moments before it glowed with whiteness, is absolutely nothing. The disappearance is almost weird in the broad daylight, as if solid stone could sink into the earth. Searching for it suddenly a village appears some way on the right – the white walls stand out bright and clear, one of the houses is evidently of large size, and placed on a slight elevation is a prominent object. But as we look it fades, grows blurred and indistinct, and in another moment is gone. The whole village has vanished – in its place is nothing; so swift is the change that the mind scarcely credits the senses.

A deep shadow creeping towards us explains it. Where the sunlight falls, there steeple or house glows and shines; when it has passed, the haze that is really there, though itself invisible, instantly blots out the picture. The thing may be seen over and over again in the course of a few minutes; it would be difficult for an artist to catch so fleeting an effect. The shadow of the cloud is not black – it lacks several shades of that – there is in it a faint and yet decided tint of blue. This tone of blue is not the same everywhere – here it is almost distinct, there it fades; it is an aerial colour which rather hints itself than shows.

Commencing the descent the view is at once lost, but we pass a beech whose beauty is not easily conveyed. The winds have scarcely rifled it; being in a sheltered spot on the slope, the leaves are nearly perfect. All those on the outer boughs are a rich brown – some, perhaps, almost orange. But there is an inner mass of branches of lesser size which droop downwards, something after the manner of a weeping willow; and the leaves on these are still green and show through. Upon the whole tree a flood of sunshine pours, and over it is the azure sky. The mingling, shading, and contrast of these colours give a lovely result – the tree is aglow, its foliage ripe with colour. Farther down comes the steady sound of deliberate blows, and the upper branches of the hedge falls beneath the steel. A sturdy labourer, with a bill on a pole, strikes slow and strong and cuts down the hedge to an even height. A dreadful weapon that simple tool must have been in the old days before the advent of the arquebus. For with the exception of the spike, which is not needed for hedge work, it is almost an exact copy of the brown bill of ancient warfare; it is brown still, except where sharpened. Wielded by a sinewy arm, what, gaping gashes it must have slit through helm and mail and severed bone!

Watch the man there – he slices off the tough thorn as though it were straw. He notes not the beauty of the beech above him, nor the sun, nor the sky; but on the other hand, when the sky is hidden, the sun gone, and the beautiful beech torn by the raving winds neither does he heed that. Rain and tempest affect him not; the glaring heat of summer, the bitter frost of winter are alike to him. He is built up like an oak. Believe it, the man that from his boyhood has stood ankle-deep in the chill water of the ditch, patiently labouring with axe and bill; who has trudged across the furrow, hand on plough, facing sleet and mist; who has swung the sickle under the summer sun – this is the man for the trenches. This is the man whom neither the snows of the North nor the sun of the South can vanquish; who will dig and delve, and carry traverse and covered way forward in the face of the fortress, who will lie on the bare ground in the night. For they who go up to battle must fight the hard earth and the tempest, as well as face bayonet and ball. As of yore with the brown bill, so now with the rifle – the muscles that have been trained about the hedges and fields will not fail England in the hour of danger.

Hark! – a distant whoop – another, a blast of a horn, and then a burst of chiding that makes the woods ring. Down drops the bill, and together, heedless of any social difference in the common joy, we scramble to the highest mound, and see the pack sweep in full cry across the furrows. Crash – it is the bushes breaking, as the first foam-flecked, wearied horse hardly rises to his leap, and yet crushes safely through, opening a way, which is quickly widened by the straggling troop behind. Ha! down the lane from the hill dashes another squadron that has eroded the chord of the arc and comes in fresher. Ay, and a third is entering at the bottom there, one by one, over the brook. Woods, field, and paths, but just before an empty solitude, are alive with men and horses. Up yonder, along the ridge, gallops another troop in single file, well defined against the sky, going parallel to the hounds. What a view they must have of the scene below! Two ladies who ride up with torn skirts cannot lift their panting horses at the double mound. Well, let us defy 'wilful damage' for once. The gate, jealously padlocked, is swiftly hoisted off its hinges, and away they go with hearty thanks. We slip the gate on again just as someone hails to us across the field to wait a minute, but seeing it is only a man we calmly replace the timber and let him take his chance. He is excited, but we smile stolidly. In another minute the wave of life is gone; it has swept over and disappeared as swiftly as it came. The wood, the field, and lane seem painfully – positively painfully – empty. Slowly the hedger and ditcher goes back to his work, where in the shade under the bushes even now the dew lingers.

So there are days to be enjoyed out of doors even in much-abused November. And when the wind rises and the storm is near, if you get under the lee of a good thick copse there is a wild pleasure in the frenzy that passes over. With a rush the leaves stream outwards, thickening the air, whirling round and round; the tree-tops bend and sigh, the blast strikes them, and in an instant they are stripped and bare.

A spectral rustling, as the darkness falls and the black cloud approaches, is the fallen leaves in the copse, lifted up from their repose and dashed against the underwood. Then a howl of wrath descends and fills the sense of hearing, so that for the moment it is hard to tell what is happening. A rushing hiss follows, and the rain hurtles through the branches, driving so horizontally as to pass overhead. The sheltering thorn-thicket stirs, and a long, deep, moaning roar rises from the fir-trees. Another howl that seems to stun--to so fill the ears with sound that they cannot hear--the aerial host charges the tree-ranks, and the shock makes them tremble to the root. Still another and another; twigs and broken boughs fly before it and strew the sward; larger branches that have long been dead fall crashing downwards;

leaves are forced right through the thorn-thicket, and strike against the face. Fortunately, so fierce a fury cannot last; presently the billows of wind that strike the wood come at longer intervals and with less vigour; then the rain increases, and yet a little while and the storm has swept on. The very fury – the utter abandon – of its rage is its charm; the spirit rises to meet it, and revels in the roar and buffeting.

By-and-by they who have faced it have their reward. The wind sinks, the rain ceases, a pale blue sky shows above, and then yonder appears a majesty of cloud – a Himalaya of vapour. Crag on crag rises the vast pile – such jagged and pointed rocks as never man found on earth, or, if he found, could climb – topped with a peak that towers to the heavens, and leans – visibly leans – and threatens to fall and overwhelm the weak world at its feet. A gleam as of snow glitters on the upper rocks, the passes are gloomy and dark, the faces of the precipice are lit up with a golden gleam from the rapidly-sinking sun. So the magic structure stands and sees the great round disk go down. The night gathers around those giant mounts and dark space receives them.

from Hodge and his Masters, 1880

The Squire's Preserves

'There are my preserves,' said the Squire of Southlands to me, pointing to several meadows that sloped down to the great brook in which Orion and I had wired the jacks [rabbit snares], long before. A little incident had led to our becoming acquainted with him and by degrees we got on very friendly terms. He was now explaining his method, and began on the upper ground near the rook trees from whence there was a view of a green hollow. Three rather large meadows went down to the brook, divided from each other by rather thick hedges. The brook itself was bordered by extensive withey beds. Further up it, there were two or three more meadows that could not be seen from here. These were very small, not above two acres each, and enclosed by well timbered mounds. Beyond these again, round to the right, was a small wood, chiefly ash, that grew partly on the slope of the hill and partly in the hollow. It was perhaps about fifteen acres in extent. 'There are my preserves,' he repeated, leading the way down one of the hedgerows, 'and you will find game in every bush and almost every tuft of grass.'

It was a beautiful day, the June roses were just opening, and the trees had the delicious fresh green of early summer. 'You are aware,' he went on, 'that this estate is only of small size, and that was one consideration that led me to this mode of preserving. It was impossible for me to have one of those broad open parks that are seen on large properties without upsetting the arrangement of the farms which had endured for generations before I succeeded. Nor could I keep up a great head of pheasants without extensive covers, a staff of keepers and a wasteful expenditure. I therefore allowed things to go on just as before, only in the case of this – the Home Farm – I undertook the supervision, in part, myself. It may be perhaps about thirty acres, exclusive of the wood. This hedgerow runs nearly straight down the slope to the brook. Here at the upper end where the ground is dry and valuable, you can see the hedge has been cut and trimmed annually in the same way as on other farms. But near the bottom of the hill, between it and the stream, the ground is naturally marshy, and is much flooded in winter. That of course could be avoided by draining, and by an engineering improvement of the bed of the stream. Now it is here that my plan comes into play. Here the land is naturally of little use, and I can have my preserve with the least possible expense and with the least possible interference with agriculture. If you will look closely at this hedgerow you will see that it has not been cut for years.'

We did look closely and found it as he said. Trailing briars and brambles grew out into the grass to such a distance and so thickly, that in places it was impossible to approach the hedge proper. The ditch was crowded – choked with grasses, sedges, flags, bunches of rushes, 'gicks' and similar plants. On the mound itself dead wood and fallen branches lay rotting in vast quantities. The stoles had sent up tall poles of withey and ash that were almost trees: every gale brought down a mass of broken dead wood out of them. The weeds of this year had to struggle hard to force their way up through the dead dry weeds of last summer. A matted, tangled mass of vegetation filled all the spaces between the stoles and the trees. Farther down towards the brook, the hedge became a small copse. The briars and brambles, the hawthorn and withey had, so to say, stepped across the ditch, and laid hold of the sward. Without the aid of a billhook it would have been impossible to get through it. Where the ditch joined the brook the sedges and flags had it all their own way. The mound between the two ditches – with the broad brook across at the end – resembled on a small scale the delta of a tropical river. Reeds, rushes, every species of aquatic weed flourished there: so much indeed that they interfered with each other, and the lesser plants could not grow because the sturdier flags and reeds overshadowed them. At a guess it must have been twenty yards across from one side to the other of the hedge here. Then the brook itself – as Orion and I knew from previous experience – was bordered with the same tangle of sedge and rush and flag. So that from this the meadow side no one could approach within many yards of the actual stream because of the marsh at the shore. Lastly across the brook the withey-beds began – another jungle. As we looked we saw the young flags – far out almost in the centre of the stream that had grown up this year, slowly waving from side to side in the current: a motion that never ceased day or night.

'This is only England in the olden time,' said the Squire. 'And not such a very olden time either. If I am right, more of the land here was open and unenclosed till about twenty years before the beginning of the present century – say a hundred years ago [c.1779]. What I have done is to bring back in a limited area the same conditions that existed then. There flows the brook, untouched and untended. It is never cleaned out and in consequence the aquatic plants have taken root: you will find many species there that you may search for in vain over half the county. The fish do just as they like, and they find an abundance of food because of these very plants and overhanging banks, bushes and trees. There are as you see great ditches opening into it – of which by-places fish are extremely fond. There are also several large ponds. My only regret is that the soil is unsuitable for trout. I should probably soon have otters here, but they have no idea that such a place exists: they cannot come up from the river because they would be shot or trapped before they could get within miles: I believe they will soon be extinct in the river.

'Water fowl come because they have wings and can rise out of reach – I get almost every species here. A swan comes now and then – not the wild swan of the estuary and the sea – but a tame swan from some mere or river. It is a sight to watch him come. He appears in the eastern sky – at first a speck, then as big as your hand, soon to enlarge, and presently sails over at an immense height. The swiftness of his progress, the strength of his wings, the noise they make, fill me with admiration. He always travels at this immense height which compels him either to begin to slope downwards at least two miles before he alights, or else to sweep round in vast circles each lower than the rest. I think he generally slopes down in a straight line, beginning as far back as the steeple yonder. Herons after a measure do the same: when they go down to the water meadows they extend their wings and slide down, down for half a mile but just above the hedgerows till they reach the desired spot. To see the swan get up is another sight – the distance he had to travel running on the land, or in the water, part swimming part flying before he can rise is astonishing. The creaking of his wings, the splashing, the efforts of the mighty bird in motion are wonderful to see. He rises by degrees and finally passes away, and as he proceeds the white glisten of his feathers is lost till he finally disappears as a black speck. He has not come recently, and I hear his wings have been clipped. What a pity if it so! The swan is beautiful to look at on the water, but the pleasure is increased when you see him in his natural state. Whatever water fowl you wish to watch you will find them all here in their season, though as I have no open sheet of water many of them only come at night. As for aquatic insects in these weeds, you may find almost every species.'

In the withey-beds the moorhens and coots found shelter: the brilliant kingfisher and the heron, alike undisturbed, came where they chose. As the kingfishers were never shot they were comparatively numerous. On this side the shore was too level for the burrows of the water-rats: on the other the banks of the withey-bed were drilled with the holes. There were almost always snipes in the winter but the woodcock rarely came. We then passed through the hedge into the next field by a narrow opening. A plank was thrown across the wide ditch, and two rough steps or rather holes led up the bank. The boughs were kept cut back here so as to leave a path through the jungle, and another plank, or slab answered as a bridge across the ditch on the other side of the mound. In this field near the brook there was a belt of grass that had not been touched by the scythe for years. It bordered the brook across the meadow for a width of forty or fifty yards. The 'bullpolls' had grown so large and strong as to usurp all the ground near the water.

Manuscript material published in *Field and Farm* (1957)

A January Night

Do not close the curtains, let the January evening, already lengthened to five o'clock, depart of itself, while Venus grows brighter in the violet Western sky. Lose not a moment's chance of contemplating beauty; each of these seconds while the day changes into night is precious; in this is life. The sleep of a winter's night is on the silent wood – the wind is still in the leafless trees, stark as if frozen.

from *Chronicles of the Hedges*, 1948

Snipes and Moonlit Sport

Regularly as the swallow to the eaves in spring, the snipe comes back with the early frosts of autumn to the same well-known spots – to the bend of the brook or the boggy corner in the ploughed field – but in most uncertain numbers. Sometimes flocks of ten or twenty, sometimes only twos and threes are seen, but always haunting particular places.

They have a special affection for peaty ground, black and spongy, where every footstep seems to squeeze water out of the soil with a slight hissing sound, and the boot cuts through the soft turf. There, where a slow stream winds in and out, unmarked by willow or bush, but fringed with green aquatic grasses growing on a margin of ooze, the snipe finds tempting food; or in the meadows where a little spring breaks forth in the ditch and does not freeze – for water which has just bubbled out of the earth possesses this peculiarity, and is therefore favourable to low forms of insect or slug life in winter – the snipe may be found when the ponds are bound with ice.

Some of the old country folk used to make as much mystery about this bird as the cuckoo. Because it was seldom seen till the first fogs the belief was that it had lost its way in the mist at sea, and come inland by mistake. Just as in the early part of the year green buds and opening flowers welcome swallow and cuckoo, so the colours of the dying leaf prepare the way for the second feathered immigration in autumn. And rarely has autumn offered the artist richer studies of colour in hedgerow and copse than this year. The maples are aglow with orange, the oaks one mass of buff, the limes light gold, the elms a soft yellow. In the hawthorn thickets bronzed spots abound; here and there a bramble leaf has turned a brilliant crimson (though many bramble leaves will remain a dull green all the winter through); the edible chestnut sheds leaves of a dark fawn hue, but all, scattered by the winds, presently resolve into a black pulp upon the earth. Noting these signs the sportsman gets out his dust-shot for the snipe, and the farmer, as he sees the fieldfare flying over after a voyage from Norway, congratulates himself that last month was reasonably dry, and enabled him to sow his winter seed.

'Sceap-sceap!' and very often the snipe successfully carries out the intention expressed in his odd-sounding cry, and does escape in reality. For there is a knack required to kill this bird which gunners accustomed to steadier game find it difficult to school their trigger-fingers into. He is the exception to the golden rule that the safest way lies in the middle, and that therefore you should fire not too soon nor too late, but half-way between. But the snipe must either be knocked over the instant he rises from the ground, and before he has time to commence his puzzling zig-zag flight, or else you must wait till he has finished his corkscrew burst. Then there is a moment just before he passes out of range when he glides in a straight line and may be hit. This singular zig-zag flight so deceives the eye as almost to produce the idea of a spiral movement. No barrel can ever be jerked from side to side swiftly enough, no hair-trigger is fine enough, to catch him then, except by the chance of a vast scattering over-charge, which has nothing to do with sport. If he rises at some little distance, then fire instantly, because by the time the zig-zag is done the range will be too great; if he starts up under your feet, out of a bunch of rushes, as is often the case, then give him law till his eccentric twist is finished.

When the smoke has cleared away in the crisp air, there he lies, the yet warm breast on the frozen ground, to be lifted up not without a passing pity and admiration. The brown feathers are exquisitely shaded, and so exactly resemble the hue of the rough dead aquatic grass out of which he sprang that if you cast the bird among it you will have some trouble to find it again. To discover a living snipe on the ground is indeed a test of good eyesight; for as he slips in and out among the brown withered flags and the grey grass it requires not only a quick eye but the inbred sportsman's instinct of perception (if such a phrase is permissible) to mark him out. If your shot has missed and merely splashed up the water or rattled against bare branches, then step swiftly behind a tree trunk, and stay in ambuscade, keeping a sharp watch on him as he circles round high up in the air. Very often in a few minutes he will come back in a wide sweep, and drop scarcely a gun-shot distant in the same watercourse, when a second shot may be obtained.

The little jack snipe, when flushed, will never fly far, if shot at several times in succession, still settling fifty or sixty yards farther on, and is easily bagged. Coming silently as possible round a corner, treading gently on the grass still white with hoar-frost in the shadow of the bushes, you may chance to spring a stray woodcock, which bird, if you lose a moment, will put the hedge between him and you. Artists used to seek for certain feathers which he carries, one in each wing, thinking to make of them a more delicate brush than the finest camel's hair.

To represent the winter as a dead time is to falsify nature. To disprove the libel let anyone hide himself in the osier-beds on the edge of a great water-meadow; for now that the marshes are drained, and the black earth of the fens yields a harvest of yellow corn, the broad level meads which are irrigated to fertilise them are among the chief inland resorts of wild fowl. When the bright moon is rising, walk in among the tapering osier-wands, the rustling sedges, and dead dry hemlock stems, and wait behind an aspen tree. In the thick blackthorn bush a round dark ball indicates the blackbird, who has puffed out his feathers to shield him from the frost, and who will sit so close and quiet that you may see the moonlight glitter on his eye. Presently comes a whistling noise of wings, and a loud 'quack, quack!' as a string of ducks, their long necks stretched out, pass over not twenty yards high, slowly slanting downwards to the water.

This is the favourable moment for the gun, because their big bodies are well defined against the sky, and aim can be taken; but to shoot anything on the ground at night, even a rabbit, whose whitetail as he hops away is fairly visible, is most difficult. The baffling shadows and the moonbeams on the barrel, and the faint reflection from the dew or hoar-frost on the grass, prevent more than a general direction being given to the gun, even with the tiny piece of white paper which some affix to the muzzle-sight as a guide. From a punt with a swivel gun it is different, because the game is swimming and visible as black dots on the surface, and half a pound of shot is sure to hit something. But in the water-meadows the ducks get among the grass, and the larger water-carriers where they can swim usually have small raised banks, so that at a distance only the heads of the birds appear above them. So that the best time to shoot a duck is just as he slopes down to settle – first, because he is distinctly visible against the sky; next, because he is within easy range; and lastly, his flight is steady. If you attempt to have ducks driven towards you, though they may go right overhead, yet it will often be too high – for they rise at a sharp angle when frightened; and men who are excellent judges of distance when it is a hare running across the fallow, find themselves all at fault trying to shoot at any elevation. Perhaps this arises from the peculiarity of the human eye which draughtsmen are fond of illustrating by asking a tyro to correctly bisect a vertical line: a thing that looks easy, and is really only to be done by long practice. To make certain of selecting the right spot in the osiers over which the ducks will pass, for one or two evenings previously a look-out should be kept and their usual course observed; for all birds and animals, even the wildest wild fowl, are creatures of habit and custom, and having once followed a particular path will continue to use it until seriously disturbed.

Evening after evening the ducks will rise above the horizon at the same place and almost at the same time, and fly straight to their favourite feeding place. If hit, the mallard falls with a thud on the earth, for he is a heavy bird; and few are more worthy of powder and shot either for his savoury flavour, far surpassing the tame duck, or the beauty of his burnished neck.

With the ducks come teal and widgeon and moorhen, till the swampy meadow resounds with their strange cries. When ponds and lakes are frozen hard is the best time for sport in these irrigated fields. All day long the ducks will stand or waddle to and fro on the ice in the centre of the lake or mere, far out of reach and ready to rise at the slightest alarm. But at night they seek the meadow where the water, running swiftly in the carriers, never entirely freezes, and where, if the shallow spots become ice, the rising current flows over it and floods another place. There is, moreover, never any difficulty in getting the game when hit, because the water, except in the main carriers, which you can leap across, hardly rises to the ankle, and ordinary water-tight boots will enable you to wade wherever necessary. This is a great advantage with wild fowl, which are sometimes shot and lost in deep ooze and strong currents and eddies, and on thin ice where men cannot go and even good dogs are puzzled.

from *The Amateur Poacher*, 1879

The Advent of Spring

Early one morning in March, awaking as the workmen's trains went rumbling by to the City, I saw on the ceiling by the window a streak of sunlight, tinted orange and crimson by the vapour through which the level beams had passed. The disk had risen, as seen from here, almost over the metropolis, illuminating with equal light the golden cross of St. Paul's and the golden grasshopper of the Exchange.

There is something in the sense of morning which lifts the heart with the sun. The light, the air, the waving branches, speak: the mind, clear as if born afresh, advances to meet them, full of joy and hope; the earth and life seem boundless at that moment. It is the same, I find, on the verge of the artificial city, as where the rays come streaming from the Downs. It is the same light, the same morning, and not all the offices, warehouses, the materialistic tone of common conversation (a very decided trait of London life) can efface the feeling of something holy in the sunrise. For the moment, the morning makes the earth a temple.

While I thus thought, looking at the streak of sunshine, suddenly there rang out three clear trumpet-like notes from a tree at the end of a little copse near the garden. A softer song followed, and then again the same three notes whose wild sweetness echoed through the trees. It was a missel-thrush, the stormcock and trumpeter of spring. His voice sounded not only close at hand but seemed to again repeat itself as it went away, as a bugle does. Lord of March, his proud call challenges the woods: there are none who can compare with him. Listen for the missel-thrush: when he sings, the snow may drift, the rain fall, but not for long; the violets are near at hand.

Next, a tiny chiff-chaff called from the top of a tall birch, and scarcely had he gone on than a titmouse began, but, busy as he was, he could not visit all the myriad buds around him. From a pine, greenfinches went by, talking to each other; a yellow-hammer called, but with shortened notes; and a lark (he had been up long since) arose again, singing, from the thin mist over the surface of an arable field by the copse. Starlings came to the spouting of the roof, whistling eagerly, full of the approaching business of nesting: how excited they get!

The sunbeam on the ceiling descended down the wall, losing the crimson and orange, and growing white as the disk left the vapour of the horizon and shone un-dimmed in the blue sky.

Blackbirds uttered low whistles in several differing directions. With the chirping of sparrows, the 'fink' of chaffinches, the 'caw, caw' of rooks, floating over, the day opened. And, day by day, looking from my window up the field beside the copse there appeared some new, slight change, some sign that the invisible forces of the sun were working here, too, as afar. The slender, drooping, birch boughs, which once reflected the light as if each twig were polished, were now thickening with opening buds. In the elms there was a reddish mist: the wind had a different sound in the trees; no longer the hollow whistle of bare branches, the network was growing and held the breeze. Near at hand, a larch was already touched with the tenderest green: the boughs of a horse-chestnut close by were enlarged at the tip where the buds were bursting. To the holly bush adjacent, though within half gunshot, a fieldfare, even the wild and untamable fieldfare, resorted for the berries in the terrible frosts of January 1880, driven by hunger almost to the door.

The glance can still penetrate some distance into the copse: but the woodbine, its green slightly tinted with dull purple, is covering the poles to which it clings. Along the enclosing hedge there runs a straggling and uncertain line of green; hawthorn and briar, the docks and nettles and parsley of the mound, each add their part.

The ploughed field is losing its brown, the innumerable blades that are springing up hiding the clods; but as they were not planted by nature, but by mechanical art, with regular spaces between, they do not yet entirely conceal the ground. The very heaps of rubbish in the corner and by the gateway are disappearing under green: weeds, if you like, but still green. The meadows on the slope almost a mile away have a much more vivid hue than a short while since. Upon one short oak in the hedgerow this side of them the leaves of last year adhere; its brown foliage is thrown out in contrast with the sward behind, and the faint green of a hawthorn bush whose lines are appearing beside it. There are spots of yellow among the furze; it will be one breadth of golden bloom shortly. Yonder, in the arable plain, white puffs of steam drift before the east wind, which dissipates it almost as quickly as it issues from the funnel of the ploughing engine. The sunshine gleams on polished brass; the black boiler and huge dull red wheels stand out clearly against the brown of the soil. These men are at work with the first note of the thrush; they cease only with the darkness. A clear blue sky extends overhead, without a cloud, but it is of a hard tint – March blue – and the furrows yonder, fresh-turned, must whiten and crumble quickly under the dry air.

from *The Old House at Coate*, 1948

The Water Colley

The sweet grass was wet with dew as I walked through a meadow in Somerset to the river. The cuckoo sang, the pleasanter perhaps because his brief time was nearly over, and all pleasant things seem to have a deeper note as they draw towards an end. Dew and sweet green grass were the more beautiful because of the knowledge that the high hills around were covered by sun-dried, wiry heather. Riverside mead, dew-laden grass, and sparkling stream were like an oasis in the dry desert. They refreshed the heart to look upon as water refreshes the weary. The shadows were more marked and defined than they are as day advances, the hues of the flowers brighter, for the dew was to shadow and flower as if the colours of the artist were not yet dry. Humble-bees went down with caution into the long grass, not liking to wet their wings. Butterflies and the brilliant moths of a hot summer's morn alight on a dry heated footpath till the dew is gone. A great rock rising from the grass by the river's edge alone looked arid, and its surface already heated, yet it also cast a cool shadow. By a copse, two rabbits – the latest up of all those which had sported during the night – stayed till I came near, and then quietly moved in among the ferns and foxgloves.

In the narrowest part of the wood between the hedge and the river a corncrake called his loudest 'crake, crake,' incessantly. The corncrake or landrail is difficult even to see, so closely does he conceal himself in the tall grasses, and his call echoed and re-echoed deceives those who try to find him. Yet by great patience and watchful skilfulness the corncrake is sometimes caught by hand. If tracked, and if you can see him – the most difficult part – you can put your hand on him. Now and then a corncrake is caught in the same way by hand while sitting on her nest on the ground. It is not, however, as easy as it reads. Walking through the grass, and thinking of the dew and the beautiful morning sunshine, I scarcely noticed the quantity of cuckooflowers, or cardamine, till presently it occurred to me that it was very late in the season for cuckoo-flowers; and stooping I picked one, and in the act saw it was an orchis – the early purple. The meadow was coloured, or rather tinted, with the abundance of the orchis, palest of pale pink, dotted with red, the small narrow leaves sometimes with black spots. They grew in the pasture everywhere, from the river's side in the deep valley to the top of the hill by the wood.

As soon as the surface of the river was in sight I stood and watched, but no ripple or ring of wavelets appeared; the trout were not feeding. The water was so low that the river consisted of a series of pools, connected by rapids descending over ledges of stones and rocky fragments. Illumined to the very bottom, every trout was visible, even those under the roots of trees and the hollow of the bank. A cast with the fly there was useless; the line would be seen; there was no ripple to hide it. As the trout, too, were in the pools, it might be concluded that those worth taking had fed, and only the lesser fish would be found in the eddies, where they are permitted by the larger fish to feed after they have finished. Experience and reason were all against the attempt, yet so delightful is the mere motion and delicate touch of the fly-line on the water that I could not but let myself enjoy that at least. The slender lancewood rod swayed, the line swished through the air, and the fly dropped a few inches too high up the rapid among the stones – I had meant it to fall farther across in the dark backwater at the foot of the fall. The swift rush of the current carried the fly instantly downwards, but not so quick as to escape a troutlet; he took it, and was landed immediately.

But to destroy these under-sized fish was not sport, and as at that moment a water-colley passed I determined to let the trout alone, and observe his ways. Colley means a blackbird; water-colley, the water-blackbird or water-ousel – called the dipper in the North. In districts where the bird is seldom seen it is occasionally shot and preserved as a white blackbird. But in flight and general appearance the water-colley is almost exactly like a starling with a white neck. His colour is not black or brown – it is a rusty, undecided brown, at a distance something the colour of a young starling, and he flies in a straight line, and yet clumsily, as a young starling does. His very cry, too, sounds immature, pettish, and unfinished, as if from a throat not capable of a full note. There are usually two together, and they pass and re-pass all day as you fish, but if followed are not to be observed without care. I came on the colley too suddenly the first time, at a bend of the river; he was beneath the bank towards me, and flew out from under my feet, so that I did not see him till he was on the wing. Away he flew with a call like a young bird just tumbled out of its nest, following the curves of the stream. Presently I saw him through an alder bush which hid me; he was perched on a root of alder under the opposite bank. Worn away by the stream the dissolved earth had left the roots exposed, the colley was on one of them; in a moment he stepped on to the shore under the hollow, and was hidden behind the roots under a moss-grown stole. When he came out he saw me, and stopped feeding.

He bobbed himself up and down as he perched on the root in the oddest manner, bending his legs so that his body almost touched his perch, and rising again quickly, this repeated in quick succession as if curtsying. This motion with him is a sign of uncertainty – it shows suspicion; after he had bobbed to me ten times, off he went. I found him next on stone in the middle of the river; it stood up above the surface of a rapid connecting two pools. Like the trout, the colley always feeds at the rapids, and flies as they swim, from fall to fall. He was bobbing up and down, his legs bent, and his rusty brown body went up and down, but as I was hidden by a hedge he gained confidence, suspended his curtsying, and began to feed. First he looked all round the stone, and then stepped on another similar island in the midst of the rushing water, pushing his head over the edge into it. Next he stepped into the current, which, though shallow, looked strong enough to sweep him away. The water checked against him rose to the white mark on his breast. He waded up the rapid, every now and then thrusting his head completely under the water; sometimes he was up to his neck, sometimes not so deep; now and then getting on a stone, searching right and left as he climbed the cascade. The eddying water shot by his slender legs, but he moved against it easily, and soon ascended the waterfall. At the summit a second colley flew past, and he rose and accompanied his friend. Upon a ledge of rock I saw him once more, but there was no hedge to hide me, and he would not feed; he stood and curtsied, and at the moment of bobbing let his wings too partly down, his tail drooping at the same time. Calling in an injured tone, as if much annoyed, he flew, swept round the meadow, and so to the river behind me. His friend followed. On reaching the river at a safe distance down, he skimmed along the surface like a kingfisher. They find abundance of insect life among the stones at the falls, and everywhere in shallow water. Some accuse them of taking the ova of trout, and they are shot at trout nurseries; but it is doubtful if they are really guilty, nor can they do any appreciable injury in an open stream, not being in sufficient numbers. It is the birds and other creatures peculiar to the water that render fly-fishing so pleasant; were they all destroyed, and nothing left but the mere fish, one might as well stand and fish in a stone cattle-trough. I hope all true lovers of sport will assist in preserving rather than in killing them.

from *The Life of the Fields*, 1884

BIBLIOGRAPHY
Previously published short extracts

A Country Walk in June (*Round About a Great Estate*, 1880)
A Defence of Sport (extracts from the essay of that title in *The Life of the Fields*, 1884)
A January Night (*Chronicles of the Hedges*, 1948)
A Shortest Day Scene (*Chronicles of the Hedges*, 1948)
An Oak Leaf in December ('The Benediction of the Light', *Chronicles of the Hedges*, 1948)
Fishing for Trout by the River Exe (*The Life of the Fields*, 1884)
Game in the Furrows (*Wild Life in a Southern County*, 1879)
Hares Boxing (*Wild Life in a Southern County*, 1879)
Hunting on the Estate (*Hodge and his Masters*, 1880)
Pheasant Poaching (*Red Deer*, 1884)
Ploughing on the Sussex Downs ('Field and Farm', *Field and Farm*, 1957)
Poaching on Exmoor (*Red Deer*, 1884)
Rook-Poachers (*Wild Life in a Southern County*, 1879)
The Advent of Spring ('The Country near London', *The Old House at Coate*, 1948)
The Farmer loves his Gun (*Wild Life in a Southern County*, 1879)
The First Gun (*The Amateur Poacher*, 1879)
The Gamekeeper's Favourite Gun (*The Gamekeeper at Home*, 1878)
The Hedgerow (*Round About a Great Estate*, 1880)
The Hunt (*Hodge and his Masters*, 1880)
The Partridge and the Hawk ('The Persecution of St. Partridge' in *Field and Farm* (1957), and *The Farmer's World*, 2015)
The Rabbit Warren (*Wild Life in a Southern County*, 1879)
The Stubbles ('Thoughts in the Stubbles', *The Farmer's World*, 2015)
The Wheat Field ('Walks in the Wheatfields', *Field and Hedgerow*, 1887)
The Wild Thyme of the Hills (*Chronicles of the Hedges*, 1948)
Young Partridges (*Wild Life in a Southern County*, 1879)

Previously published full-length articles

A Plea for Pheasant Shooting (The Farmer's World, 2015)
An English Deer Park (*Field and Hedgerow*, 1887) subdivided into: 'The Old Manor-House', 'The Window-seat in the Gun Room', 'The Coomb', 'Shooting in the Forest', 'The Deer, and 'The Life of the Forest'
An English Homestead (*Toilers of the Field*, 1892)
Choosing a Gun (*Hills and the Vale*, 1909)
Hedge Miners (*Chronicles of the Hedges*, 1948)
Notes on the Year (originally published in the *Pall Mall Gazette* and included in *Wild Life in a Southern County*)
Poaching as a Profession (two parts, originally published in the *Pall Mall Gazette* and included in *The Gamekeeper at Home* as part of a larger chapter)
Shooting a Rabbit (*Chronicles of the Hedges*, 1948)

The Art of Shooting (*Field and Farm*, 1957)
The Horse as a Social Force (*Field and Farm*, 1957); *The Farmer's World* (2015)
The Place of Ambush (*Field and Farm*, 1957)
The Single-barrel Gun (*The Open Air*, 1885)
The Squire's Preserves (*Field and Farm*, 1957)
The Water Colley (*The Life of the Fields*, 1884)
Technique in Game-Shooting ('The Squire and the Land', *The Old House at Coate*, 1948)

Uncollected

About the Hedges (published in the *Standard* and included in *Hodge and his Masters* (1880) with one sentence omitted)
Early in March (published in the *Standard* and most of the text is included in *Hodge and his Masters*, 1880)
November Days (published in the *Standard* and most of the text is included in *Hodge and his Masters*, 1880)
Sleight-of-Hand Poaching Parts I and II (the majority of the text appears in *The Gamekeeper at Home* (1878) as part of chapters V and VII)
Snipes and Moonlit Sport (published in the *Pall Mall Gazette* and the majority of the text is included in *The Amateur Poacher* (1879) as part of a larger chapter)
Willow Tide (published in the *Standard* and half of the text is included in *Hodge and his Masters* (1880))

Uncollected and not since republished full-length articles

Ironbound December (*Pall Mall Gazette*, 26 December 1878)
Partridges in 1880 (*St. James's Gazette*, 29 June 1880)
Rabbiting (*Pall Mall Gazette*, 8 March 1873)
Rabbit-Shooting (*St. James's Gazette*, 3 February 1882)
Snipe Shooting at Home (*Pall Mall Gazette*, 19 January 1874)
Snow Shooting (*Pall Mall Gazette*, 19 January 1874)
The Country in November (*Graphic*, 25 November 1871)
The Use of Dogs in Shooting (*Pall Mall Gazette*, 30 August 1879)
Wild-Fowling (*St. James's Gazette*, 4 December 1885)
Wild Fowl Shooting (*The Times*, December 1877, reprinted in the *Leeds Mercury*, 21 December 1877)

Bibliographical Note

Evidence for Jefferies' authorship of the 10 newly republished items is published online: www.richardjefferiesarticles.com

Other countryside and sporting literature from Merlin Unwin Books

full details: www.merlinunwin.co.uk

The Countryman's Bedside Book BB £18.95

The Naturalist's Bedside Book BB £17.99

The Best of BB £18.95

The Shootingman's Bedside Book BB £18.95

The Way of a Countryman Ian Niall £16.99

The BASC Gameshooter's Pocket Guide Michael Brook £7.99

The Sporting Gun's Bedside Companion Douglas Butler £15.99

A Countryman's Creel Conor Farrington £14.99

The Poacher's Handbook Ian Niall £14.95

That Strange Alchemy Pheasants, trout and a middle-aged man
Laurence Catlow £17.99

The Black Grouse Patrick Laurie £20

Geese! Memoirs of a Wildfowler Edward Miller £20

The Airgun Hunter's Year Ian Barnett £20

Advice from a Gamekeeper John Cowan £20

The Gamekeeper's Dog John Cowan £20

Vintage Guns for the Modern Shot Diggory Hadoke £30

The British Boxlock Gun & Rifle Diggory Hadoke £30

Hammer Guns Diggory Hadoke £30

The Stalking Party A fieldsports thriller D. P. Hart-Davis £14.99